An Ordinary Mission of God Theology

An Ordinary Mission of God Theology

Challenging Missional Church Idealism, Providing Solutions

Andrew R. Hardy

FOREWORD BY
Dr. Clare Watkins

WIPF & STOCK · Eugene, Oregon

AN ORDINARY MISSION OF GOD THEOLOGY
Challenging Missional Church Idealism, Providing Solutions

Copyright © 2022 Andrew R. Hardy. All rights reserved. Except for brief quotations in critical publications or reviews, no part of this book may be reproduced in any manner without prior written permission from the publisher. Write: Permissions, Wipf and Stock Publishers, 199 W. 8th Ave., Suite 3, Eugene, OR 97401.

Wipf & Stock
An Imprint of Wipf and Stock Publishers
199 W. 8th Ave., Suite 3
Eugene, OR 97401

www.wipfandstock.com

PAPERBACK ISBN: 978-1-6667-3626-7
HARDCOVER ISBN: 978-1-6667-9437-3
EBOOK ISBN: 978-1-6667-9438-0

Table of Contents

List of Tables viii
Foreword ix
Acknowledgments xii
Abbreviations xiii
Glossary of Key Terms xiv

Chapter 1 Introduction 1
  Introduction 1
  1.1 Phoenix's Background 7
    1.1.1 Characterizing Ministry and Mission in Phoenix of the Past 9
    1.1.2 Changes in Congregational Ways of Life 12
  1.2 Background to *Missio Dei* Theology 14
  1.3 Researcher Positionality 20
  1.4 Limited Literature 21
  1.5 Structure 27

Chapter 2 Methodology 31
  Introduction 31
  2.1 Research Question and Objectives 31
  2.2 Practical Theology 32
  2.3 Rescripting Methodology 34
  2.4 Four Voices 39
  2.5 Reflexivity 41
  2.6 Research Design and Process 41
    2.6.1 Initial Processes 42
    2.6.2 Semi-Structured Interviews 44
    2.6.3 Participant Observations 45
    2.6.4 Questionnaire 47
    2.6.5 Congregational Consultations 48
  2.7 Summary 49

Chapter 3 Characteristics of a Newbigin-like *Missio Dei* Theology 50
  Introduction 50
  3.1 Characteristics of a Newbigin-like *Missio Dei* Theology 52
    3.1.1 Theocentric Community-Focused Mission 52
    3.1.2 The Kingdom of God and the Goal of the *Missio Dei* 54
    3.1.3 Representatives of the Kingdom of God 55
    3.1.4 Missio Dei: Reframing Ecclesial Theology and Practices 56
    3.1.5 The Sending Nature of the Trinity 60
    3.1.6 A Missional Hermeneutic of the Bible 61
  3.2 Summary 63
Chapter 4 Congregational Changes 64
  Introduction 64
  4.1 Extent of Espousal of *Missio Dei* 66
  4.2 Indicators of *Missio Dei* Awareness 69
    4.2.1 Characteristic 1: Theocentric Concentration on the Community 69
    4.2.2 Characteristics 2 and 3: Kingdom as Destination and Representation 76
    4.2.3 Characteristics 4 and 5: The *Missio Dei* and the Trinity 81
    4.2.4 Characteristic 6: A Missional Hermeneutic of the Bible 86
  4.3 Summary 87
Chapter 5 Experiences of Change 90
  Introduction 90
  5.1 Group 1's Testimonies 91
  5.2 Group 2's Testimonies 101
  5.3 Analysis of Group 1 and 2's Testimonies 106
    5.3.1 Potential Causes of an Activist Theology of Mission 107
    5.3.2 Challenging Misunderstandings of Missional Ecclesiology 110
  5.4 Rescription 111
  5.5 Summary 114
Chapter 6 Discernment and Participation 116
  Introduction 116
  6.1 Prophetic Words in Context 116
  6.2 Analysis of Testimonies 119
    6.2.1 Prophetic Words of Comfort, Disruption, and Challenge 121
    6.2.2 Prophetic Words of Caution 126
    6.2.3 A Prophetic Word of Encouragement 133
    6.2.4 A Prophetic Impression 136
  6.3 Summary and Rescription 137

Chapter 7 Cost and Conflict 143
  Introduction 143
  7.1 Cost of Change Themes 144
    7.1.1 Differences in Theological Values 144
    7.1.2 Conflict and Coup Attempt 145
    7.1.3 Discouragement 149
    7.1.4 Churches-within-a-Church 150
    7.1.5 Deficits in Pastoral Care and Isolation 151
    7.1.6 Sacrifice and Burnout 151
  7.2 Analysis of Key Themes 153
    7.2.1 Potential Causes of Tension and Conflict 153
    7.2.2 Competing Ecclesial Frames 157
  7.3 Rescription 161
  7.4 Summary 163

Chapter 8 Conclusions and Recommendations 164
  Introduction 164
  8.1 Rescripting Missional Ecclesiology 165
    8.1.1 Rescripting a Social Trinitarian Version of Participation 165
    8.1.2 Rescripting Theologies of Being and Doing 170
    8.1.3 Rescripting Theologies of Discernment and Participation 174
    8.1.4 Rescripting Constraining Missional Ecclesiologies 179
  8.2 Recommendations 181
    8.2.1 Enriching Congregational Praxis 181
    8.2.2 Future Research 184
  8.3 Personal and Professional Development 184
  8.4 Research Contributions 188
  8.5 Concluding Remarks 188

Appendix A: Ethics Consent Confirmation 191
Appendix B: Congregational Interviews and Consultations 193
Appendix C: Sample Interview Questions 195
Appendix D: Qualitative Data 197
Appendix E: Congregational Questionnaire 200
Appendix F: Field Notes Template 209
Appendix G: Summary of Missional Projects 211
Appendix H: Churches of Christ Background 215
Bibliography 217

Tables

Table 1: Desired Direction of Congregational Change
Table 2: Members First Heard of *Missio Dei* at Phoenix
Table 3: Members Felt Inspired to Share their Faith because of *Missio Dei*
Table 4: Missional Projects

Foreword

By Dr. Clare Watkins,
University of Roehampton

We are living in a time and context in which the realities of church decline, variously understood, are an apparently enduring feature of our social landscape. Whether we consider the vibrancy of Christianity in terms of numbers of people actively engaged with churches, or with regard to the place of Christian voices in the public realm, institutional church decline is evident. Yet, as is increasingly well recognized, this (apparent) decline —which may more authentically be understood as a radical shift in the meaning and expression of faith in our context—also marks a creative and enlivening moment for many Christian communities, as the foundational call to *mission* is, yet again, rediscovered, and explored, in theology and practice, in new ways. This return to mission as what the church is *for* can be seen across all major Christian traditions. For all that we may have different ways of speaking—evangelism, evangelization, mission, liberation, service—the call on all church communities to reach out in new ways into a wider society in which the gospel is increasingly unknown is a point of profound ecumenical convergence and learning. At the same time, for all the wealth of literature, academic and pastoral, on how to be "mission-shaped" or "make missionary disciples," there appears on the ground to be a certain reluctance, even resistance, from a great many ordinary Christians. Church leaders and missiologists seek to find ever-more exciting, creative, and innovative ways to engage the whole people of God in mission; but in truth this is often an uphill struggle.

Andy Hardy makes an important contribution to this reality and its accompanying theologies by seeking, in his research as described in this book, to move precisely into that place of the church-in-ordinary which is so often presented as the problem for enthusiastic mission leaders and ministers: the church of the ordinary Christian, the lay person, the person in the pew. It is from these people—the vast majority of Christians—that he sets out to learn more than is formally taught in colleges training missionary leaders; and he is not disappointed. This inquiring of ordinary Christians' missiologies is not only an important pragmatic step from which Hardy is able to make important practical recommendations; but it is also, to my mind, a crucially theological step, and one which ultimately leads the attentive reader to questions of spirituality as an essential practice of mission. The theological rescripting which Hardy carries out (for all that, as he knows, I have significant problems with anything that looks like a social doctrine of the Trinity!) offers a way in which the ordinary theology of faithful lay people can be the genuine and fertile ground for a healthy, home-grown missiology. Such a missiology, because it is true to its context, can grow, be sustained, and flourish in ways that things learned from books and programs—however good and helpful—cannot.

In all this I am aware that I come form a very different theological and specifically ecclesiological tradition from that which is the context for this book and its research. As a result, I read it as something of an outsider: Hardy's own professed Free Church Catholic Ecclesiology is significantly different from my own Roman Catholic ecclesiology, especially when details of ecclesial embodiment of theologies of church, ministry, and mission are considered. Related to this, our different assumptions around mission, scripture, and ontology were things I felt in my reading, sometimes acutely. However, it is precisely this awareness of difference that makes the deep connection that is also there so significant; for it is in the attending to the voices of congregants, what I would call ordinary lay people, and reading these in challenging ways alongside the activities and rhetoric of formal leaders and their normativities, that our common, thoroughly ecumenical vision of mission and church for today's world can be felt. In this place—the testimonies, experiences, hurts, and inspiration of the person in the pew—there is something of the Spirit to be discerned, which is needed to refresh our ecclesial, missiological, and academic practices.

This is, I suggest, the real treasure of Andy Hardy's work here; it is, in the end, the treasure which is the *sensus fidei*—the "sensitivity to the faith"—which we can hear in the voices of lay Christians in the world.

What we learn here is the danger of any "blueprint missiology" (as Hardy describes it, in a nod to Nick Healy and his criticism of "blueprint ecclesiologies"). It is in the messy, real-life people who make up the church that we can learn from an authentic mission which draws on the realities of how faith is actually lived and understood in ordinary ways, in ways that are sustainable, and which do not drive people to activism and, ultimately exhaustion, disillusionment, or conflict. For if *missio Dei* missiology—to which both our ecclesial traditions would subscribe in some way—is about attention first to God's agency in God's mission, to the Holy Spirit, then this careful practice of attending and discernment must also be a primary characteristic of the Christian community itself, and shape its own inner relations and decision-making. Hardy has described for us the great wealth and wisdom that is to be discovered in the ordinary theology of Christian people, even in our mess, muddle, and struggles with one another.

I am, of course, something of a lay person myself, though perhaps not entirely ordinary in sociological terms! My great hope is that Christian leaders might read this book and allow themselves and their received practices and thinking to be challenged by it; and that lay people may recognize here our own essential wisdom, and be encouraged to participate fully in the complicated, messy work of discerning what the Spirit is calling us to. Then we might, as Christians together, take a step or two closer to participation in that mission of love and life which is God's own for and in our world.

Acknowledgments

THIS IS THE CULMINATION of five years of research. It would have been impossible to complete it without the input and support of numerous individuals and organizations. I want to thank them all, whether they are named here or not. I would like to thank my wife Jenny for her continuous support and encouragement. Without her backing I could not have completed it. I would also like to thank Phoenix church members and leaders for allowing me to undertake this investigation within their community. I appreciate the time they have sacrificed so that I could interact with them and learn from them.

I would also like to acknowledge the invaluable support that my supervisors, Dr. Andrew Rogers and Dr. John Moxon, have given to me. They have been helpful critical conversation partners who have enabled me to keep on pushing myself to investigate important angles to enhance my research, as well as to avoid pitfalls that would have undermined its potential credibility. I also acknowledge the helpful insights of Mr. Donald Morton and Dan Yarnell.

I am grateful to ForMission college for giving me the time to engage in and complete this investigation. One of the aims of my research has been to enhance college academic programs and my professional practice as the college's Director of Research. I believe the college's generosity has helped me to make an important contribution to the development of its courses.

I dedicate this research to all churches and faith-based organizations that faithfully seek to publicly engage in Christian witness and service to society for the common good.

Abbreviations

CWME	Commission of World Mission and Evangelism
FCC	Fellowship of Churches of Christ
FIEC	Fellowship of Independent Evangelical Churches
GOCN	Gospel and Our Culture Network
IMC	International Missionary Council
WCC	World Council of Churches

Glossary of Key Terms

Term	Explanation
Christology	The branch of theology that studies the person, role, and nature of Christ
Economic Trinity	The study of what God does
Emic Analysis	Seeks to analyze the insider perspectives of members of a particular community
Eschatology	Is concerned with the death, judgement, and final destiny of the human soul and humanity
Etic Analysis	Seeks to analyze emic categories of data with reference to other sources
Free Church Catholic Ecclesiology	The belief that all Free Churches are united through their confession of Christ as one catholic body. Churches from this tradition actively seek to remove barriers to Christian unity between differing ecclesial traditions
Missio Dei	Latin Phrase translated "mission of God" - God is understood to be the source, agent, and guide of all mission
Missional	A specific way some Christians identify themselves, which involves adopting the posture, thinking, and practices of a missionary so that they might influence others to become Christians
Missional Church	A church that seeks to equip congregants to participate in the *Missio Dei*, as well as to operate as a community that supports mission-minded people and new converts.

Missional Ecclesiology	The academic and theological study of churches that identify themselves as engaged in mission in their local contexts
Missional Leader	A person who aims to enable Christians to conceive of themselves as called to participate in the *Missio Dei* and who seeks to develop organizational structures to support the work of mission
Missional Project	A project that aims to engage in some form of Christian mission which involves social action for the common good and the promotion of the benefits of the Christian faith, and which meets specific needs in a community
Missional Theology	The process of critical theological reflection, integration, and contextualization of the elements of Christian mission into practice
Newbigin-like Theology	A theology that has strong similarities to Newbigin's theology. It need not be framed in Newbigin's actual words or phrases, but it must have identifiable links to a mediated theology that is based on Newbigin's theology. It must also be conceptually related to Newbigin's theology
Ontological Trinity	The study of who God is as a being
Ordinary Theology	Jeff Astley, the inventor of this phrase, defines it thusly: "Ordinary Christian theology is my phrase for the theologising of Christians who have received little or no theological education of a scholarly, academic, or systematic kind. 'Ordinary,' in this context, implies . . . non-academic."[1]
Perichoresis	Relates to the mutual relational interactions of the persons of the Trinity (Father, Son and Holy Spirit)
Soteriology	The study of the doctrinal formulations of salvation by a divine being, and how humans can cooperate with the saving work of God in their lives

---

1. Astley, *Ordinary Theology*, 56.

Theological Rescription	Mark Cartledge, who adapted Martin's use of this term, defines it as the investigator's efforts "to maintain a tension between a revised script that is both in continuity with and in discontinuity with the existing script. It seeks to move ordinary theology forward through a deeper analysis of its testimony mode and broader dialogue with the Christian theological tradition, illuminated by the insights of the social sciences."[2]
Works Righteousness	Is a kind of self-righteousness that believes human salvation can be earned and maintained by a person doing good works. It is also a righteousness thought to come by obedience to God

---

2. Cartledge, *Testimony in the Spirit*, 18; cf. Martin, "Undermining the Old Paradigms."

Chapter 1

Introduction

Introduction

THIS BOOK CONCENTRATES ON the impact of the communication of a Mission of God theology to a congregation named Phoenix. I will explain in this chapter why it is important to concentrate on this kind of theology because of its growing influence on congregations, that are seeking to equip congregants to come to view themselves as participants in God's mission. It will become evident in what follows that churches, like Phoenix, that have not historically concentrated on equipping their members for mission in the public square can face serious challenges when they seek to equip them for mission. I will argue that these challenges have not been given sufficient attention in the missional church literature. By paying attention to them much may be learned to avoid such challenges negatively impacting congregations in the future. I see my research as a contribution, made in all humility, to help enhance the work of respected forerunners who have been researching and writing in the field for much longer than I. My investigation seeks to provide a useful, detailed case example of what some of these challenges seem to be.

This book is based on my doctoral thesis, which I successfully completed by God's grace in 2021. I have sought to write it in an accessible style so as to make it relevant to a wider readership, not just specialists in the field.

Stated as a question, my research asks: What impact did the communication of a *Missio Dei* (meaning "mission of God") theology to Phoenix[1] church have on its members? This investigation concentrates on

---

1. A pseudonym.

the efforts of college[2] graduates at work in this British Reformed church, who completed BAs and MAs in mission and leadership (at the college for which I worked, henceforth termed "my college"[3]). These graduates sought to equip members to view themselves as Christian missionaries in their church's locality (2009–18).

It is important to note that until the employment of their new minister, Bill, in 2009, Phoenix did not seek to equip its members to engage in missionary work in its neighborhood. Bill (the senior pastor) and three other graduates (Jake, Lynda, and Becky) at work in Phoenix, learned their theology of *Missio Dei* from participation in my college's missional leadership programs. I engaged in fieldwork at the church from 2016–18.

I was part of my college's academic faculty at the time of the research and wanted to investigate the impact of *Missio Dei* theology, learned in its programs, on ordinary church members when it was communicated to them by college graduates. My research led to some key insights which made it clear that college programs, and much of the missional church literature, potentially need to be challenged for making some rather idealistic assumptions about the ease with which churches can be helped to become focused on local mission.

As a pilot study I initially engaged in research at Phoenix to evaluate if college programs were enabling graduates to equip congregations to become focused on mission. I noticed that a third of Phoenix's members had left the church seemingly because some of them had reacted negatively to the experience of the congregation becoming focused on mission. Based on pilot research I found that complex tensions had developed between members because of the church's new missional focus. This challenged a common assumption, often found in the missional church literature, that churches that become mission-focused will generally benefit because

---

2. The college I work for first began in 2002 with an MA program in Missional Leadership, through an organization called Together in Mission (TiM). It has about 200 students enrolled in its undergraduate and postgraduate programs at any given time (source anonymized to protect identity of college). It has trained about 1,200 leaders since it began. Most students are not part of the college's Fellowship of Churches of Christ denomination.

3. I anonymize the name of my college, as I do not believe it is fair to draw attention to it. Moreover, what I write regarding enhancements that might be made to its curriculum could be applied to other Christian colleges which offer similar programs in the areas of mission and leadership. Hence, not officially naming the college does not impact the value of what I write about its theology, and its courses because of the potential broader application.

they will help their members engage in contextually relevant ministry in society.[4] The evidence provided by some of Phoenix's members suggested the need for a critical rereading of overly optimistic assumptions of this kind. In later chapters, it will become evident that my research challenges idealistic assumptions found in the formal literature, which seem to miss the difficulties congregations face when they change from being inwardly focused to becoming outwardly focused on local mission. In-depth accounts of congregants' theological reasons for leaving churches due to missional changes taking place in them are missing for British-based churches.[5]

The need for churches to concentrate on mission has become a matter of the survival of the Christian faith itself in Britain, especially among its British-born population.[6] For example, the *British Social Attitudes Survey* predicts that Anglicanism will disappear in Britain by 2033 if current trends continue.[7] Rich's account of the *Grace Project's* findings indicates that Anglican churches are growing where they serve their local communities, but current growth rates are not making enough impact to halt the more general trend of decline.[8] The overall rate of decline in church attendance has remained constant at between 6 percent and 7 percent per decade since the 1950s.[9] Brierley Consultancy predicts that if current trends continue, then by 2064 no British-born person will attend a Christian church.[10] However, the book, *UK Church Statistics,* indicates that it is likely that a smaller Christian presence will remain in Britain—probably

---

4. Cf. Barrett et al., *Treasure in Clay Jars*; Guder, *Missional Church*; Rich, *Growing Good*; Thiessen et al., "What Is a Flourishing Congregation?"; Van Gelder and Zscheile, *Missional Church in Perspective*; Van Gelder and Zscheile, *Participating in God's Mission*, 38.

5. Having made this critique, it needs to be noted that Barrett et al.'s research has the merit of indicating that some churches had experienced tensions as a result of engaging in a missional change process; cf. Barrett et al., *Treasure in Clay Jars*, 12–17. It was weakened by not giving voice to members' theological views about these changes.

6. Cf. Faith Survey, "Christianity in the UK."

7. Cf. Faith Survey, "Christianity in the UK."

8. Rich, *Growing Good*; cf. Faith Survey, "Christianity in the UK."

9. Brierley Consultancy, "Where Is the Church Going?," 4; Robinson and Smith, *Invading Secular Space*, 15–38. It is to be noted that one-third of traditional churches are declining in membership in Britain (i.e., Anglican and Catholic congregations). Two-thirds are growing, among which are Pentecostal and new churches; cf. Brierley Consultancy, "Where Is the Church Going?," 8.

10. Faith Survey, "Christianity in the UK."

made up of Christians who have migrated here.[11] Predictions of this kind have led most denominations to turn their attention to engaging in some form of church growth program or mission work.[12] Yet, is there enough of a will among Christian churches to pay the price for missional change to occur within them if it means losing members that do not want to engage in missionary activity, as was the case at Phoenix (cf. §4.1; 7.1.2)?[13]

Further research will be required if we want to learn more about the relative impacts of differing versions of missional ecclesiology on congregations. There are increasing numbers of empirical studies that concentrate on Fresh Expressions of church or Emerging churches, but there are none that concentrate on the impact of a Newbigin-like *Missio Dei* theology on the theological views of Reformed church members.[14] Lesslie Newbigin's work has had quite a strong influence on much of the missional church thinking of practitioners and writers over the past forty to fifty years. Hence, it seems relevant to consider how Newbigin-like versions of *Missio Dei* theology have influenced churches like Phoenix, given its pervasive influence. Due to a lack of concentration on the influence of Newbigin-like theologies on church members, my investigation seeks to start filling this gap.

This is important to do, as there is evidence that some influential Reformed scholars are building on Newbigin's missional ecclesiology to help congregations become mission focused.[15] My investigation provides a critical assessment of the impact that a Newbigin-like theology has been having on this particular Reformed church, which may help Reformed networks of churches to evaluate the strengths and weaknesses of a Newbigin-like missional ecclesiology and its potential value to them.

---

11. Brierley Consultancy, "Where Is the Church Going?," 3, 4.

12. Moynagh and Harrold, *Church for Every Context*, ix–xvii; Greene and Robinson, *Metavista*, xvi–xxi; Cray, *Mission-Shaped Church*.

13. Mission work is no longer only about going overseas but also focuses on Britain as a mission field; cf. Robinson and Smith, *Invading Secular Space*, 15–38; Kimball, *Emerging Church*, 57–66.

14. Tueno, "Built on the Word"; Wigner, "Spiritual Borrowing"; Gibbs and Bolger, *Emerging Church*.

15. Cf. §1.4; Franke, "Teaching Missional Theology"; Stetzer, *Planting Missional Churches*, 23; Paas, "Leadership in Mission"; Smith, Evangelical Evaluation of Key Elements. It is to be noted that there are numerous Reformed churches in Britain which makes my research relevant to help them; cf. Faith Survey, "Christianity in the UK."

My investigation concentrates on the ordinary theologies of Phoenix's members. Astley coined the term "ordinary theology" and explains it as follows:

> Ordinary Christian theology is my phrase for the theologizing of Christians who have received little or no theological education of a scholarly, academic, or systematic kind. "Ordinary," in this context, implies . . . non-academic.[16]

I argue that the research literature needs to be tempered by more investigations into the ordinary theologizing of congregants regarding the *Missio Dei* to provide sources of grassroots evidence of what members in missional churches believe, value, and practice. This will arguably contribute to the development of the understanding of a variety of local ordinary missional theologies, Newbigin-like or otherwise. A body of pieces of research of this kind might then make it possible to predict which versions of missional ecclesiology are best suited to differing ecclesial traditions.[17] This is important to do, as my research account indicates that it can take a number of years for congregants to integrate an alien missional church theology into their ordinary theologies. I will argue that by paying attention to a church's members' ordinary theologies, that develop in reaction to the communication of a *Missio Dei* theology to them, it will become possible to help them integrate this kind of theology into their existing espoused theologies. It is important to highlight that my research is only concentrating on the impact of a Newbigin-like version of *Missio Dei* on a Reformed church, not on other expressions of this theology.

My college, and its denomination—Fellowship of Churches of Christ (FCC)[18]—draw on the missiology of Bishop Lesslie Newbigin[19] and developments of Newbigin scholarship in organizations like the Gospel and Our Culture Network (GOCN).[20] Newbigin's ecumenical theology

---

16. Astley, *Ordinary Theology*, 56; cf. Astley and Francis, *Exploring Ordinary Theology*; Ward, *Introducing Practical Theology*, 58–60.

17. Cf. Tueno, "Built on the Word"; Wigner, "Spiritual Borrowing"; Barrett et al., *Treasure in Clay Jars*; Gibbs and Bolger, *Emerging Church*.

18. http://fellowshipofchurchesofchrist.wordpress.com. It is worth noting that at the time of going to press, this website was in the process of being redone, and so readers might or might not be able to access it right away.

19. Newbigin was not an FCC minister.

20. Cf. Guder, *Missional Church*; Van Gelder and Zscheile, *Missional Church in Perspective*; Van Gelder, *Missional Church in Context*. It is to be noted that I am an

is attractive to FCC and my college because it emphasizes the need for partnerships between different denominations to be forged so that they might work together in the task of mission in the West (§1.3; appendix H).[21] Both organizations share the conviction that missional churches need to present the claims of the gospel of Christ as a public truth to postmodern society.[22] This requires a critique of postmodern assertions that all truth claims are relative.[23] This is probably one reason why Newbigin's version of *Missio Dei* theology proved attractive to graduates at work in Phoenix, because it resonated with their evangelical Christology and soteriology, which makes Christ central to human salvation.[24]

According to Van Gelder and Zscheile, the Newbigin-like version of GOCN challenges churches to become *completely* focused on mission in "everything they do."[25] It is this emphatic universal call for *every* Christian to view themselves as missionaries which has proved challenging to some of Phoenix's members.[26] My investigation reveals valuable insights that come from congregants' ordinary theologies that have reacted to a mediated theology of participation in the *Missio Dei*.[27]

---

ordained minister in the FCC.

21. Cf. Newbigin, *Open Secret*, 150–53, 159; Newbigin, *One Body*; Weston, "Lesslie Newbigin," 14, 15. It is to be noted that this is also a feature of the theology of Fresh Expressions of the church; cf. Moynagh and Harrold, *Church for Every Context*, ix–xxi.

22. Newbigin, *Mission and the Crisis*, 103–15.

23. Newbigin, *Mission and the Crisis*, 14–26.

24. Cf. Grudem, *Systematic Theology*, 569–70. It is to be noted that Grudem's Christology and soteriology are based on evangelical theology, which places Christ as the only means of human salvation; cf. Grudem, *Systematic Theology*, 569–70. Debates regarding inclusivist and exclusivist views of salvation are a common part of missiology; cf. Karkkainen, *Trinity and Religious Pluralism*, 2–4; D'Costa, *Christianity and World Religions*, 3–33; Tennent, *Invitation to World Missions*, 191–228. Grudem's view is exclusivist, which broadly aligns with Reformed evangelical churches which are part of the FIEC; cf. Grudem, *Systematic Theology*, 569–70; FIEC, "Beliefs."

25. Van Gelder and Zscheile, *Missional Church in Perspective*, 4.

26. Cf. Van Gelder and Zscheile, *Missional Church in Perspective*; Van Gelder, *Missional Church in Context*, 12–43; Guder, *Missional Church*; Roxburgh and Romanuk, *Missional Leader*, 143–64.

27. I suggest that other versions of missional ecclesiology, such as those espoused by Fresh Expressions of church, need to evaluate the impact of their versions of *Missio Dei* on congregants' ordinary theologies. A key question may be: What negative and positive impacts has *Missio Dei* had on them? cf. Moynagh and Harrold, *Church for Every Context*, 104–7; Tueno, "Built on the Word."

Newbigin-like versions of missional ecclesiology are increasingly becoming influential with leaders of differing church traditions in Britain,[28] Australia,[29] and North America.[30] [31] This increase in influence makes my research relevant to the broader field of missional church studies. Future research will hopefully reveal how the impact of this particular Newbigin-like version compares and contrasts with other versions.

This chapter provides an explanatory framework and rationale that will clarify the aims of this investigation related to my professional practice context and the academic literature. I hope the reader will obtain important insights into the value of focusing on the professional practice context, as it is important to keep in mind how our perspectives about our work can impact the way we interpret what we believe we know about the things we investigate and write about. In this book, I aim to be highly reflexive so as to reveal how my perspectives impacted my interpretation of what I found out about Phoenix's members' reactions to the communication of *Missio Dei* theology to them. Reflexivity is important to congregational research of this kind, as it hopefully will enable the reader to become more aware of how and why I interpreted the research data in the way I did. In my view, research requires an ongoing conversation with research subjects to ensure it represents perspectives other than the investigator's.

This chapter aims to: (1) provide a background to Phoenix church; (2) explain the background to Newbigin's *Missio Dei* theology; (3) explain my subject-position to the research; (4) discuss limitations in the GOCN research literature, and (5) explain the structure of the book.

1.1 Phoenix's Background

As is common in congregational studies, the background to Phoenix church will be provided.[32] Phoenix is located on the boundary between two contrasting wards of a city in the United Kingdom. One of the wards

---

28. For instance, through FCC and my college and their partnerships with churches and Christian organizations from other traditions.

29. Through Churches of Christ.

30. Through GOCN, which is not a Churches of Christ organization.

31. Greene and Robinson, *Metavista*, 178–79; cf. Van Gelder and Zscheile, *Missional Church in Perspective*.

32. Cf. Ammerman et al., *Studying Congregations*; Rogers, *Congregational Hermeneutics*; McClintock Fulkerson, *Places of Redemption*.

is middle class and affluent, the other is among the top 5 percent of the most poverty-stricken city-wards in Britain. There were approximately 120 members on the church's books during my fieldwork (cf. §4.1). Membership was evenly balanced between men and women, ranging from eighteen to ninety years of age. Approximately seventy children and young people also attended. The congregation's demographic was mainly middle class and white Caucasian.

The evangelistic campaigns of Edward Jeffreys (1928–38) led to Phoenix being established during the 1930s.[33] It, like some other congregations planted by Jeffreys, chose to align itself with the Reformed Evangelical tradition.[34] Phoenix eventually settled within the Fellowship of Independent Evangelical Churches (FIEC), which serves a large constituency of over 600 Reformed congregations.[35] Warner characterizes FIEC as a "leading" Reformed "Calvinist-exclusivist network of churches."[36] It is exclusive in the sense that it promotes separation between the church and the world, and is suspicious of other theological traditions. However, Phoenix seems to be moving away from this kind of exclusivism, with some members perhaps becoming "cautiously open conservatives," whilst others are perhaps "progressives."[37] Some of those who were exclusivists have left the church (cf. §7.1.2). It is important to recognize this shift because it may be argued that this exclusivist outlook had an unexpected impact on the congregation of the past. It had been much more suspicious of welcoming outsiders into its community. This may be one reason why the pastor and elders were positioned as the only ones responsible for ministry and mission within and outside of the congregation.[38] This practice apparently helped Phoenix to maintain tight control of who could join the congregation, by making leaders primarily responsible for the conversion and vetting of newcomers.

During my fieldwork, I encountered a complex range of responses to the missional changes that had occurred, and were occurring, in Phoenix. It is this complexity of reactions that make this investigation valuable (cf. §3.1). Some longstanding members reacted strongly to changes in the

33. Watts et al., *Edward Jeffries, Healing Evangelist*, 104.
34. Cf. Watts et al., *Edward Jeffries, Healing Evangelist*, 104–5.
35. FIEC, "Who We Are"; Warner, *Reinventing English Evangelicalism*, 40, 247.
36. Warner, *Reinventing English Evangelicalism*, 40, 247.
37. Cf. Warner, *Reinventing English Evangelicalism*, 247.
38. A few members occasionally posted tracts through the letterboxes of local homes as a form of evangelism.

approaches to ministry and mission in the congregation. These changes will be explored by comparing and contrasting the approaches in old and new Phoenix to ministry and mission.

1.1.1 *Characterizing Ministry and Mission in Phoenix of the Past*

Caspian, a member for forty years, indicated that in old Phoenix (pre-2009) missional activities were not considered to be something that every member should practice. It was primarily the role of the paid pastor, or those sent to engage in missionary activities elsewhere. The few members that were considered to have an aptitude for mission were treated fascinatingly. Caspian commented:

> gifted members were sent away from the congregation to serve elsewhere rather than in the congregation. We used our resources to train them and then sent them out (Appendix B:4).[39]

Phoenix's version of a Reformed model of pastoral leadership seemingly contributed to distancing its members from personal missionary engagement in their local community. Belinda had grown up in the church and remembered old Phoenix's way of life well. She commented, "Before we were a lot more closed off because we were part of this community." By "this community" she meant the church as an exclusive group, not the wider neighborhood. Desmond, a member for ten years, remembered some longstanding members standing up during services saying:

> The Great Commission[40] isn't for everyone, it just applied to the apostles as missionaries. (Appendix B:28)

Views like this were a common feature during the early years of the church's missional change process (2009–15). Caspian provided an interesting portrayal of how members of the past had understood their roles and those of leaders:

> at the time the picture was, "This is a fellowship, in the fellowship there will be some who are equipped to preach, there will be some who are equipped to be missionaries [i.e. overseas missionaries], and then there's everybody else. Everybody else's

---

39. Members like this were sent to train as pastors in other British churches, or as overseas missionaries.

40. Matt 28:16–20 is most often referenced as an example of the "Great Commission" (cf. John 20:19–23; Luke 24:45–49).

job is to bring people here so they can hear the gospel." So, for example, that was my mentality. (Appendix B:4)

Apparently, congregants understood their role to be that of suppliers of potential recruits for the professionally trained pastor to convert to Christianity at visitors' services. It was also his role to catechize new converts. Members acted as supporters of the professional pastor but not as actual participants in the work of conversion. They were not encouraged to view themselves as personally responsible to engage in local mission, except to invite potential recruits to the church. At visitors' services members would also fulfill the roles of providing food for meals, hot drinks, and a hospitable welcoming atmosphere. Once newcomers became members of the church, they would then take part in similar kinds of activities. Caspian explained the impact this model of ministry had on him:

> Once I had got married our nephew came to stay with us and went with us to a visitors' service. He spoke to us afterward and said, "I really experienced God in the service today." I didn't have anything to help him with, because my model was come to the church and get saved. So we took him to a local church near where he lived, which was a disaster. And, you know, that highlighted to me the inadequacy of that model. The mentality of the church was, "We pay someone to do everything." (Appendix B:4)

One consequence of this model seemed to be that preaching concentrated on what Caspian termed a "needs-based gospel," which focused on meeting the needs of the congregation.[41] Caspian commented on its impact on members:

> It is sort of a childlike thing, "Here are my needs—fulfill them." This is a sort of consequence of having a very needs-based gospel in the past (Appendix B:4).

Caspian seemed to interpret this needs-based gospel to mean that members were not equipped by leaders to view themselves as ministers in their own right.[42] Members were expected to get their spiritual needs met

---

41. Having a paid pastor need not lead to developing this situation in a church.

42. The priesthood of all believers is commonly associated by many evangelicals with all Christians having responsibility for engaging in a ministry of some type. Interestingly, Edward Jefferies did not espouse the doctrine of the "priesthood of all believers," which may explain why Phoenix had not in the past equipped members

by church leaders through preaching, worship, and pastoral care.[43] This view of ministry had made a significant impact on members like Belinda. She commented:

> Ultimately, I feel that it is not my job to convert people. If Jesus is going to move in their lives he will find a way of doing it. (Appendix B:16)

Belinda did not want to take part in the church's missional activities. She wanted the church to return to its former model of ministry, which did not focus on members becoming local missionaries. She had positive memories of the close-knit family atmosphere that the church had particularly enjoyed before the changes. Based on her testimony, and others like it, it was evident that some members were content with the church's old way of life and did not want to embrace the newer missional church outlook (cf. §7.1.2).

However, a married couple named Drummond and Jessica were pleased about the missional changes in the church. They provided an insight into how they had sought to engage in witnessing activities before the church's change journey. They provided an interesting contrast between what they had done in terms of Christian witness in their old church compared to when they first joined Phoenix in the 1980s. They had both been raised in a Reformed church in another city. This other church had encouraged them to use their children's ministry abilities in local work with children. When they joined Phoenix, they sought to engage in outreach with unchurched children in the church's immediate neighborhood. Interestingly, they were sent by the pastor to work on a Sunday school project in another ward of the city that specialized in this area of children's work. They commented:

> *Drummond:* The Sunday school used to bring in children from the poor estate by minibus .(Appendix B:10)
>
> *Jessica:* Yes, but not to Phoenix but the other one, didn't they? So that was separate from Phoenix. (Appendix B:11)

Their comments indicated how in the past Phoenix had generally distanced itself from integrating local unchurched children or their families into its congregation. From what I could gather, this was because the

---

to act as local missionaries; cf. Watts et al., *Edward Jeffries, Healing Evangelist*, 67, 68.

43. It included the traditional evangelical practice of members reading the Bible in their daily devotionals; cf. Foster, *Streams of Living Water*, 185–234.

church's version of Reformed theology was very narrowly concentrated on only official officeholders, like the pastor and elders, engaging in ministry or local mission work. Paas's research indicates that the structures of some Reformed churches can be very much like this because they do not recognize other forms of ministry except those of the pastor, elders, or deacons.[44] According to Lucy, there was also another reason why members were not engaged in local mission work:

> Ten years [ago] we had a commuter church in an interesting position on the edge of a very deprived estate, and it had always been a commuter church, including myself. And you had some keen people, well mostly me, and one other, who were keen about reaching the area. And that was really it, I was out on the estate chatting with people, but really no one else was. (Appendix B:7)

I came across other testimonies similar to Lucy, Caspian, Drummond, and Jessica's, which indicated that members were deliberately not encouraged by leaders to engage in local mission work. It was only a few in the past who had seemed keen to do something in the church's neighborhood, or the actual city. This situation significantly changed during Bill's tenure.

1.1.2 Changes in Congregational Way of Life

Table 1: Desired Direction of Congregational Change		
Members Not Engaged in Local Mission	→	Members Engaged in Local Mission
Leaders Solely Responsible for Local Mission	→	Leaders Equip Members to be Responsible for Local Mission
Church Inwardly, Not Outwardly, Focused	→	Church Outwardly, Not Inwardly, Focused

Table 1 illustrates the kind of changes that graduate leaders aspired to bring about at Phoenix in the roles of members and leaders (i.e., moving from left to right). However, it would be far too simplistic to suggest the table represents what actually occurred within the church. This is because members reacted in complex ways to the mediation of *Missio Dei*

---

44. Paas, "Leadership in Mission."

theology. Subsequent data chapters will indicate how some congregants seemed to shift from left to right, as they began to focus on missionary work in their neighborhoods. Later analysis will also illustrate sources of tension and conflict that seem to be traceable to changes in the roles of leaders and members, due to changes in the *modus operandi* of the congregation (cf. chs. 5–7).

The left-hand column of Table 1 seeks to partially summarize the situation that existed in older Phoenix before Bill's ministry. A particular comment made by Bill summarized well the changes in the ethos of ministry represented in the table:

> The first thing I had to get to grips with . . . was, that it was not my purpose to be chaplain to the dynasty.[45] It was to equip God's people for works of service. So, these two things started to emerge in the first year, which was pushed back by several key people. I wasn't paid to do all of the work . . . and to look after the dynasty while I did that. So those two things needed to be challenged before any missional conversation could even have a hope. (Appendix B:5)

Bill challenged the church's tradition, which had theologically positioned the pastor and elders as solely responsible for ministry and local mission. It took time for some congregants to develop a new understanding of the roles of leaders and members. A significant number did not accept them (cf. §4.1; 7.1.2). Bill believed that a new leadership structure was necessary, which required the development of a church culture that concentrated on participation in local mission. Leaders would be repositioned as collaborators with members. They would need to encourage congregants to explore their abilities to help them to discern what God might be calling them to do in mission. This required that members develop a new missional mindset, which placed the focus on congregants participating with God in mission in society. It challenged the dynasty to release control of the church's local mission work so members could engage in work in the neighborhood. Later data chapters will provide thick accounts that will trace congregants' reactions to change.

---

45. By dynasty, Bill meant some of the elders of the congregation who wanted to maintain the ethos of ministry practiced in old Phoenix.

1.2 Background to *Missio Dei* Theology

The historical story of how *Missio Dei* became linked to the work of the church is important to outline in terms of the aims of this book. There are some excellent accounts of how this came about. Flett's published PhD thesis is one of the most recent contributions.[46] It draws on the historical theological roots of Trinitarian theology, and twentieth-century missiological developments that led to the *Missio Dei* becoming linked to the church.[47] *Missio Dei* can be traced back to Augustine (354–430) as well as Aquinas (1224–74), who, in the *Summa Theologica*, portrayed mission as a matter of divine agency alone.[48] Aquinas's understanding of *Missio Dei* meant that it was not associated with the churches' work or the activities of missionaries, because it was assumed to be only God's work.[49] However, Neill points out that this assessment is not fully accurate as the Jesuits in the sixteenth century used the term *Missio Dei* to speak of engaging in mission.[50] Yet this was unusual, and overall the language of *Missio Dei* was not used during the Reformation in terms of the church and its missionary work.

However, this did not mean that churches planted by colonial missionaries during the eighteenth and nineteenth centuries failed to concentrate on engaging in mission with non-Christian peoples in the mission fields.[51] Yet, these churches struggled to successfully communicate the Christian faith to indigenous peoples because they were modeled on an emerging form of cultural Christianity which was better suited for the Christendom context of Europe.[52] Arguably, this made their European version of Christianity difficult to relate to for non-Western peoples. This partly explains why William Carey called in 1806 for world missionary conferences to be held every ten years, to place more emphasis on the

---

46. Flett, *Witness of God*; Bosch, *Transforming Mission*; Engelsviken, "*Missio Dei*."

47. Flett, *Witness of God*.

48. Thomas Aquinas, "Summa Theologica" 1.43.2; cf. Spencer, *SCM Studyguide*, 9, 10; Wesley, "Church as Missionary," 22, 23; Engelsviken, "*Missio Dei*"; Kirk, *What Is Mission?*

49. Cf. Spencer, *SCM Studyguide*, 9, 10.

50. Neill, *History of Christian Missions*, 202–4; cf. Spencer, *SCM Studyguide*, 9, 10.

51. I only include a discussion of mission history in the eighteenth through twenty-first centuries because references to key events, beliefs, and practices in them helped to demonstrate how missional ecclesiology became linked to *Missio Dei* theology. In §1.4 there will be a discussion of mission related to the Reformation.

52. Cf. Latourette, "By Way of Inclusive Retrospect," 26.

actual context of the work of mission in the mission fields themselves.[53] Carey's vision for world mission conferences was not realized in the nineteenth century. But in 1825, some regional conferences began to be hosted.[54] These regional conferences helped to highlight the need for the planting of indigenous churches. For example, Henry Venn, the General Secretary of the Church Missionary Society (1841–73), formulated an approach to mission which focused on the planting of mission churches, based on what was termed "the three-self principle."[55] The three principles were, "self-governance," "self-propagation," and "self-support," which aimed at enabling indigenous churches to become more independent of Western mission-sending organizations.[56]

By 1877, Livingstone Nevius, a missionary at work in China, adapted Venn's formula, leading to it being officially adopted in 1892 at the Shanghai Conference of Christian Missions.[57] It required that Chinese churches be planted and led by indigenous Chinese leaders. This new focus contributed toward the development of a local ecclesiocentric view of mission. Missionary thinking was changing from mission being a specialist subdivision of the churches' work, carried out by parachurch missionary organizations, toward it becoming more central to the churches' local work.[58]

In 1910, the first World Missionary Conference (WMC) was hosted in Edinburgh.[59] Out of this meeting a Continuation Committee was commissioned to plan and implement what was to become International Missionary Councils (IMC).[60] During the early IMC councils, a localized ecclesiocentric view of mission was adopted in a way that it had not been during the nineteenth century. For example, at the 1928 IMC in Jerusalem the theme of the conference was described thus: "the task of the Christian Church . . . both to carry the message of Christ to the

---

53. Cf. Haldar, "Towards Convergence," 1.

54. Cf. Haldar, "Towards Convergence," 1.

55. Cf. Ott and Strauss, *Encountering Theology of Mission*, 115.

56. Cf. Ott and Strauss, *Encountering Theology of Mission*, 115.

57. Cf. Terry, "Indigenous Churches," 483–85.

58. Cf. Beaver, "History of Mission Strategy," 58–72; Latourette, "By Way of Inclusive Retrospect," 26. It is to be noted that §1.4 highlights that Anabaptists sought to engage in mission in Europe.

59. Cf. Kim, *Joining in with the Spirit*, 20, 21.

60. Cf. Haldar, "Towards Convergence," 1, 2.

individual soul and to create a Christian civilization."[61] In the following IMC conference, held in Tambaram (Madras) in India in 1938, this view of mission was reinforced and developed further.[62] Yet there were concerns about this perspective. For example, the Methodist theologian E. Stanley Jones was deeply troubled that making the church responsible for mission would undermine the work of missionary organizations.[63] He was concerned that their concentration would move from focusing on the coming of the kingdom of God to the political affairs of the church.[64] Reactions like this were amplified by the time of the Whitby IMC meeting in Canada in 1947.[65] The delegates at this conference, in the aftermath of World War II, were much less enthusiastic about espousing the superiority of Western Christian mission-sending churches or organizations. This was because delegates were concerned about public perceptions that Western Christian nations had failed to avoid the evils of the war. Hence, how could they claim Christian moral superiority to the peoples of non-Western cultures?[66] Instead, the council acknowledged that mission did not belong to the church but to God.[67] By the time of the IMC meeting held in Willingen, Germany in 1952, concerns about promoting an ecclesiocentric view of mission were intensified. In the Protestant tradition, this led to strengthening the perspective that all mission was in the hands of God and not human institutions such as the church.[68]

It was at Willingen that the sending nature of the Trinity was first linked to the church as one of the instruments of the *Missio Dei*, rather than the church being solely responsible to promote it.[69] This was an important shift because the church was now not placed in the controlling

---

61. Cf. Kim, *Joining in with the Spirit*, 23, 24; Hogg, *Ecumenical Foundations*, 297–98; Davies and Conway, *World Christianity in the 20th Century*, 19.

62. Cf. Briggs, "Tambaram Conference," 928.

63. Cf. Jones, "Where Madras Missed the Way," 86–89.

64. Cf. Jones, "Where Madras Missed the Way," 86–89.

65. Kim, *Joining in with the Spirit*, 24.

66. Cf. Kim, *Joining in with the Spirit*, 24.

67. Cf. Kim, *Joining in with the Spirit*, 24.

68. Cf. Kim, *Joining in with the Spirit*, 24, 25; Bevans and Schroeder, *Prophetic Dialogue*, 57.

69. Bevans and Schroeder, *Prophetic Dialogue*, 57, 58; Bosch, *Transforming Mission*, 389–93; Engelsviken, "Missio Dei"; Flett, *Witness of God*, 17, 18.

position to direct missionary work. Instead, the church was to be a participant in what God was already at work doing in the world.[70]

The received history of how *Missio Dei* influenced Willingen suggests that Barth's theology of the Trinity was mediated to its delegates by his student Hartenstein. It is argued by notable scholars like Bosch that Barth's theology helped to forge a participatory theology of the *Missio Dei*.[71] For example, the final report of Willingen linked *Missio Dei* to the Trinity, positing: (1) that the ownership of mission needed to shift from the church to the triune God, it was God's mission; (2) *Missio Dei* was at the heart of God's nature, and that the "obligation of the church comes from the love of God in His active relationship with" humanity;[72] and (3) participating in the *Missio Dei* makes the church an instrument of the divine mission, but not its owner.[73]

This received history regarding Barth's influence is challenged by Flett.[74] He argues that up until the time of Willingen, and for seven years afterward, Barth did not once use the term *Missio Dei*,[75] nor did he ever claim that God was a missionary being by nature.[76] Indeed, Hartenstein, who attended some of the IMC meetings before Willingen, as well as the ones at Willingen, claimed that Barth was not a "friend" of mission.[77] In fact, Barth's dialectical Trinitarian theology refused to acknowledge that humans had any part to play in the reconciling work of God, as this would compromise divine agency.[78] Flett claims there is no evidence that Hartenstein introduced *Missio Dei* to the Willingen delegates.[79] Newbigin, who wrote the final Willingen report as part of a small working committee, may have been largely responsible for its Trinitarian language.[80] Whichever version is adopted, it seems doubtful that Barth's dialectical

---

70. Cf. Flett, *Witness of God*, 44, 45; Bevans and Schroeder, *Prophetic Dialogue*, 57, 58.

71. Bosch, *Transforming Mission*, 390; Kim, *Joining in with the Spirit*, 28.

72. Cf. Kim *Joining in with the Spirit*, 28.

73. Cf. Kim *Joining in with the Spirit*, 29.

74. Flett, *Witness of God*.

75. In fact, he never used it.

76. Flett, *Witness of God*, 12.

77. Cf. Flett, *Witness of God*, 13.

78. Cf. Flett, *Witness of God*, 16.

79. Cf. Flett, *Witness of God*, 15.

80. Cf. Flett, *Witness of God*, 15.

theology of the time would have favored the missiology of the conference's final report, which was drafted by Newbigin.[81]

Indeed, the view of the church as a participant in the *Missio Dei* was not the only missiology version discussed at Willingen. The Dutch theologian Hoekendijk introduced another view which fundamentally separated the *Missio Dei* from the work of the church.[82] Hoekendijk's view obtained dominance in the conferences that followed Willingen, such as at the 1958 IMC meeting held in Achimota, Ghana. It also influenced the 1963 World Council of Churches (WCC) meeting in Mexico City.[83] Bassham argues that at the 1963 New Mexico conference, it was said that Christians must "discover a shape of Christian obedience being written for them by what God is already actively doing in the structures of the city's life outside of the Church."[84] The churches' role in mission was being minimized in favor of mission becoming concentrated on improving society, rather than on communicating the gospel to its peoples.[85]

This rejection of the ecclesiocentric view, or the Willingen view of the church as an instrument of the *Missio Dei*, meant that the churches' role in mission was seriously undermined in future conferences. Evangelicals increasingly disassociated themselves from the WCC and CWME because of what they thought of as theological liberalism.[86] Instead, they became part of an evangelical equivalent known as the Lausanne Movement, following its first inaugural congress in 1974.[87] Lausanne's evangelical model of participation in the *Missio Dei*, unlike the secular cosmocentric view of Hoekendijk, was Christocentric.[88] It emphasized the communication of the gospel to all peoples of the world, as well as the importance of seeking to promote justice when injustice and evil were promoted by human institutions.[89] The church needed to play a

---

81. Cf. Flett, *Witness of God*, 12–18.

82. Hoekendijk, "Church in Missionary Thinking."

83. Cf. Flett, *Witness of God*, 36–38; Hoekendijk, "Church in Missionary Thinking." It is to be noted that by 1963 IMC was affiliated with the WCC and its Commission on World Mission and Evangelism (CWME).

84. Bassham, *Mission Theology*, 65.

85. Cf. Arthur, "*Missio Dei* and the Mission of the Church"; Davies, "Ecumenism," 127–31.

86. Cf. Davies, "Ecumenism," 130, 131.

87. Cf. Lausanne Movement, "Lausanne Movement's Unique Calling."

88. Cf. Davies, "Ecumenism," 130, 131.

89. Cf. Woolnough and Ma, *Holistic Mission*.

primary role in the formation of disciples, who were themselves called to participate in the divine mission.[90]

Interestingly, the development of the Lausanne Movement led to evangelicals and the ecumenicals (of the WCC) increasingly working together because evangelicals began to develop a holistic understanding of mission.[91] This holistic version did not simply focus on conversion, but also on seeking to improve the lives of people in the world.[92] Thus, a theology of holistic mission which concentrated on social and political issues as well as the communication of the Christian faith helped some evangelicals and ecumenicals to join forces in the work of mission.[93]

Catholic mission-focused theology also significantly influenced ecumenicals and evangelicals alike. Vatican II (1962–65) made a substantial contribution, not only to Catholic mission-concentrated theology but also to the broader ecumenical understanding of the church as "the people of God" called to participate in the "universal *Missio Dei*."[94] It also contributed to the holistic mission theology of the Lausanne Movement. Bevans and Schroeder comment:

> The church is "missionary by its very nature," Vatican II taught. If the church is to be the church today, it must also share and continue in God's healing, fulfilling, challenging, and redemptive work. It must truly be God's missionary people, the Body of Christ in the world, the presence of the Spirit as God's Temple, God's building.[95]

The portrayal of the church as "the people of God" was a vital contribution, making participation in the *Missio Dei* the work of every Christian, rather than limiting it to the control of ecclesial institutions.

This outline indicates three principle views of *Missio Dei* that still influence missiology: (1) a mission theology focused on the church as the agent of mission, i.e., human agency; (2) a view that concentrates on divine agency that distances itself from the church to political and social

---

90. Cf. Woolnough and Ma, *Holistic Mission*.

91. Cf. Haldar, "Towards Convergence," 1–14; Woolnough and Ma, *Holistic Mission*.

92. Cf. Haldar, "Towards Convergence," 1–14; Woolnough and Ma, *Holistic Mission*.

93. Cf. Haldar, "Towards Convergence," 1–14.

94. Cf. Bevans and Schroeder, *Prophetic Dialogue*, 1–4; Faggioli, *Vatican II*.

95. Bevans and Schroeder, *Prophetic Dialogue*, 1.

engagement in the world; and (3) a theology that makes the church a participant in the *Missio Dei* but not its owner.[96] It is holistic, as it focuses on conversion as well as political and social engagement. It is the third of these perspectives that Newbigin particularly developed, and further applied when he returned to Britain after his retirement in 1974.[97] It is his version that will be investigated in chapter 3 because of its foundational importance to most missional church ecclesiologies that are developing in the Western context.

1.3 Researcher Positionality

As I engaged in fieldwork at Phoenix, I became increasingly aware of how my Free Church Catholic Ecclesiology (FCCE) impacted my research perspective.[98] Arguably, to some extent, my precommitments to this ecumenical tradition frame, inform, and constrain my theological approach. Phoenix's Reformed theology is quite different from my outlook, which means I have often had to remind myself of differences in my viewpoint and congregants' theological perspectives. I have sought to take into account all theological perspectives whether they cohere with my own or not.

FCC, the college, and I draw on the FCCE theology of William Robinson and other similar formulations.[99] FCCE theology is well known in the Free Church sector in Britain, which is made up of congregations that share a common conviction that all Christian churches are part of the universal (catholic) body of Christ.[100] Robinson was the first Principal of the British Churches of Christ training college, which was called Overdale (1920–70). My college is a successor of Overdale. I believe this focus on ecumenical unity makes it important to equip non-FCC churches, like Phoenix, to become more open to working in partnership with other denominations in mission projects. What made research at Phoenix

---

96. Cf. Flett, *Witness of God*, 38, 39.

97. Cf. Weston, "Lesslie Newbigin," 15. It is to be noted that Newbigin adopted this position during the Willingen Conference as his final written report for the conference demonstrates.

98. For a discussion of the broader concerns of Free Church Catholic Ecclesiology see Bullard, *Re-membering the Body*; Harvey and Hollon, "Series Preface."

99. Cf. Gray, *W.R.*

100. FCCE theology began with the Churches of Christ movement in the nineteenth century.

enticing was that the church had gone through a journey from once being quite inward-looking toward becoming more outward-looking. It captured my theological interest because its Reformed theology was arguably in tension with FCC's, the college's, and my ecumenical outlook. It was particularly fascinating that the ecumenical dimension of the college's/Newbigin's *Missio Dei* theology seemed to have enabled some of Phoenix's members to become more outward-looking when compared to their former inwardly focused *modus operandi* (cf. §1.1.1).

My association with FCC's theological tradition at times made it harder for me to understand aspects of Phoenix's theological tradition.[101] I do not embrace Phoenix's FIEC Reformed theological perspective. However, I respect those in the congregation who aver it. At times I have found it difficult to understand the theological views of some of the members, such as not allowing women to exercise a preaching ministry in the church.[102] I have kept similarities and differences in perspectives like these in mind as I have analyzed empirical data. In chapter 2 there will be a discussion of how my mixed-methods approach to research has helped me to be attentive to the theological perspectives of congregants and their tradition (cf. §2.6). I have been cautious throughout the fieldwork at Phoenix to be reflexively attentive for biases arising from differences in my perspective and those of the congregation (as far as possible; cf. §2.5). I have also kept in mind, as one of the designers of my college's programs, that I may be prejudiced against representing findings that reflect badly on college courses. I have tried to remain reflexively attentive to my reactions to data that do not conform to my expectations. I represent negative and positive findings alike in the data chapters (cf. chs. 4–7). I feel comfortable about doing this because I am committed to the critical enhancement of the college's academic programs, as well as the formal missional church literature. I am also aware that inevitably personal bias can never be fully overcome.

1.4 Limited Literature

There is an absence of published research on congregants' ordinary theologies that have developed in reaction to the mediation of a Newbigin-like theology of *Missio Dei*. However, three empirical congregational

---

101. For a discussion of the origins of Churches of Christ, see Appendix H.
102. Cf. Bolt, "Eschatological Hermeneutics."

investigations will be reviewed below, which give attention to the impact of GOCN-like *Missio Dei* theology on churches' missional practices. In addition to these investigations, there is a review of literature that discusses the relevance of mission to Reformed ecclesiologies. I believe it is important to give a voice to it because it highlights an interest of Reformed churches in the international missional church dialogue. Later chapters will draw on findings in the literature reviewed here, as well as other relevant collateral research to critically analyze Phoenix's congregational data.

First of all, three pieces of *Missio Dei*-related research will be considered. Barrett et al.'s investigation provides ethnographic testimony to the impact of the *Missio Dei* and missional ecclesiology on some denominations in North America.[103] It characterizes eight patterns of missional ecclesiology which inform churches that are undergoing a process of missional transformation. There were three dimensions of this investigation that proved useful to mine which: (1) included analysis of a group of Reformed churches that were exploring missional church praxis; (2) investigated how missional churches discern their missional vocation, which helped me to analyze a similar trend at Phoenix; and (3) was based on ethnographic research which partly resonated with my approach (cf. §2.2).[104] Its strength was that it drew on practical theology by utilizing theological reflection to investigate findings—although it did not draw on ordinary theology.[105] Its main weaknesses were: 1) it relied on the views of congregational leaders to gather its empirical data, and 2) its data was gathered during short one-day visits to congregations. This was a particular weakness because longer-term participant research in congregations enables researchers to get a deeper understanding of a church's beliefs, values, and practices (cf. §2.2). It was also of limited value because it was based on research in a North American rather than British context.

The second piece of research is that of Branson, which investigates the transformation of several congregations that were seeking to enable their members to engage in mission activities.[106] His research is based on a Doctor of Ministry program (DMin) offered by Fuller Theological

---

103. Barrett et al., *Treasure in Clay Jars*.
104. Barrett et al., *Treasure in Clay Jars*, 33–58.
105. Cf. Barrett et al., *Treasure in Clay Jars*.
106. Branson, "Missional Church Process."

Seminary.[107] Postgraduate students were allowed to develop expertise as missional change management agents within their congregations whilst on the Fuller program. An important goal of this piece of research was to determine how the missional change process that was taught, as the primary content of the DMin, had impacted change in three churches.

These churches had agreed to participate in a longitudinal preintervention and postintervention research experiment over three years.[108] Branson's research methodology was based on a quantitative survey approach.[109] Its overall weakness was the impossibility of determining any real qualitative understanding of the views of members regarding the impact of missional changes on them. Its overall strength was that it sought to demonstrate that mission-focused change management processes seem to positively influence changes in congregations' readiness to engage in local mission.[110]

The third piece of research conducted by Niemandt investigates twelve churches that were part of the South African Partnership of Missional Churches.[111] These congregations provided evidence of the impact of the application *of Missio Dei* theology on changes in the way they approached local mission.[112] There is evidence that missional changes occurring within them were equipping them to discern and participate in the *Missio Dei*.[113] A weakness of Niemandt's research is that there is no thick description of data represented, but a simple articulation of findings.[114] It is, therefore, impossible to assess the credibility of his qualitative data.

Niemandt's methodology is based on action research.[115] It utilizes critical theological reflection to analyze findings.[116] He pays attention to what he terms "movements" at work in these congregations by identifying

107. Branson, "Missional Church Process," 99.
108. Branson, "Missional Church Process," 118.
109. Branson, "Missional Church Process," 118–22.
110. Branson, "Missional Church Process"; cf. Cronshaw, "Reenvisioning Theological Education and Missional Spirituality."
111. Niemandt, "Five Years of Missional Church."
112. Niemandt, "Five Years of Missional Church."
113. Niemandt, "Five Years of Missional Church," 397–98.
114. Thick description is a method that provides detailed descriptions and insights into social situations observed by an investigator.
115. Niemandt, "Five Years of Missional Church," 400–404.
116. Niemandt, "Five Years of Missional Church," 400–404.

changes in members' and leaders' perspectives and practices related to church life and local mission.[117] He comments:

> Movements give expression to the organic change and dynamics through which the missionary nature of the church emerges. It is a clear indication of a change in direction, a new way of being a church, and a different culture. Four movements were identified: a new experience of the presence of God; a new focus on the work of the Holy Spirit; a new focus on the incarnation; and a new language.[118]

Niemandt identifies how these movements were becoming more normative to the twelve congregations. Indeed, some of these so-called movements were evident at Phoenix (cf. chs. 4–6).

None of these pieces of research took place in the British ecclesial context, which may be termed a constraint because it reduces the possibility to relate findings made in one cultural context compared to another. Yet there is some correspondence between them in terms of their secular contexts, i.e., all of the congregations investigated were seeking to engage secular peoples through their mission endeavors.[119] Each piece of research was also based on a participatory *Missio Dei* theology like mine, which means that their theological starting points are not dissimilar to my own.

Attention now turns to the fourth category of literature. Paas provides a historical and theological background to the development of Reformed theologies of leadership and membership in the European context.[120] He indicates that in some traditional Reformed churches the ministries of the official officeholders, namely pastors and elders, are the only officially recognized ministries.[121] This means little to no recognition is given to lay ministries, such as local mission work.[122] This is similar to the approach to ministry espoused in Phoenix before its mission change journey (cf. §1.1.1).[123] Paas argues there is a need for traditional

---

117. Niemandt, "Five Years of Missional Church," 397, 398.

118. Niemandt, "Five Years of Missional Church," 407; cf. Niemandt, "Trends in Missional Ecclesiology."

119. Cf. Barrett et al., *Treasure in Clay Jars*; Branson, "Missional Church Process"; Niemandt, "Five Years of Missional Church."

120. Paas, "Leadership in Mission"; Paas, "Discipline of Missiology in 2016."

121. Paas, "Leadership in Mission," 112–14.

122. Paas, "Leadership in Mission," 112–14.

123. Paas, "Leadership in Mission," 112–14.

Reformed churches like this to be helped to extend their understanding of ministry to include members as lay ministers and missionaries.[124] This is so church leaders might equip congregants for mission work in society. Importantly, he draws on some of Newbigin's missiology to make the case for Reformed churches to do this.[125]

It is relevant to note, at this early stage of the discussion, that I am not going to be arguing that the Protestant Reformed tradition is responsible for making laypeople uninvolved in mission in Europe (cf. §1.1.1). I will instead suggest that some very traditional Reformed churches, like those indicated by Paas, interpret their theology of official officeholders to mean that only the clergy should be recognized as ministers or local missionaries.[126] In other words, it is not the Reformed tradition, but the local interpretation of Reformed clerical practices which is responsible for not equipping some Reformed congregations to engage in local mission.

Reference to Paas's research helps to explain why some contemporary Reformed churches have not equipped members to engage in local mission. Paas provides a brief historical background to what led to their existing ministry practices.[127] He theorizes that during Christendom most Europeans were at least nominal Christians by culture. Hence, the clergy did not feel the need to equip congregants to act as missionaries to their peers.[128] This view of Christendom is also a common assumption found in GOCN missional ecclesiology.[129] The consequence was that Europe was not considered to be a mission field by Reformers like Calvin and Luther.[130]

Randall critiques assumptions like those of Paas.[131] He traces how the Anabaptist Radical Reformation sought to actively engage in mission with what was perceived to be a largely non-Christian Europe.[132] Murray avers a similar line of argument, as does Kreider.[133] Wachsmuth similarly

124. Paas, "Leadership in Mission," 112–14.
125. Paas, "Leadership in Mission."
126. Paas, "Leadership in Mission."
127. Paas, "Leadership in Mission."
128. Paas, "Leadership in Mission," 111–14.
129. Guder, *Missional Church*, 6, 7; Van Gelder and Zscheile, *Participating in God's Mission*, 82–88; Ott and Strauss, *Encountering Theology of Mission*, 198.
130. Paas, "Leadership in Mission," 113–16.
131. Randall, "Mission in Post-Christendom."
132. Randall, "Mission in Post-Christendom," 230–32.
133. Murray, *Post-Christendom*; Murray, *Church after Christendom*; Kreider,

argues that Luther and Calvin at least made some links to mission in bringing the Reformation to Europe, but not through the efforts of the laity.[134]

Paas, like Wachsmuth, stresses that Calvin's[135] understanding of clerical leadership made the clergy responsible for the governance, care, and support of churches rather than performing as enablers of the laity for missionary service to their fellow citizens.[136] Wachsmuth indicates that this was largely a product of the prevailing expectations about the role of the clergy during the Reformation.[137] This is because only the authorized ordained clergy could preach, teach, and catechize.[138] Similar to Paas, she also indicates that in many Reformed churches this has remained the culture of leadership down to the contemporary era, but not for all.[139]

Williams makes an interesting observation about the nature of the classical evangelical Christian tradition,[140] positing that it was suited to one context in a past generation but not the present postmodern one.[141] He comments, "traditions are not reified 'things' that can be known apart from practice" or their contemporary context.[142] Similar to Bevans, Williams argues that tradition has to be reinterpreted to each new context if it is to be passed on to new generations.[143] This suggests that there has been a failure in some Reformed churches to contextualize their theology of official officeholders to allow for congregants to be viewed as ministers and missionaries in their own right. Importantly, at Phoenix, graduate

---

Change of Conversion, 99.

134. Wachsmuth, "Mission and the Reformation," 146.

135. For a discussion of Calvinism and Reformed faith cf. Holt, "Calvinism and Reformed Protestantism," 214–32.

136. Paas, "Leadership in Mission," 110; cf. Wachsmuth, "Mission and the Reformation," 144–45.

137. Wachsmuth, "Mission and the Reformation," 144–46.

138. Wachsmuth, "Mission and the Reformation," 144–46.

139. Wachsmuth, "Mission and the Reformation," 144–46.

140. Williams, *Evangelicals and Tradition*.

141. Williams, *Evangelicals and Tradition*, xxi–xxiii.

142. Williams, *Evangelicals and Tradition*, xxi.

143. Williams, *Evangelicals and Tradition*, xxi–xxii; Bevans, *Models of Contextual Theology*; Niemandt, "Five Years of Missional Church"; Niemandt, "Trends in Missional Ecclesiology"; Cronshaw, "Australians Reenvisioning Theological Education and Missional Spirituality"; Cronshaw, "Reenvisioning Theological Education, Mission and the Local Church"; Dreyer, "Missional Ecclesiology," 4.

leaders contextualized the theology of official officeholders to include all members as potential lay ministers and missionaries.[144]

Paas argues that Reformed churches should not downplay the important role that nonofficeholders need to play.[145] They need to be equipped to act as authentic lay ministers in the context of the mission work of the local church.[146] He argues that Reformed churches need to learn from missional church theory and praxis how to mobilize congregations for the work of local mission.[147] Although his work provides no testimony from leaders or members of actual congregations, it is important as it stresses an increasing groundswell of interest within the Reformed tradition for leaders to equip members for local mission—especially to help in the planting of new churches.[148]

Although the Reformed academic literature is limited in terms of its discussion of *Missio Dei* theology, there are hopeful signs that there is growing interest in concentrating attention on planting missional churches, as well as Newbigin's contributions to their understanding of missional ecclesiology.[149] My research seeks to add an empirical account of some Reformed members' reactions to the mediation of a participatory *Missio Dei* theology.

1.5 Structure

This book has eight chapters. A summary of each chapter's aims is provided below.

Chapter 1 provides the context of my research regarding the impact of the communication of a Newbigin-like participatory *Missio Dei* theology on members of Phoenix church. The main impetus for the work

---

144. Bill indicated that *Missio Dei* had been largely communicated through the medium of biblical preaching.

145. Paas, "Leadership in Mission."

146. Paas, "Leadership in Mission." For instance, in helping to plant new churches.

147. Paas, "Leadership in Mission"; Paas and Vos, "Church Planting and Church Growth"; Paas, "Discipline of Missiology in 2016"; Paas, "Case Study of Church Growth."

148. Paas, "Leadership in Mission."

149. Stetzer, "Planting Missional Churches," 23; Smith, "An Evangelical Evaluation of Lesslie Newbigin's Apologetics"; Paas, "Leadership in Mission"; Paas and Vos, "Church Planting and Church Growth"; Paas, "Discipline of Missiology in 2016"; Paas, "Case Study of Church Growth."

is that there is no published research regarding the ordinary *Missio Dei* theologies of members of Reformed churches in the research literature. Indeed, there has been no significant research conducted in the field of ordinary *Missio Dei* theologies that I am aware of at the time of writing this account. I argue that missional church literature needs to start learning from the ordinary theologies of church members on the receiving end of the communication of *Missio Dei* theology, if they are to be enabled to integrate missional theology into their ordinary theologies. This will require urgent attention being given to the question of how ordinary theology can be used to help congregations negotiate missional change processes occurring within them.

Chapter 2 explains the research design. It examines Cartledge's innovation of rescripting methodology and how it is used to analyze, and then rescript, the ordinary theologies of members of Phoenix, as well as aspects of missional ecclesiology.[150] I will be arguing that rescripting of formal missional church theology and the theologies of differing congregations needs to be facilitated with reference to what can be learned from congregants and their ordinary theologies, which have developed in reaction to the mediation of missional ecclesiology to them.

Chapter 3 examines six characteristics of a Newbigin-like theology of participation in the *Missio Dei*. The goal is to provide a critical framework to analyze the ordinary theologies that congregants have developed in reaction to the communication of *Missio Dei* theology to them.

Chapter 4 provides a critical overview of members' reactions to facets of a Newbigin-like *Missio Dei* theology. The goal is to ascertain the impact of this theology by measuring it in terms of practical changes that have occurred in the church's missionary practices. It will become evident that not everyone has welcomed the missional changes that have impacted the congregation, although a significant proportion of members seem to have been positively motivated by them.

Chapter 5 begins a process of digging more deeply into the life of the congregation to characterize the complex relationships that helped to inform members' reactions to *Missio Dei* theology. It also provides important contextual background that is required to engage in meaningful theological rescription of congregants' ordinary theologies. It investigates two out of three interest groups that I identified during my fieldwork. One of these groups has seemingly been transformed by *Missio Dei*

---

150. Cartledge, *Testimony in the Spirit*.

theology, and has become engaged in the church's missional projects. The other group has reacted against *Missio Dei* theology, and seems to have felt increasingly marginalized by the church. I engage in analysis of these two groups' ordinary theologies and then theologically rescript their testimonies with a mediating theology.

Chapter 6 investigates the data of a third group. It provides a profile of the complex relationships which existed between members in the church that had seemingly developed because of the mediation of *Missio Dei* to the congregation. This group's testimonies further complexify the analysis of reactions of congregants to missional changes that have impacted Phoenix. Their ordinary theology of prophetic discernment will be used to suggest theological rescription of the church's approach to the discernment of the *Missio Dei*.

Chapter 7 concentrates on the cost of missional change to the congregation. The word "cost" is not used to measure the financial impact of these changes on Phoenix, but rather changes to members' experiences of life in the church. It will become evident that missional change has caused significant strains in the congregation. It will seek to demonstrate that for a Reformed church like Phoenix significant changes in its way of life seem to have forced members to make hard choices. These choices have, at times, meant that they have needed to end close relationships with people they have known for many years. Arguably, members' voices need to be heard to challenge what at times seem to be overly idealistic preconceptions found in the academic literature regarding the benefits of missional changes on churches.

Chapter 8 aims to draw conclusions from the research and make recommendations. It will synthesize members' ordinary theologies and modify key concepts found in the academic literature focused on missional churches. These suggested rescriptions of the formal missional church literature provide some working examples by which future researchers might seek to use ordinary theology to rescript missional ecclesiology. Recommendations will also be made to rescript aspects of the ordinary theologies of congregants, as well as features of my college's academic programs and assumptions made in the academic literature. It will discuss some of the impacts of this research on me, and how I have come to think of some new ways of engaging in professional practice. It is to be remembered that this reflexive component to my work is provided to help the reader understand the importance of how our perspectives can impact our professional practice, as well as how new hermeneutical horizons revealed by research can transform the way we go about our professional praxis. Chapter 8 will also recommend topics for future research and indicate the key contributions my investigation makes to the field of missional ecclesiology.

Chapter 2

Methodology

Introduction

THIS CHAPTER EXPLAINS MY research methodology. I quite recognize that some nonresearch-focused readers will not want to read this chapter because of its technical academic concentration on methodology. If this is the case, then moving on to chapter 3 will help the reader to understand the theological baseline that is used to analyze my findings in later chapters. Having said this, much can be learnt from the discussion of rescripting methodology that might help the practitioner in the application of ordinary theology to their professional practice contexts. For the student engaged in missional church research I believe it will be of importance to understand my use of methodology. This chapter is divided into six sections which examine: (1) the research question and objectives; (2) practical theology and its relationship to empirical research; (3) rescripting methodology; (4) the analytical use of four theological voices; (5) the researcher's position in the research; and (6) the research design and process.

2.1 Research Question and Objectives

My investigation asks: What impact has the communication of a Newbigin-like *Missio Dei* theology had on Phoenix's church members?[1] As I explained in chapter 1, my research interest arose from my professional practice context as an ordained minister in the FCC, as well as my

---

1. Phoenix is a pseudonym, as are names assigned to its members.

academic work with church leaders who engage in undergraduate and postgraduate programs at my college (cf. ch. 1). I will not repeat here what led me to ask this question (cf. ch. 1). The book's objectives that follow indicate the contributions that my investigation seeks to make to the field of missional church studies, and to my professional practice context. There are five objectives, namely, to:

1. analyze congregants' ordinary theologies which have seemingly arisen in reaction to *Missio Dei* theology;
2. rescript their ordinary theologies in critical conversation with the scholarly literature;
3. rescript some aspects of Newbigin's and GOCN's missional ecclesiology by insights arising from rescriptions of congregants' ordinary theologies;
4. provide a basis to begin a broader scholarly conversation about the impact of ordinary *Missio Dei* theologies on a variety of church traditions and versions of the *Missio Dei*; and
5. contribute to the intellectual capital that frames and informs college academic programs.

My chosen methodology seeks to facilitate how I answer the research question and meet these objectives.

2.2 Practical Theology

My investigation is situated within the discipline of practical theology and engages in a detailed examination of Phoenix's members' beliefs, values, and practices. Ballard and Pritchard suggest that congregational praxis is motivated by more than theology, it also draws on other kinds of cultural beliefs, values, and norms.[2] In other words, Phoenix's theological expressions do not exist in a vacuum but are also influenced by outside cultural and ideological forces. This is a well-known phenomenon in the fields of contextual theology and congregational hermeneutics.[3] Like

---

2. Cf. Ballard and Pritchard, *Practical Theology*, 70, 71; Cartledge, *Testimony in the Spirit*, 179; Swinton and Mowat, *Practical Theology and Qualitative Research*, 17–25; Mager, "Action Theories," 256–59.

3. Cf. Bevans, *Models of Contextual Theology*; Rogers, *Congregational Hermeneutics*, 41–55; Schreiter, *Constructing Local Theologies*, 98.

Swinton and Mowat, I assume it is possible to reflect theologically on the value-laden practices of believers, to help the church better engage with "faithful participation in God's redemptive practices—to and for the world."[4] One of the key ways my research seeks to facilitate faithful participation is by rescripting,[5] and thus modifying, aspects of missional ecclesiology by being attentive to congregants' emic perspectives.[6]

The concentration on emic categories of data relates to an ethnographic interpretivist methodology, which seeks to uncover aspects of the insider perspectives of those being investigated.[7] A thick description of data is required to uncover a range of congregational emic perspectives.[8] An important goal of the gathering of thick data is to capture as much as possible of the theological perspectives of insiders.[9] Like Cartledge, I also employ "etic . . . concepts to rescript . . . emic or ordinary ideas and expressions" (cf. §2.3).[10] Of course, emic and etic analyses cannot be fully separated because there is an interaction between them in the research process. I will seek to avoid producing a reductionist account of emic data when engaging in etic analysis.

Cartledge's approach to practical theology engages in interdisciplinary dialectical conversations with sociology and philosophy, whilst seeking to make ordinary theology its primary methodology.[11] Given

---

4. Swinton and Mowat, *Practical Theology and Qualitative Research*, 6; McClintock Fulkerson, *Places of Redemption*, 48.

5. Rescription treats what is transcribed from participant data as a script, which is then rescripted in dialectical *conversation* with other sources.

6. Cf. Astley, *Ordinary Theology*; Anderson, *Shape of Practical Theology*, 47–60; Cartledge, *Testimony in the Spirit*, 18, 19; Hiebert, *Transforming Worldviews*, 89; Hiebert, *Gospel in Human Contexts*; Hiebert and Hiebert-Menses, *Incarnational Ministry*.

7. Cf. Hammersley and Atkinson, *Ethnography*, 124–56.

8. Cf. Phillips, "Charting the 'Ethnographic Turn,'" 95–106.

9. Hopewell called a congregation a "thick gathering" to be understood through thick description (*Congregation*, 3–18).

10. Cartledge, *Testimony in the Spirit*, 19; Cartledge, "Pentecostal Experience"; Hiebert, *Transforming Worldviews*, 89.

11. Cartledge, *Testimony in the Spirit*; Cartledge, "Pentecostal Experience." Cf. Bennett, "Britain," 480; Mercer and Miller-McLemore, *Conundrums in Practical Theology*. It is to be noted that Astley's understanding of ordinary theology is progressively becoming an accepted part of practical theology. New pieces of research are revealing vital insights into the nonacademic theological discourse of Christians (cf. Perrin, *Bible Reading of Young Evangelicals*, 15; De Wit, *Through the Eyes of Another*, 10; Rogers, *Congregational Hermeneutics*, 17; Astley, *Ordinary Theology*, 56; Cartledge,

that I adapt Cartledge's interdisciplinary rescripting methodology, these ethnographic methods of data-gathering and analysis will arguably assist me to posit critical theological findings for my research (cf. §2.2).[12]

This research relates to the phenomenon of missional change discussed in the field of missional *ecclesiology*, which is claimed to arise from the mediation of a participatory *Missio Dei* theology to congregations.[13] Like Rogers, my adoption of theological ethnography is based on the notion that church members' beliefs, values, and practices are laden with theological meaning.[14] It is their rhetoric that helps to reveal what their ordinary theologies mean to them, which can then be related to the wider field of missional ecclesiology.[15] Not everything discussed in this book will have a direct correspondence with the experiences of other congregations, but some of it may.[16] Relatability is not to be confused with positivistic research frames which seek to generalize findings to a larger population.[17] My adaptation of rescripting methodology seeks to relate the research at Phoenix to the larger academy.

2.3 Rescripting Methodology

The methodology is founded upon Cartledge's revision of Martin's approach to theological rescription.[18] It will be used with some adaptations

---

"Pentecostal Experience"; Cartledge, *Testimony in the Spirit*; Astley and Francis, *Exploring Ordinary Theology*). Perrin helpfully points out challenges related to the use of the term "ordinary" in her published PhD thesis (*Bible Reading of Young Evangelicals*, 15–17). For example, she points out that it is important not to assume that Christians without formal theological training are theologically illiterate, as, for instance, they may have some knowledge of academic theology based on their own reading (*Bible Reading of Young Evangelicals*, 15–17). Hence, the practical theologian will need to determine to what extent a believer's theological knowledge might be thought of as nonacademic (*Bible Reading of Young Evangelicals*, 15–17; cf. Astley, *Ordinary Theology*, 56, 102). My experience on the ground at Phoenix revealed that members generally did not seem to express academic knowledge of theology in their discourse.

12. Cf. Cartledge, *Testimony in the Spirit*; Cartledge, "Pentecostal Experience"; Ward, *Perspectives on Ecclesiology and Ethnography*, 6, 7.

13. Cf. Barrett et al., *Treasure in Clay Jars*; Guder, *Missional Church*; Niemandt, "Five Years of Missional Church."

14. Rogers, "Ordinary Biblical Hermeneutics," 78.

15. Rogers, "Ordinary Biblical Hermeneutics," 77.

16. Cf. Rogers, *Congregational Hermeneutics*, 3.

17. Cf. Swinton and Mowat, *Practical Theology and Qualitative Research*, 41–44.

18. Cartledge, *Testimony in the Spirit*, 16; Cartledge, "Pentecostal Experience";

METHODOLOGY   35

to rescript Phoenix members' ordinary *Missio Dei* theologies (or other theologies). This section will not reiterate in detail Cartledge's whole methodology. Key components of it will be outlined to make my adaptations of it intelligible.[19] Rescripting methodology treats what congregants theologically communicate as a script[20] (based on transcripts of their testimonies). These scripts may then be modified by other mediating sources that relate to them. Cartledge explains that the rescripting process:

> . . . seeks to maintain a tension between a revised script that is both in continuity with and in discontinuity with the existing script. It seeks to move ordinary theology forward through a deeper analysis of its testimony mode and broader dialogue with the Christian theological tradition, illuminated by the insights of the social sciences.[21]

Rescripting is a way to look at what a person (or group) communicates, and then to analyze and modify it based on other perspectives. Cartledge's rescripting entails a dialectical conversation between the ordinary theological testimonies of believers, and critical interaction with denominational tradition and specific theological doctrines.[22] This dialectical conversation may lead to modification of congregants' ordinary theologies. Rescripting seeks to create a critical conversation between ordinary theological beliefs, values, and practices, and other mediating sources—to modify perspectives. For example, later in the book I use social Trinitarianism as a mediating source to rescript a communal and activist ordinary theology (cf. §5.4). It is important to note, that by "testimony" Cartledge refers to "the telling of Pentecostal believers" personal stories about their encounters with God, which are "central to the ordinary expression of" their "faith."[23] Astley's characterization of ordinary theology provides the basis to Cartledge's and my understanding of it (cf. §1.1).[24] In essence, my experience on the ground at Phoenix was of congregants who largely relied on oral testimonies to tell their stories,

---

Martin, "Undermining the Old Paradigms."

19. Cf. Cartledge, *Testimony in the Spirit*; Cartledge, "Pentecostal Experience."
20. Rescripting is also used to modify participant data in other fields of study like politics.
21. Cartledge, *Testimony in the Spirit*, 18.
22. Cartledge, *Testimony in the Spirit*, 17.
23. Cartledge, *Testimony in the Spirit*, 17.
24. Astley, *Ordinary Theology*, 58.

or those of the congregation, meaning Cartledge's rescripting approach could be used.[25]

Cartledge, like Martin, utilizes theological rescription to modify ordinary theology, whilst seeking to remain true to the original script of congregants' testimonies.[26] In the case of my research, I will begin by paying attention to the verbatim testimonies of church members regarding how *Missio Dei* theology was mediated to them. Based upon these testimonies, their apparent ordinary interpretations of *Missio Dei* will be mapped, including those that react negatively to *Missio Dei* theology. Similarities and differences between members' ordinary theologies will then be viewed in the context of the larger congregational and denominational stories. I will aim to provide a picture of the impact of *Missio Dei* theology on congregants' beliefs, values, and practices. Opportunities for theological rescription will be identified based on tensions between members' ordinary theologizing and the academic literature. Rescription of members' ordinary theologies may help to reduce congregational tensions (cf. §5.4).

Like Cartledge, I pay attention to interrelated theological narratives[27] that inform congregants' theological perspectives.[28] Cartledge analyzes the relationships between three theological narratives: (1) members' testimonies; (2) the larger congregational story; and (3) the denominational story.[29] He then theologically rescripts (1) in relation to (2) and (3). According to Wilkinson, it is this approach that integrates congregational studies into Cartledge's approach.[30] Indeed, Cartledge's concentration on these theological narratives relates to similarities with Ammerman's classic approach to theological reflection on a congregation's story.[31] Like Cartledge, I argue that paying attention to these theological narratives will take the authentic witness of the ordinary theologizing of Phoenix's members into serious account when engaging in theological rescription

---

25. Cartledge, *Testimony in the Spirit*, 17, 18.

26. Cartledge, *Testimony in the Spirit*, 179; Martin, "Undermining the Old Paradigms."

27. Cartledge terms them modes (*Testimony in the Spirit*, 17, 18).

28. Cartledge, *Testimony in the Spirit*, 179; Martin, "Undermining the Old Paradigms."

29. Cartledge, *Testimony in the Spirit*, 17.

30. Wilkinson, *Testimony in the Spirit*.

31. Ammerman et al., *Studying Congregations*, 26, 27.

of congregants' ordinary theologies.[32] As is common to practical theology, I will engage in rescription by theologically reflecting on these narratives.[33]

Additionally, I adapted several of Cartledge's approaches. Cartledge investigates three levels of discourse[34] to facilitate rescription of ordinary theology. He splits the third level into two parts.[35] He begins, as above, with: (1) ordinary theological testimonies; (2) the denominational story; and then adds (3a) academic theological discourse and (3b) sociological discourse.[36] He rescripts the discourse of (1) in critical conversation with (2), (3a), and (3b). This means the denominational story, academic theology, and sociological discourse can then be used to suggest the rescription of ordinary theology. Unlike Cartledge, I pay less attention to sociological analysis of scripts and instead focus more attention on the discourse found in the missional church and practical theology literature—to rescript ordinary theology. Cartledge assigns academic theology and sociology to an equal third-order level of analysis in his scheme, i.e., (3a) and (3b). They are separated by the differences between these two disciplines. I instead will distinguish two discipline subtypes: (a) practical theology; and (b) missional church theology. The kinds of literature associated with these two disciplines both contain sociological analysis. Hence, sociology will not be absent from my method but integrated into the sources I use as conversation partners.

Furthermore, I do not structure my data chapters in the same manner as Cartledge. He uses an unwavering formulaic approach, where each chapter has the same sections: transcripts, sociological discourse, denominational discourse, academic theological discourse, and rescription.[37] I concentrate on these categories of analysis but not in a rigid formulaic manner. I mix discussion of several of these categories in a single section or may discuss each one in different places as is appropriate for the topic being addressed. Emphasis is placed on the discourse partners that seem to make the best sense of the emic data being analyzed. Like Cartledge, I

32. Cartledge, *Testimony in the Spirit*, 17, 18.
33. Cf. Ballard and Pritchard, *Practical Theology*; Thompson et al., *SCM Studyguide*; Graham et al., *Theological Reflection*.
34. Discourse criticism is also known as rhetorical criticism - cf. Foss, *Rhetorical Criticism*.
35. Cartledge, *Testimony in the Spirit*, 20.
36. Cartledge, *Testimony in the Spirit*, 18, 19.
37. Cartledge, *Testimony in the Spirit*.

will analyze and rescript using three levels of discourse: (1) the ordinary theology of congregants; (2) Reformed theology/denominational story; and then (3a) practical theology, and (3b) missional ecclesiology. Like Cartledge, I will rescript (1) in critical conversation with (2), (3a), and (3b).

However, unlike Cartledge, I investigate how a new incoming missional church tradition has impacted the current/former tradition of Phoenix. Interestingly, the GOCN research literature has neglected the ordinary dimension in terms of developing theory related to missional church praxis. I will take the step of rescripting some dimensions of missional ecclesiology, based on insights determined by a comparison of the ordinary theologies of Phoenix's members with Newbigin-like/GOCN theology. My concentration on congregants' ordinary theologizing will arguably challenge some theoretical assumptions made in this literature. For example, GOCN research literature does not explore the inherent tensions that are caused when members' ordinary theologies cause them to reject *Missio Dei* theology, or cause them to misunderstand the significance of divine agency in mission (cf. §5.3; 8.1.1).[38] Barrett et al.'s research has the merit of highlighting a few tensions that arose in some congregations because of missional changes, but it gave no theological voice to members' ordinary theological accounts of these tensions.[39]

Cartledge's book, *Testimony in the Spirit*,[40] is critiqued by Kelly for not assessing the impact of theological rescription on the congregation he investigated.[41] I could not assess the impact of theological rescription on Phoenix either, as it would require several years to pass after my research finished for this to be meaningfully possible. This may help to explain why Cartledge did not investigate its impact on the church he investigated.

Like Cartledge and Martin, I will seek to avoid, as far as possible, overly strong rescriptions, so as not to misrepresent the evidence provided by the ordinary theologizing of congregants.[42] Cartledge's version of rescription seems to have navigated a balanced route between the poles

---

38. Cf. Barrett et al., *Treasure in Clay Jars*.

39. Barrett et al., *Treasure in Clay Jars*, 12–16.

40. Cartledge, *Testimony in the Spirit*.

41. Kelly, "Testimony in the Spirit," 69, 70; cf. Gladwin, "Testimony in the Spirit"; Wilkinson, "Testimony in the Spirit"; Flynn, "Testimony in the Spirit."

42. Cartledge, *Testimony in the Spirit*, 17; Martin, "Undermining the Old Paradigms," 23.

of weak and strong rescriptions so that it is founded on the ordinary theological voices of those it investigates.[43] I will be attentive to charting a similar course in my application of rescription methodology.

Because I am rescripting the ordinary theologies of church members, I have: (1) the opportunity to make suggestions to modify the congregation's hermeneutical horizons,[44] meaning (2) that I am placed in a position of power, which, ethically speaking, means I have needed to handle rescription methodology carefully.[45] The consultative approach I have utilized throughout the research process has made it possible for congregants to discuss and contribute to the key themes which make up this research narrative. Members have, at times, also challenged my ideas in terms of the sense I have sought to make of the congregation's missional change journey, and have tried to help me understand alternative perspectives (cf. chs. 4–7). Because of this, I would suggest there has been a sense of collaboration between the congregation and myself. I will seek to suggest rescriptions that arise from the most prominent themes in congregants' testimonies, whilst paying close attention to how members have challenged or confirmed key themes. Indeed, this relates to Rogers's approach to the analyses of congregational hermeneutical horizons.[46] Rogers recommends that the researcher needs to pay attention to "affirmative" and "disruptive" interpretations of a congregation's ordinary theologies.[47] By doing this it may become possible to obtain insights into the hermeneutical lenses that different parties within a church espouse.[48] It will also provide insights into what might motivate theological tensions between different parties within a congregation.

2.4 Four Voices

As already explained, my primary approach to research is rescripting methodology. But I also adapted[49] Cameron et al. and Watkins's "four

43. Cartledge, *Testimony in the Spirit*.

44. Congregants have access to findings based on a short, readable summary of them.

45. Cf. Rogers, *Congregational Hermeneutics*, 28, 29. I have written about analysis of power structures in Hardy et al., *Power and the Powers*, 75–92.

46. Rogers, *Congregational Hermeneutics*.

47. Rogers, *Congregational Hermeneutics*, 39, 90–93, 212.

48. Cf. Rogers, *Congregational Hermeneutics*, 39, 90–93, 212.

49. I adapted it by not using their theological action research approach; cf.

voices" concept to provide insights into members' reactions to *Missio Dei* theology.[50] Their concept offered the first step to analyze thematic data before using rescripting methodology. Their understanding of the four voices may be characterized as the:

- Normative voice—based upon "what the practicing group names as its theological authority";
- Espoused voice—which concentrates on believers' own theological expressions;
- Operant voice—which is the theology embedded within the actual practices of a group; and
- Formal voice—which relates to the academic theology of theologians.[51]

By first paying attention to theological tensions that existed between these voices and which were found in members' testimonies to varying degrees, I identified what appeared to be differing interest groups within the congregation. It was then possible to characterize differing interest groups' ordinary theologies (cf. chs. 5–6). These characterizations were used to engage in rescripting differing groups' ordinary theologies (cf. §2.3; chs. 5–8).

The combination of Cameron et al./Watkins's concept and Cartledge's approach fulfills a twofold purpose. It provides: (1) a nuanced way of determining differing groups' ordinary theologies; and (2) a means to rescript these ordinary theologies. Cartledge's dialectical method[52] coheres with my use of the four voices concept, because the formal voice allows the theology of the academy to become a critical conversation partner with the normative, espoused, and operant voices.[53] The aim is not to overpower these voices, but rather to bring the church and academy into critical dialogue.

Cameron et al., *Talking about God in Practice*; Watkins, *Disclosing Church*.

50. Cameron et al., *Talking about God in Practice*; Watkins, *Disclosing Church*, 39–54.

51. Cameron et al., *Talking about God in Practice*, 54–56; Watkins, *Disclosing Church*, 39–54.

52. Cf. Gladwin, "Testimony in the Spirit."

53. Cf. Cameron et al., *Talking about God in Practice*, 55–60.

2.5 Reflexivity

In chapter 1, I discussed my subject position in this research and use of reflexivity. I will not repeat what was previously articulated. Instead, I draw attention to my position as a reflexive practitioner. I am drawing on an interpretivist frame rather than a positivist epistemology.[54] I assume a critical realist perspective that empirical research can reveal approximate authentic knowledge of how others interpret the world.[55] Dreyer helpfully characterizes the epistemological dilemma that confronted me throughout the research process:

> ... all knowledge is mediated knowledge, that there is a conflict of interpretations, and that bias, researcher subjectivity, and positionality play a role in these interpretations.[56]

Throughout the book, I seek to locate my subject-position with my views and in critical conversation with other views that diverge from my own. My goal is to identify other perspectives that my viewpoint may otherwise conceal.[57] Galdas stresses that the researcher's perspective plays a vital role in helping to reveal his or other viewpoints when differences in outlook are reflexively contemplated.[58] I have found contemplation of this sort revealing and challenging to my views, as well as leading me to change some of my theological outlooks (cf. §8.3). Researcher reflexivity has also helped me to address questions of bias and power, by enabling me to be more transparent about my subject-position. Reflexivity has enabled me to critically self-reflect on the impact of my "preconceptions, relationship dynamics and analytic focus" on the research.[59]

2.6 Research Design and Process

The combination of methods discussed below was adopted because I needed to investigate empirically the emic voices of congregants to

---

54. Cf. Dreyer, "Knowledge, Subjectivity, (De)Coloniality," 91; Clark Moschella, "Ethnography," 225.
55. Cf. Bryman, *Social Research Methods*, 692–93.
56. Dreyer, "Knowledge, Subjectivity, (De)Coloniality," 91.
57. Cf. Dreyer, "Knowledge, Subjectivity, (De)Coloniality," 91.
58. Galdas, "Revisiting Bias in Qualitative Research," 2.
59. Cf. Galdas, "Revisiting Bias in Qualitative Research," 2; Swinton and Mowat, *Practical Theology and Qualitative Research*, 62–63.

obtain insights into their perspectives. In brief: (1) semistructured interviews helped me to obtain thick data regarding members' ordinary theologies;[60] (2) participant observations helped me to interact in the life of the congregation, to obtain indicators of how *Missio Dei* theology was impacting the church's communal and missional activities; (3) the use of a congregational questionnaire helped me to establish how many of the congregation had first heard of *Missio Dei* during the tenure of graduate leaders from my college; and (4) congregational consultations enabled me to crosscheck the validity of key themes that emerged from the investigation. The combination of these methods was designed to crosscheck my research findings.

In what follows, I will begin with a discussion of the process that led to my research at Phoenix, and then provide a more detailed examination of the research methods outlined above.

2.6.1 Initial Processes

The church pastor and elders discussed the research with me, and then gave me written consent to engage in this investigation.[61] Ethics clearance was obtained from the university, which also required a risk assessment process that I conducted with Bill's input (cf. Appendix A). Only those above the age of eighteen years old were permitted to take part in the research.[62] All participants were required to provide written consent before taking part in interviews, completing a questionnaire, or participating in congregational consultation groups.[63] Each participant was also informed that they could request that their data be withdrawn.

Pilot research was carried out at Phoenix from 2016–17 to evaluate the viability of my investigation and to test the feasibility of interview questions.[64] Comprehensive fieldwork commenced late in 2017 and was completed in September 2018. Thirty members took part in interviews (out of about 120 possible participants); forty-three members completed

---

60. Cf. Ward, *Introducing Practical Theology*, 161.

61. Cf. Swinton and Mowat, *Practical Theology and Qualitative Research*, 137–38.

62. Because I could not interview those under eighteen years old I had to rely on adult accounts of mission with younger people; cf. Kirsty and Leah's testimonies §6.2.3–6.2.4.

63. Cf. Kimmel, *Ethical Issues in Behavioral Research*, 319.

64. Cf. Bryman, *Social Research Methods*, 247, 248.

questionnaires; thirty-two took part in four separate congregational consultations; and six leaders participated in a final leader's consultation.[65] Roughly an equal number of males and females participated in this research.

As I did not personally know most individual members, [66]I tried to select randomly those I interviewed.[67] The youngest participant was eighteen years old and the oldest eighty-seven years of age. My role as participant-observer helped to mitigate researcher selection bias, to some extent, because I intentionally interacted with almost all congregants throughout the two years of fieldwork.[68] This meant I was exposed to a range of negative and positive views about the impact of the missional changes on the congregation, which had the effect of challenging some of my preconceived ideas. I reflexively draw attention to instances of this kind throughout the book.

As I thought through the challenges of checking the validity of congregational data related to my perceptions, I developed a strategy to employ a mixed-methods approach to data collection.[69] It would enable the crosschecking of the data derived from interviews, the questionnaire, and consultation groups.[70] Correspondences between data types would provide a potential indicative opportunity to confirm, or disconfirm, key research findings.[71]

My research methodology incorporates strategies to determine its internal and external validity. In terms of internal validity, I have employed reflexivity, thick description, the mixed-methods approach, deviant case analysis, and respondent validation.[72] In terms of external

---

65. There was some unavoidable overlap between who took part in each of these research processes, but new participants were included in each process.

66. Occasionally a leader or member might suggest speaking to a named individual. As I got to know members better, I became proficient at identifying members who represented differing group perspectives.

67. Cf. Bryman, *Social Research Methods*, 38, 39, 167–73.

68. I took part in church services, social gatherings, prayer meetings, the church's Bible school, and some leaders' meetings. I also visited the church's various missional initiatives.

69. Cf. Holmes and Lindsay, "In Search of Christian Theological Research Methodology," 5.

70. Cf. Bryman, *Social Research Methods*, 604–10.

71. Cf. Swinton and Mowat, *Practical Theology and Qualitative Research*, 50, 70–71; Bryman, *Social Research Methods*, 379, 611–12; Hussain, "Use of Triangulation."

72. Cf. Silverman, *Doing Qualitative Research*, 384–96; Bryman, *Social Research*

validity, my research enters into critical conversation with relevant aspects of congregational research and missional church research.

Given that my research was mostly based on qualitative data, I utilized QSR NVIVO11 to code it thematically.[73] Raw data were analyzed and key themes were determined and used in data chapters (cf. chs. 5–7). I used the constant comparative method to analyze congregants' testimonies.[74] When a point of data saturation was reached for each theme, I then engaged in a process of emic and etic analyses, comparing and contrasting categories, and relating findings to the relevant academic literature.[75] Based upon this analytical process, I determined chapter outlines for the book which arose from the key thematic categories of coded data.

2.6.2 Semi-Structured Interviews

I chose to begin the research process with audio recorded fifty-minute, semi-structured interviews with congregants, which provided an opportunity to obtain thick emic data, as well as valuable insights into the experiences of the congregation (Appendices B and C).[76] Bryman suggests that semi-structured interviews provide flexibility to the researcher, which: (1) gives the interviewer a small list of key questions, meaning participants discuss some of the same matters of topical importance in common; and (2) they provide interviewees with "a great deal of leeway in how to reply," thus meaning they feel less constrained than by an unwieldy interview.[77] I was cautious not to use leading questions that set up interviewees to give particular answers.[78]

Methods, 376–79.

73. https://www.qsrinternational.com/nvivo-qualitative-data-analysis-software/home.

74. Cf. Bryman, *Social Research Methods*, 542.

75. Cf. Weller et al., "Open-Ended Interview Questions and Saturation," 6; Hiebert, *Transforming Worldviews*, 89.

76. Cf. Partington, "Qualitative Research Interviews"; Bryman, *Social Research Methods*, 438.

77. Bryman, *Social Research Methods*, 438; Partington, "Qualitative Research Interviews."

78. Cf. Bryman, *Social Research Methods*, 242; Partington, "Qualitative Research Interviews", 35.

2.6.3 Participant Observations

I also engaged in participant observations from the beginning of the fieldwork process. I found Hammersley and Atkinson's discussion of how to formulate fieldnotes particularly useful, as the questions that structure a notebook enable the observer to engage in some consistent observations and reflections on the data (cf. Appendix F).[79] I was not a "complete-participant" because I did not engage in covert observations.[80] Instead, I acted as a "participant-as-observer" because members were aware of my research.[81] This had the disadvantage of making my role as researcher obvious, which could make members wary of interacting with me. Hence, building rapport was important so trust could be built between us.[82] Members seemed to be more relaxed when I explained to them that my ethics clearance precluded me from quoting congregants' words without obtaining written consent from them. During my participation in the congregation's life, I was able to identify members who seemed to avoid contact with others, as well as possible interest groups within the church.[83]

As I engaged in research at Phoenix over the two years, I took part in a range of mission-focused projects in the local community. I regularly visited the missional café project, and was able to engage in what might be termed "fly on the wall" observations of conversations that took place between clients and café staff. I was also able to observe some of the key practices that staff engaged in, in terms of how they sought to share their Christian faith with local people. I also visited the missional allotments, and interacted with members who were at work there. I was surprised[84]

---

79. Hammersley and Atkinson, *Ethnography*, 175–86.

80. Cf. Bryman, *Social Research Methods*, 410.

81. Cf. Bryman, *Social Research Methods*, 410; Shah, "Ethnography?"

82. Cf. Hammersley and Atkinson, *Ethnography*, 142–45.

83. I also relied on the keeping of memos to record what I observed; cf. Bryman, *Social Research Methods*, 256; Charmaz, *Constructing Grounded Theory*, 3.

84. My sense of surprise arose from the idea that working at an allotment could be seen as an instance of actual mission work, given that it is often associated with a form of recreation based on my experience with family members and friends who keep them. Given that at one of the church's allotments it was felt that they were planting a rather novel kind of church there, this really challenged my own ideas about what might be termed "mission." However, in terms of the theses' concentration on ordinary theology, I have come to think of these missional allotment projects as a kind of ordinary ecclesiology, with the church becoming the people of God rather than as a building, with all its formal ecclesiastical paraphernalia. It subverts grand notions of

by the amount of enthusiasm some members had for the allotment work, and their evident convictions that what they were doing there was part of the church's mission work. I also visited the missional youth group several times, and had opportunities to speak with members at work there, as well as to young people. I took part in Sunday morning worship services, and took copious field notes based on the sermons I heard, and the reactions of members to them, as well as comments made by congregants after services. I also took part in a number of the church's numerous house groups, and made copious notes on what I observed—particularly in terms of both negative and positive reactions to the church's concentration on mission. It was also valuable to attend a number of sessions of the church's in-house Bible school. I obtained valuable insights into what leaders were teaching members about mission and ministry. I also was able to read assignments written by members, which gave me insights into their understanding of mission.

My overall aim in taking part in these various activities was to learn as much as I could about congregants' ordinary theological beliefs, values, and practices related to mission. Being a full participant and observer also gave me opportunities to theologically reflect on the ways of life of congregants as they engaged in mission-focused activities, as well as other kinds of practices in the life of the church. My participation in a variety of differing events provided important opportunities for me to discern evidence of the degree of acceptance by congregants of the church's mission activities and the call for them to participate in them. I realized quite early on in the fieldwork process that participant observations provided an invaluable opportunity for me to capture snapshots of ordinary congregational life, which revealed positive and negative reactions of members to the church's concentration on local mission. I kept on reminding myself that my presence as a full participant would inevitably have some influence on the behavior of members. As far as I could determine, once congregants had gotten used to my presence at different events, and had gotten to know me better, they seemed to make genuine efforts to treat me as part of the church, and seemed to feel relaxed with respect to what they talked about together in my presence. My overall participation in the life of the congregation seemed to be appreciated by members, although it took time for some of them to feel relaxed around me as my role as a researcher was communicated to members at quite a

---

planting formal churches, and instead replaces them with a small community sharing life together in something they love doing with Christians and non-Christians alike.

few services, as well as in the church's newsletters. Many members were interested in what I was investigating, and were also interested in my own Christian faith journey. As far as I could tell, they accepted me as a genuine Christian, and this seemed to help them feel more relaxed about accepting my involvement in the life of the church.

2.6.4 Questionnaire

I ended the fieldwork process with two procedures to crosscheck fieldwork data: (1) a questionnaire; and (2) five consultations with small groups of members and leaders. The questionnaire was designed to crosscheck how many members claimed to have been influenced by an understanding of *Missio Dei* theology, or to have engaged in local missionary work, as well as to obtain other congregational metrics (cf. §4.1–4.2). Two questions found in the questionnaire, 9c and 9d, proved to be especially helpful when it came to making sense of the extent of the espousal of a *Missio Dei* theology by congregants (cf. §4.1; Appendix E). Bryman's discussion of the categories of qualitative data that can be included in a questionnaire helped me identify the need to investigate congregants' beliefs, values, knowledge, and norms.[85] The questionnaire approach also provided me with a means to posit quantitative findings.[86] Hermans and Schoeman discuss the range of data categories that congregational surveys can investigate.[87] Some of these categories are to be found in my questionnaire, such as the way it seeks to measure attitudes and perceptions of members (cf. Appendix E).[88] I particularly found a questionnaire produced by the practical theologian Andrew Rogers very helpful, and I adapted the metrics section to suit it to the context of Phoenix.[89] Results from my questionnaire are discussed in chapter 4, and inform the analysis of data in other chapters.

---

85. Bryman, *Social Research Methods*, 239, 644, 691.
86. Cf. Hermans and Schoeman, "Survey Research," 47.
87. Hermans and Schoeman, "Survey Research."
88. Hermans and Schoeman, "Survey Research," 52.
89. With his permission.

2.6.5 Congregational Consultations

A participatory consultative framework characterized the whole research process. I began the research design process by consulting with the church's leadership team and some members about the methods I would use to conduct the investigation. There was a desire for the research process to be consultative. Consultations were both informal and formal. The informal approach meant I could take time with a range of small groups of members during church lunches, social gatherings, or after services to discuss themes that were arising with them. I found these conversations informative because members felt free to challenge my views, or those of their peers, while providing me with new insights into congregants' views about the church's change journey.

Five formal consultations concluded the fieldwork. They also provided a means to crosscheck congregational thematic data to confirm, or disconfirm, the relevance of themes.[90] These formal consultations lasted sixty to ninety minutes. Approximately eight members, both male and female, were included in each of the five groups, with about six leaders in one group. These consultations did not function as focus groups, but they did share some characteristics in common. Bryman characterizes the focus group method as a targeted approach, enabling the researcher to examine how people in conjunction with one another "construe the general topics in which the researcher is interested."[91] For instance, group conversations revealed prominent differences in perspectives, or were indicative of why members might feel and think the way they did, which helped me to understand points of tension that existed in the larger congregation better.[92]

During each formal session, I gave a short verbal and written summary of key research themes to each member. Congregants were then invited to discuss themes, to suggest new themes, or challenge themes. I also gave participants my contact details so that if they had anything they wanted to add they could contact me. I explained that I welcomed as much critique as possible because I needed to ensure that what seemed to be key themes were representative of the views of groups in the wider

---

90. Cf. Bennett, "Britain," 480.
91. Bryman, *Social Research Methods*, 475.
92. Bryman, *Social Research Methods*, 475.

congregation (as far as possible). I audio recorded these consultations and engaged in analysis of transcripts of them.[93]

2.7 Summary

The book is structured to provide a coherent discussion of how the methodology and methods of this research are applied, and how it aims to arrive at specific provisional results. Other congregations wanting to explore a similar kind of missional change process may learn much from the theological rescripting of congregants' ordinary theologies explored in this book. Hence, understanding how it works is important. Indeed, I suggest it is of foundational importance for formal missional church studies to engage in a root-and-branch reevaluation of its missional ecclesiology in light of listening carefully to the ordinary theological voices of congregants on the receiving end of missional change processes. I also suggest rescripting methodology will not only help members to develop their own kinds of missional theology, but will also challenge much of the received wisdom portrayed in the formal missional church literature.

---

93. In later data chapters the key emic findings of these consultations are discussed.

Chapter 3

Characteristics of a Newbigin-like *Missio Dei* Theology

Introduction

A FUNDAMENTAL AIM OF my research is to investigate the impact on members of a Newbigin-like theology of the *Missio Dei*. *Missio Dei* and the missionary role of the church are inseparably linked in Newbigin's theology.[1] Guder's introduction in the book, *Missional Church*, identifies six characteristics of Newbigin's thought which provide a convenient framework for the analysis of Phoenix's members' ordinary theologies.[2] Van Gelder and Zscheile argue that *Missional Church* provides a contextualized articulation of a "missiological consensus" regarding the key concepts of Newbigin's missional ecclesiology.[3] It might be thought of as a standardized understanding of these concepts. I chose to use the term *Newbigin-like* instead of *Guder-like* to refer to these six characteristics because Guder attributes them to Newbigin.[4] The team of scholars who helped to write *Missional Church* with Guder collaborated, to some extent, with Newbigin in the formulation of GOCN ecclesiology. I will draw

---

1. Cf. Weston, "Ecclesiology in Eschatological Perspective," 70–87.

2. Guder, *Missional Church*, 3–11; cf. Van Gelder and Zscheile, *Missional Church in Perspective*, 6, 7.

3. Van Gelder and Zscheile, *Missional Church in Perspective*, 6; Guder, *Missional Church*, 3–4.

4. Guder, *Missional Church*, 3–10; cf. Van Gelder and Zscheile, *Missional Church in Perspective*, 1–9.

on references to Newbigin's own works, and those found in Newbigin scholarship, to flesh out some key aspects of these "six characteristics."[5]

Missional Church has proved highly influential in the development of GOCN's missiology, and upon the thinking of scholars from a range of Christian traditions in North America and the wider world.[6] It is particularly useful because it aims to critically explore how congregations might reconcentrate their efforts on mission suited to their contexts.[7]

I recognize that a work designed to address the North American situation is not contextualized to the British setting. I will bear in mind the differences between these situations when later analyzing data. The work of British Newbigin scholars, like Weston, also helps to adjust for potential cultural biases that might affect Guder's interpretation of Newbigin's missional ecclesiology.[8] It is also important to recollect that Newbigin was involved in the establishment of GOCN in Britain, which provided the model for its North American counterpart. Hence, the fundamental substrate of the North American version of the GOCN is founded on a theology of mission first developed in the United Kingdom by Newbigin.

Garrett critiques *Missional Church* for being overly theoretical, and particularly for not offering discussion of how to bring about the missional transformation of congregations. Despite this critique, Van Gelder and Zscheile indicate it has led to the development of other theoretical works, as well as a groundswell of interest in the establishment of missional churches.[9] Interestingly, Raiter offers a Reformed critique of *Missional Church*.[10] He argues that it fails to prioritize the gospel's challenge to repent of sin, to find salvation in Christ, and to pursue holy living and righteousness.[11] He also critiques it for only viewing the life practices of the church through a missional lens, leading to not enough attention being concentrated upon the formation of other forms of Christian

---

5. Cf. Goheen, *Church and Its Vocation*; Goheen, "As the Father Has Sent Me"; Laing and Weston, *Theology in Missionary Perspective*; Weston, *Lesslie Newbigin, Missionary Theologian*; Hunsberger, *Bearing the Witness of the Spirit*.

6. Cf. Van Gelder and Zscheile, *Missional Church in Perspective*.

7. Guder, *Missional Church*, 1–17.

8. Cf. Laing and Weston, *Theology in Missionary Perspective*; Weston, *Lesslie Newbigin, Missionary Theologian*.

9. Van Gelder and Zscheile, *Missional Church in Perspective*, 1–10.

10. Raiter, "Missional Church."

11. Raiter, "Missional Church."

ministry.¹² It will be important to evaluate the extent to which these common Reformed concerns are expressed by Phoenix's members. Having noted these critiques, they do not take away from *Missional Church* providing a summary of the key concepts of Newbigin's missional ecclesiology, which will help me to analyze congregational emic data.¹³

3.1 Characteristics of a Newbigin-like *Missio Dei* Theology

This section investigates the six characteristics of a Newbigin-like *Missio Dei* and missional ecclesiology (cf. §3.1). These characteristics will be used later to analyze members' ordinary theologies (cf. §4.2).¹⁴

3.1.1 Theocentric Community-Focused Mission

Guder, like Newbigin, connects ecclesiology to missiology, positing that Western society is a mission field, and that the church needs to act as an instrument of the divine mission in its context.¹⁵ In other words, its focus needs to be theocentric rather than ecclesiocentric by concentrating congregations on joining with what God is guiding them to do, rather than them determining their own direction. Guder posits that the Western church of the post-Christendom era has generally lost sight of its missionary nature, although things are changing in this regard in the United Kingdom.¹⁶ Like Newbigin, Guder argues that the church has concentrated too much attention on maintaining practices which were understood within civil society during Christendom, but which are not understood in the post-Christendom Western context.¹⁷ As a result, Christianity has

---

12. Raiter, "Missional Church."

13. Guder, *Missional Church*.

14. Cf. Guder, *Missional Church*; Franklin, "Missionaries in Our Own Back Yard," 185–86.

15. Guder, *Missional Church*, 3–8, 110–43; Newbigin, *Gospel in a Pluralist Society*, 222–41; Weston, *Lesslie Newbigin, Missionary Theologian*, 59, 117–20, 207–17.

16. Guder, *Missional Church*, 6–8, 48–55; McNeal, *Missional Communities*, 1–13; cf. MacIlvaine, "How Churches Become Missional"; Moynagh, *Church in Life*; Moynagh and Harrold, *Church for Every Context*; Cray, *Mission-Shaped Church*.

17. Cf. Newbigin, *Gospel in a Pluralist Society*, 1–13; Guder, *Missional Church*, 6–8, 48–55; McNeal, *Missional Communities*, 1–13. It is to be noted that Newbigin was critiqued for wanting to bring about a new Christendom; cf. Heneise, "Critical

largely lost its preferred status as the religion of the masses, and has to work hard to obtain a voice within Western society.[18] This means a "missiological ecclesiology" is required to equip Christians to become missionaries in the secular communities within which they live and work.[19] Guder emphasizes that the focus of Newbigin's ecclesiology was to join with what it discerned God was doing in its local neighborhood and within a wider Western social context.[20]

Goheen stresses that Newbigin's missional ecclesiology was premised on equipping the laity to engage in local missionary witness.[21] This would require that the church invest its resources in equipping them for this kind of "witness."[22] Christian witness was to be grounded on "renewal of" human "minds and a radical transformation of" their "way of being."[23] Thus, believers needed to learn how to model what it meant to belong to God based on their participation in a congregation that was committed to faith and obedience in God. Newbigin believed a church of this kind would also need to enable Christians to help people in society engage in a spiritual formation process to develop a Christian faith for themselves.[24]

The first characteristic of a Newbigin-like theology may be summarized as: a church that views society at large as a mission field and concentrates its efforts on engaging in mission alongside God in its local community. It, therefore, has a theocentric focus and seeks to enable new believers to develop a deep faith in God.

Evaluation," 51, 52.

18. Cf. Newbigin, *Gospel in a Pluralist Society*, 1–13; Guder, *Missional Church*, 18–22, 48–55; Roxburgh, *Missional Map-Making*, 19–40, 73–86.

19. Guder, *Missional Church*, 142–82; cf. Stevens, *Abolition of the Laity*, 3–23.

20. Guder, *Missional Church*, 3–4, 110–43; Newbigin, *Gospel in a Pluralist Society*, 222–33.

21. Goheen, *Church and Its Vocation*, 206–9; Newbigin, *Gospel in a Pluralist Society*, 234–41; cf. Henderson Callahan, "Forming Lay Missional Leaders," 120–46; Barrett et al., *Treasure in Clay Jars*, 33–58.

22. Goheen, *Church and Its Vocation*, 209.

23. Cf. Rae, "Congregation as Hermeneutic of the Gospel," 189.

24. Newbigin, *Gospel in a Pluralist Society*, 222–24; cf. Franklin, "Missionaries in Our Own Back Yard," 183–86; Hunsberger, *Bearing the Witness of the Spirit*, 156–93.

3.1.2 The Kingdom of God and the Goal of the Missio Dei

Guder stresses that Newbigin's theology focuses on the coming of the kingdom of God as the goal of the *Missio Dei*.[25] Newbigin's version of "reign of God" theology is premised on an *already* and *not yet* tension, which challenges believers to live as if they already were part of the kingdom of God, whilst also living with the tension of awaiting its full eschatological arrival.[26] Newbigin's theology of the kingdom could be neatly characterized in a phrase conceived by Fee, that Christians may view themselves as beginning to live "the life of the future in the present" world (cf. §4.2.2).[27]

Newbigin's theology of the kingdom is proleptic as it reflects on the hope of the future life and projects it back onto the present world. Thus, believers may develop a consciousness of themselves as already spiritually being part of the kingdom of God into which others might be invited.[28] This awareness of the imminence of the kingdom may then spur Christians on to have confidence in their status as already belonging to the future eschatological kingdom, as well as helping new converts discover this belief for themselves. It may be thought of as a motivating theology that can enable Christians to participate in the *Missio Dei*.

The second characteristic of a Newbigin-like theology may be summarized thus: the proleptic theology of the coming kingdom concentrates the outlook of the missionary-sending church on the goal of the *Missio Dei* (i.e., the full arrival of the kingdom.)[29]

---

25. Guder, *Missional Church*, 10, 77–109; Newbigin, *Open Secret*, 40–65; cf. Sarisky, "Meaning of the *Missio Dei*," 262.

26. Newbigin, *Open Secret*, 40–65; Guder, *Missional Church*, 10; Hunsberger, *Bearing the Witness of the Spirit*, 173, 206, 236.

27. Fee, *Paul, the Spirit, and the People of God*, 99; cf. Weston, *Lesslie Newbigin, Missionary Theologian*, 138–40; Weston, "Ecclesiology in Eschatological Perspective," 70–87.

28. Cf. Weston, "Ecclesiology in Eschatological Perspective," 70–87; Newbigin, *Open Secret*, 40–65.

29. Newbigin, *Open Secret*, 40–65; Weston, "Ecclesiology in Eschatological Perspective," 70–87.

3.1.3 Representatives of the Kingdom of God

In Newbigin's view, the church was to represent a prophetic "sign and foretaste" of a restored harmony between God and humanity.[30] Believers were to model the influence of God's kingdom on their lives to people outside the church.[31] In other words, Newbigin's missional ecclesiology is interpreted in the light of the future society that will come about when the kingdom of God fully arrives. Guder, like Newbigin, asserts that the church's missionary nature needs to be redefined by placing it as a representative community of God's reign to wider society.[32] Similar to Guder, Grenz and Smith relate how the motif of the kingdom of God calls for a challenging journey of ecclesial change because:

> The Spirit forms us into a people through whom he can bring about the completion of God's work in the world.[33]

This means the local congregation will need to act as the "hermeneutic of the gospel."[34] Newbigin taught that those in society who did not espouse the Christian faith might be influenced by the virtuous lives of Christians, thereby providing society with embodied representations of the impact of the gospel on the beliefs, values, and practices of believers.[35]

Guder, like Newbigin, believes "the church of Jesus Christ is not the purpose or goal of the gospel but rather its instrument and witness."[36] The church is to exist so that the quality of humanity's spiritual life might be advanced in wider society, rather than the church just concentrating on maintaining its own inner life.[37]

---

30. Newbigin, *Gospel in a Pluralist Society*, 222–33; cf. Weston, "Ecclesiology in Eschatological Perspective," 70–87.

31. Newbigin, *Gospel in a Pluralist Society*, 222–33; cf. Weston, "Ecclesiology in Eschatological Perspective," 70–87.

32. Guder, *Missional Church*, 5, 77, 78, 93–104; Newbigin, *Gospel in a Pluralist Society*, 222–33.

33. Grenz and Smith, *Created for Community*, 173.

34. Cf. Newbigin, *Gospel in a Pluralist Society*, 229; Newbigin, *Open Secret*, 56; Rae, "Congregation as Hermeneutic of the Gospel," 189–202; cf. Guder, *Missional Church*, 77, 78; Hastings, *Missional God, Missional Church*, 140–41.

35. Newbigin, *Gospel in a Pluralist Society*, 228–31. It is to be noted that this is not just a theology espoused by Newbigin. It is, for example, identifiable in Wesleyan Methodism; cf. Raser, "Compassion," 158–67.

36. Guder, *Missional Church*, 5.

37. Cf. Van Gelder and Zscheile, *Participating in God's Mission*, 38.

Newbigin stressed that a church could only act as a representative community of the kingdom if it were itself committed to uniting all peoples through Christ.[38] The church needed to represent:

> a living demonstration of the gospel which it proclaims, because "a gospel of reconciliation can only be communicated by a reconciled fellowship."[39]

A church that consisted of disunited groups that fragmented its inner life could not function sufficiently as a representative community of the coming kingdom.[40]

Interestingly, according to Sheridan and Hendriks, a mission-focused representative theology can harm the church.[41] It can lead to less attention being concentrated on the quality of the church's inner life, which in turn may negatively impact its witness to the world. They comment:

> *Missio Dei* . . . tend[s] to marginalize the place of the church: it either serves the larger purposes of the kingdom of God or if it is unable or unwilling to do so, is bypassed.[42]

In later analysis of the data, I will be attentive to ways that missional ecclesiology might have impacted the communal life of Phoenix and, therefore, the kind of image the congregation projects to represent its Christian faith to others.

The third characteristic of a Newbigin-like theology may be summarized as: the church's missionary nature is redefined, placing it as a representative community of God's reign to wider society.

3.1.4 Missio Dei: *Reframing Ecclesial Theology and Practices*

As already mentioned, Guder, like Newbigin, theorizes that participation in the *Missio Dei* needs to become the focus of missionary-equipping churches.[43] The purpose is to enable congregants to discern God's

---

38. Newbigin, *Household of God*, 141; Weston, "Ecclesiology in Eschatological Perspective," 79–81. It is to be noted that this raises issues of inclusion and diversity.
39. Weston, "Ecclesiology in Eschatological Perspective," 79.
40. Weston, "Ecclesiology in Eschatological Perspective," 79–81.
41. Sheridan and Hendriks, "Emergent Church Movement," 319.
42. Sheridan and Hendriks, "Emergent Church Movement," 319.
43. Guder, *Missional Church*, 3–4; Newbigin, *Open Secret*, 56.

missionary activity in the world, and then to participate in it by seeking to convey the gospel to them.[44] According to Bevans,[45] Newbigin's missionary gospel needs to be contextualized so it can be understood by post-Christian peoples. For Newbigin, contextualization of the gospel was counter-cultural and culture-critical, meaning it:

> offends . . . because there is always something in a communication of the gospel that calls a particular human experience, a particular culture, a particular social location and historical situation to judgement.[46]

Goheen, as well as Hunsberger, stresses that Newbigin's version of the missionary gospel concentrates on the transformation of culture, which arises from his culture-critical theology.[47] There is a deliberate creation of tension that is a characteristic of it because it assumes God is active in the church and world to bring about radical change. For example, it seeks to challenge evil or unjust structures in society, or within the church.[48] This implies a deconstruction of a church's preexisting structures if they are considered to be resistant to the development of a missional church that needs to critique evil.[49] It is, in this sense, critical of preexisting ecclesial corporate cultures. This is an important matter for serious theological reflection. For example, congregational cultures that cause Christians to keep their religion private need confronting, according to Newbigin, because they accommodate secular ideology, which goes against Newbigin's assertion that the gospel is for public consumption.[50] Hence, Newbigin's *Missio Dei* theology challenges the church to critique its own culture if it does not equip it to participate in public missionary activity.[51]

Weston, like Guder, concurs that a culture-critical *Missio Dei* theology was of pivotal importance to Newbigin's missionary ecclesiology,

---

44. Guder, *Missional Church*, 3–4, 81; Newbigin, *Open Secret*, 56; cf. Davies, "Mission and Spirituality for Life"; Kaggwa, "Mission and the Spirit"; Dehmlow Drier, *Created and Led by the Spirit*.

45. Bevans, *Models of Contextual Theology*.

46. Bevans, *Models of Contextual Theology*, 117; cf. Thomas, "Role of the Church."

47. Goheen, *Church and Its Vocation*, 90, 91; Hunsberger, *Bearing the Witness of the Spirit*, 173, 206, 236.

48. Bevans, *Models of Contextual Theology*, 117–19.

49. Cf. Van Gelder and Zscheile, *Missional Church in Perspective*, 51, 52.

50. Cf. Goheen, *Church and Its Vocation*, 170–72; Kaiser, "From Biblical Secularity to Modern Secularism," 79–112; Karkkainen, *Holy Spirit*, 136–38.

51. Newbigin, *Open Secret*, 150–53, 159.

as well as to the development of missional ecclesiology.[52] In Newbigin's pamphlet, *The Other Side of 1984*, he made the case for the church to engage in what it had been sent to do by seeking to address the challenges of living in a post-Christian culture.[53] He frequently questioned if the West could be rewon for Christ if the church rediscovered its missionary calling.[54] Guder postulates that the *Missio Dei* requires that the church's missionary nature must arise as a direct "result of God's initiative, rooted in God's purposes to restore and heal creation."[55] *Missio Dei* is normally understood to concentrate on divine agency and guidance. Hence, if the church follows God's guidance then it must not seek to plan mission as if it owns the rights to it, or use it to promote its own agenda (i.e., human agency). Everything it does must be based on discerning divine activity so the church can participate in it alongside God.[56]

The concentration on divine agency arguably protects the church from abusing the rhetoric of mission to promote its own agenda, which has been a critique leveled at overseas missions that occurred during the colonial period.[57] Newbigin's version of participation in the *Missio Dei* challenges Christians to engage in costly public missionary witness in society.[58] Newbigin's sacramental theology concentrates on the church modelling its life on the costly sacrifice of Christ, which is at the center of the gospel as "public truth."[59] Newbigin challenged versions of evangelical theology that limited salvation to the forgiveness of sins only and a

---

52. Weston, "Ecclesiology in Eschatological Perspective," 70–87; Karkkainen, *Holy Spirit*, 125–54; Guder, *Missional Church*, 3–4; cf. Bevans and Schroeder, *Prophetic Dialogue*, 9–18.

53. Newbigin, *Other Side of 1984*,

54. Newbigin, "Can the West be Converted?" (1985); Newbigin, *Foolishness to the Greeks*; Newbigin, "Can the West be Converted?" (1987); Newbigin, *Mission and the Crisis*.

55. Guder, *Missional Church*, 3–4; cf. Newbigin, *Gospel in a Pluralist Society*, 131, 226.

56. Cf. Newbigin, *Open Secret*, 56, 60.

57. Cf. Song, "Freedom of the Human Spirit," 15–34; Akrong, "Deconstructing Colonial Mission," 63–75; Hanciles, *Beyond Christendom*, 83, 93–104.

58. Newbigin, "Gospel as Public Truth."

59. Newbigin, "Gospel as Public Truth," Goheen, "*As the Father Has Sent Me*," 278. It is to be noted that Newbigin also portrayed the doctrine of the Trinity as a public truth for the world, not just the church; cf. Newbigin, "Trinity as Public Truth."

future life in heaven.⁶⁰ Instead, it was to equip believers to participate in missionary witness in the present world.⁶¹

Newbigin believed that this kind of missionary theology required church leadership approaches to be changed so leaders would need to focus on equipping congregations for costly missionary service.⁶² Guder, and some other missional church scholars, similarly emphasize the need for universities and colleges to concentrate more attention on educating more Christian leaders to equip their congregations for this sort of influential mission praxis.⁶³

The need for empirical research is, therefore, intensified as more colleges and universities develop missional leadership programs. For example, Niemandt's practical theology concentrates on the church's embodied missional life in the context of South Africa.⁶⁴ Reflective practical theologies like Niemandt can help to inform the academic debate about the impact of differing versions of missional ecclesiology on congregations, and help students in the academy to grasp what it will require of them as missional leaders.⁶⁵ Cameron et al. highlight that theological reflection on the *Missio Dei* is vital if the church is to be enabled to fulfill its missionary role.⁶⁶ Later analysis of data will provide examples of how Phoenix members' reflections on *Missio Dei* have seemingly influenced them in positive and negative ways (cf. §4.2; 5.3.1–5.3.2). I hope Phoenix's story will inform academic pedagogical debate and the work of missional leaders who graduate from higher-level educational programs.

The fourth characteristic of a Newbigin-like theology may be summarized thus: *Missio Dei* theology is understood to make God the sole agent and guide of all mission in the world.

---

60. Cf. Goheen, "*As the Father Has Sent Me*," 277–79.

61. Cf. Goheen, "*As the Father Has Sent Me*," 277–79.

62. Newbigin, *Gospel in a Pluralist Society*, 234–41.

63. Guder, "Investigating Theological Formation for Apostolic Vocation"; cf. Cronshaw, "Australians Reenvisioning of Theological Education"; Banks, *Reenvisioning Theological Education*; Shaw, *Transforming Theological Education*. It is to be noted that in Britain, it is encouraging to see evidence of Christian colleges and some universities focusing on educating leaders in this manner.

64. Niemandt, "Five Years of Missional Church"; Niemandt, "Trends in Missional Ecclesiology"; cf. Love and Niemandt, "Led by the Spirit."

65. Niemandt, "Five Years of Missional Church"; Niemandt, "Trends in Missional Ecclesiology"; Gibbs and Bolger, *Emerging Church*.

66. Cameron et al., *Talking about God in Practice*, 7–17, 63.

3.1.5 The Sending Nature of the Trinity

Guder, like Newbigin, emphasizes there is a need to refocus the church on identifying itself as an instrument of the Trinity's mission.[67] Instrumental language of this sort arises from what is termed by systematic theologians as "economic Trinitarianism."[68] The concept of the economy can suggest that the triune persons fulfill different functions. The Father is portrayed as the source of all life and mission, the Son is sent to redeem humankind, and the Spirit is sent to universally bring about the reconciliation of the entire cosmos to the Father.[69] It, in other words, can segment the roles of Father, Son, and Spirit to the performance of different functions (or to functional modes of action in the divine economy). Newbigin conceives of the Trinity as the primary agent of all mission, and understands the church to be a secondary instrument.[70] The church only acts as an instrument insofar as it rightly discerns what God is calling and empowering it to do. Hence, in Newbigin's view, the church itself has no agency of its own.[71]

Grenz emphasizes that the doctrine of the Trinity went into virtual eclipse in Western theology before its reemergence in the twentieth century, but with its reappearance, Guder indicates it became foundational to understanding the missionary nature of God and the church.[72] This eclipse impeded the Western church from making an earlier connection of the sending nature of God to the work of the church.[73] Its rediscovery is of vital importance to emphasizing God's sending-missionary activity in and through the church.[74]

Guder, like Newbigin, is enthusiastic about affirming that the "Trinitarian point of entry into" the "theology of the church necessarily shifts

---

67. Guder, *Missional Church*, 4–5; Newbigin, *Open Secret*, 56–65; Newbigin, *Relevance of Trinitarian Doctrine*.

68. Cf. McGrath, *Historical Theology*, 54–58.

69. Cf. Newbigin, *Open Secret*, 56–65; Guder, *Missional Church*, 4–5; McGrath, *Historical Theology*, 54–58.

70. Guder, *Missional Church*, 5.

71. Newbigin, *Open Secret*, 56–66.

72. Grenz, *Rediscovering the Triune God*, 6–32; Guder, *Missional Church*, 4–5.

73. Guder, *Missional Church*, 4–5; Grenz, *Rediscovering the Triune God*, 6–32; cf. Bosch, *Transforming Mission*, 389–93.

74. Cf. Newbigin, "Sending of the Church."

all the accents" of "ecclesiology."[75] In other words, it arguably magnifies the functional role of congregants, who are sent to engage in missional activities by the triune God.[76] Interestingly, Fergusson discusses how Newbigin's theology "stresses the extent to which the Christian community" rests "upon the" theology of the "prior work of Father, Son and Spirit," especially in terms of modelling its life on fulfilling the function of what it has been sent to do.[77] Newbigin's Trinitarian theology does not develop a relational communal theology of the Trinity, which one writer of *Missional Church* recognized was missing and needed developing.[78] The danger of any theology that emphasizes mission as a function of participation in the *Missio Dei* is that it may lead to too much emphasis being placed on a theology of missional *doing*, to the detriment of a communal theology of the church's relational *being* (cf. §5.4; 8.1.2).

The fifth characteristic of a Newbigin-like theology may be summarized as: the sending nature of the triune God enables the missional church to conceive of itself in functional terms of being sent to participate in the triune mission.

3.1.6 Missional Hermeneutic of the Bible

Guder develops Newbigin's missional hermeneutics, suggesting it provides an interpretative lens through which Christians may see themselves as called to act as missionaries.[79] The Bible is interpreted by Newbigin as a revelation of God's missionary activity in the world.[80] Newbigin drew on Barth's theology of God's self-revelation in the person of Christ, believing that God had revealed God's self in history, and that the Bible was a primary source of offering testimony to God's presence in the world arena.[81] He understood divine revelation to be part of the sending nature

---

75. Guder, *Missional Church*, 4–5; Newbigin, *Open Secret*, 30–65.

76. Guder, *Missional Church*, 4, 5; cf. Fergusson, "Ecumenism and the Doctrine of the Trinity Today," 552, 553; McKnight, *Kingdom Conspiracy*, 115–17.

77. Fergusson, "Ecumenism and the Doctrine of the Trinity Today," 552; cf. Ott and Strauss, with Tennent, *Encountering Theology of Mission*, 63–89.

78. Cf. Guder, *Missional Church*, 77–109; Van Gelder and Zscheile, *Missional Church in Perspective*, 54, 55.

79. Guder, *Missional Church*, 183; cf. Newbigin, *Open Secret*, 12–29.

80. Newbigin, *Gospel in a Pluralist Society*, 52–65; Guder, *Missional Church*, 10–11, 212–14; cf. Bauckham, "Mission as Hermeneutic," 228–44.

81. Newbigin, *Gospel in a Pluralist Society*, 66–79; cf. Weston, *Lesslie Newbigin*,

of God. Wagner, like Newbigin, posits that the church needs to obtain its missionary self-understanding from what he terms an "apostolic reading of Scripture."[82] He comments:

> "... the church as the community of the reconciled" is "called into fellowship with the triune God as active participants in God's own work of reconciliation."[83]

Guder, like Newbigin, stresses that the Bible provides a framework to help the church to identify and discern the missionary-reconciling work of the triune Spirit in contemporary society.[84] Newbigin's missional pneumatology posited that the sovereign Spirit guides the church, and that it is for the church to discern the Spirit's preecclesial activities in the world and then to participate in them.[85] His rational approach to discernment was not based on a charismatic theology of divine prophetic guidance, although he was not without sympathy toward a charismatic theology of the gifts of the Spirit (§8.1.3).[86] Neither did he believe it would be easy for the church to always rightly discern the Spirit's work in the world.[87] It would require believers to fully indwell the biblical story, as well as their cultural stories, in order to seek God's guidance for how to respond to the needs of society.[88] Based on this kind of deep living within the biblical and cultural stories, Newbigin considered that the Spirit's missional work could be discerned by believers identifying similar patterns of God's influence on non-Christians' lives to their own, which would put them in a position to cooperate with what God might be doing in others' lives.[89] The key to discernment was to be observant for a correspondence between the biblical story with the stories embedded in

---

Missionary Theologian, 5, 12; Goheen, *Church and Its Vocation*, 15–40.

82. Wagner, "*Missio Dei*"; cf. Newbigin, *Gospel in a Pluralist Society*, 89–102; Wright, *Mission of God's People*, 23–32.

83. Wagner, "*Missio Dei*."

84. Guder, *Missional Church*, 10–11; Newbigin, "Can the West be Converted?" (1987), 355–68; cf. Van Gelder and Zscheile, *Missional Church in Perspective*, 151–52; Goheen, *Church and Its Vocation*, 158, 159.

85. Newbigin, *Open Secret*, 56.

86. Newbigin, *Open Secret*, 56.

87. Cf. Goheen, "As the Father Has Sent Me," 355.

88. Cf. Newbigin, *Gospel in a Pluralist Society*, 128–40; Goheen, "As the Father Has Sent Me," 355.

89. Cf. Goheen, "As the Father Has Sent Me," 156, 299, 300; Newbigin, *Open Secret*, 56; Hughes, "Life in the Spirit," 2013.

movements occurring in society.⁹⁰ Goheen suggests that Acts 10, which records the Spirit's guidance of the early church's work with the first gentile converts, was the paradigm for Newbigin's understanding of how the church should continue to discern its mission.⁹¹ It would involve identifying indicators of similar patterns of God's missionary work in modern peoples' lives compared to those found in the Bible, and then joining with that work.

The sixth characteristic of a Newbigin-like theology may be summarized as: a missional interpretation of the Bible provides a framework to indicate how God works in mission in the world with and through believers.

3.2 Summary

In summary, these interlinked Newbigin-like theological characteristics will be utilized to critically analyze the fieldwork data derived from my research at Phoenix. Two key questions will be used to analyze data in subsequent chapters: How have these Newbigin-like characteristics influenced Phoenix's members' ordinary theologies (if at all)? And how are these theological outlooks represented in congregants' espoused and operant theologies (if at all)?

---

90. I.e., in people's lives; Newbigin, *Gospel in a Pluralist Society,* 65; Goheen, "As the Father Has Sent Me," 129–34; 299–300.

91. Goheen, "As the Father Has Sent Me," 156, 157; cf. Van Gelder and Zscheile, *Missional Church in Perspective,* 151–52. It is to be noted that Goheen stresses that Newbigin's pneumatology was not well developed, making it "ambiguous" ("As the Father Has Sent Me," 299, 300).

Chapter 4

Congregational Changes

Introduction

THIS CHAPTER CONCENTRATES ON an overview of missional changes that occurred at Phoenix church among its members, in terms of their growing awareness of themselves as called and sent by God to participate in God's mission. Phoenix's journey of change may be depicted as a work-in-progress. Graduate leaders from my college sought to transform members' self-consciousness to view themselves as participants in the *Missio Dei*.[1] I characterize this change in perspective as congregants developing and adopting a theological self-awareness that God had called and sent them to participate in the divine mission.

The research literature suggests understanding *Missio Dei* encourages congregants to discern their missional vocation.[2] This chapter investigates how members' ordinary theologies were seemingly undergoing modification, leading some of them to exhibit a sense of personal calling to participate in the *Missio Dei*.

As I listened to individual accounts of the church's change journey, I noticed there seemed to be two distinct phases of change identified by congregants. They were what might be termed: (1) a consciousness development phase; and (2) a consciousness adoption phase. During the first

---

1. My research does not engage in the philosophical investigation of human consciousness; cf. Tye, "Philosophical Problems of Consciousness," 17–31; Searle, "Irreducibility of Consciousness," 700–708; Legrand, "Phenomenological Dimensions," 204–27. Schleiermacher was the first to base his dogmatic theology on God-consciousness; cf. *Christian Faith*; McGrath, *Historical Theology*, 232.

2. Cf. Barrett et al., *Treasure in Clay Jars*, 33–58; Bosch, *Transforming Mission*, 389–93; Ott and Strauss, with Tennent, *Encountering Theology of Mission*, 217–37.

phase, it seems members were helped by graduate leaders' preaching to understand what participation in the *Missio Dei* meant to them. As far as I could determine, this development phase began in the latter part of 2012 and predominated until about 2015.[3] A few missional projects were implemented during this period, but they were not the main focus of congregational activity. This was primarily a teaching phase, and only a small number of congregants began to explore how they might engage in local mission activities.[4] Then, from 2015–18, a second phase of change emerged. More members seemed to adopt a self-understanding of being sent by God to participate in mission (cf. §4.2.3). This resulted in an increasing number of congregants supporting the church's concentration on local mission (cf. §4.1).[5]

This chapter investigates quantitative and qualitative congregational data. It consists of two main sections: (1) quantitative data is analyzed to gauge the extent to which members had become conscious of themselves as participants in the *Missio Dei*; and (2) qualitative data is evaluated to assess which of the six characteristics of a Newbigin-like theology of *Missio Dei* were informing members' ordinary theologies (if at all).[6] Given that GOCN academic literature asserts that congregations will adopt these six characteristics, if they are to equip members to engage in mission it will be important to evaluate which of them seemed to inform the ordinary theologies of congregants.[7] Concentrating on an overview of congregational data will provide a wide canvas on which to later sketch more detailed aspects of the larger congregational landscape (cf. chs. 5–7). Providing a canvas on which to trace out the bigger congregational picture is a vital part of mapping the responses of congregants to the development of their self-consciousness of themselves as participants in God's mission.

---

3. During 2009–2012, Bill's preaching laid the foundations for the later communication of *Missio Dei* theology. He began to preach about *Missio Dei* whilst doing an MA program of my college (2012/2013).

4. I obtained this data from Bill and other leaders.

5. Some members resisted it, which impeded the launching of missional projects.

6. I listened to numerous sermons that included aspects of these six Newbigin-like characteristics. Hence, those who had been members for two years or more had the chance to learn about them.

7. Cf. Guder, *Missional Church*, 2–10.

4.1 Extent of Espousal of *Missio Dei*

This section aims to investigate: (1) the extent of members' espousal of *Missio Dei* theology; and (2) how it may have influenced them to engage in missional projects. At the conclusion of fieldwork at Phoenix (in September 2018) I gave out questionnaires to members during a Sunday morning service (cf. Appendix E). The aim of this questionnaire was primarily to determine answers to two key questions: (a) How many members first heard the term *Missio Dei* during the time of their new pastor (Bill), and (b) Had an understanding of the *Missio Dei* inspired members to act in new ways in how they sought to share their faith? Tables 2 and 3 indicate the results related to these questions.

Table 2: Members First Heard of Missio Dei at Phoenix (N is the symbol for sample size)				
	Frequency	Percent	Valid Percent	Cumulative Percent
Valid Yes	27	63	69	69
No	12	28	31	100
Total	39	91	100	100
Missing No Response	4	9		
Total	4	9		
Total	N = 43	100		

Table 3: Members Felt Inspired to Share Their Faith because of Missio Dei (N is the symbol for sample size)				
	Frequency	Percent	Valid Percent	Cumulative Percent
Valid Yes	34	79	90	90
No	4	9	10	100
Total	38	88	100	100
Missing No Response	5	12		
Total	5	12		
Total	N = 43	100		

There were forty-three members who completed the questionnaire. There were approximately 120 adult members/attendees of the congregation during 2016–18.[8] I investigated possible reasons why only forty-three congregants completed it. Most often only one member of a family completed it because: (a) one adult was looking after children;

---

8. Including visitors, Sunday morning attendance could be up to 160 adults.

(b) couples claimed to share similar views to their life partners; (c) some members left directly after the service, and (d) one person disagreed with *Missio Dei* theology and refused to complete it.[9]

According to church records, fifty-eight (48 percent) adult members had left Phoenix since the missional change journey had begun (2013–18). Ten (8 percent) congregants had left because they disagreed with the new missional focus.[10] Others had left because of moving home, finding a job, etc. Importantly, an unofficial grassroots view suggested more than twenty members (16 percent) had departed due to negative reactions to missional changes in the church. It was impossible to determine the exact figures. The figure of twenty seemed more likely, as members who remained in touch with those who had left said it was because they did not agree with the new missional focus. During some interviews, it was indicated that yet more members were feeling discouraged and thinking of leaving. Soon after completing my fieldwork, another fifteen members left (i.e., 12 percent). Based on my observations, the fifteen who departed were among members I had spoken to who were not in favor of the church's missional emphasis (cf. Group 2's data in §5.2).[11] In total, thirty-five (29 percent) left because they did not agree with the missional changes.[12] About sixty new members joined Phoenix during 2009–18 which indicated a decline in the congregation's size by about thirteen members. This means the congregation's membership was reduced to about 107.

Based on responses to the question in Table 2, 63 percent of members had first learned about *Missio Dei* during Bill's tenure. Another 28 percent of members had heard of it elsewhere (this 28 percent consisted of the newer members). In interviews with some of the sixty newer members, I discovered they had been attracted to Phoenix partly because of its missional focus. It was a significant finding that an extrapolated 79 percent of the congregation claimed that understanding *Missio Dei* had inspired them to share their faith with others (cf. Table 3). I recognize that

---

9. I followed Bryman's advice that when people choose not to participate in a survey caution needs to be exercised regarding the value of the data, as sampling errors may occur (*Social Research Methods*, 168–70).

10. I think a more credible explanation for differences between members' estimates and the official record was due to congregants not feeling comfortable about telling leaders the real reasons for their departure.

11. Based on my conversations, I found no evidence that members left because of my research with them.

12. Less conservative estimates may raise this number to as many as fifty members/attendees leaving.

members simply feeling inspired to share their faith cannot be equated with them doing so. Hence, I tried to substantiate this rather high figure in other ways.[13] I crosschecked it with the perceptions of members who participated in the five congregational consultations. I asked them what their views were about this high figure. There was a general consensus that more than half of the congregation were in favor of the church's missional focus. They also pointed to the significant number of members who were supporting the church's missional projects as evidence of this view. Based on my interactions with Bill and leaders of missional projects I was able to obtain the data found in Table 4.

Table 4: Missional Projects		
Description of Missional Initiative	Number of Members Involved	Year of Launch
Community Support Group (the lonely and those with mental health issues)	3	2015
Missional Café	5	2016
Missional Allotment 1	6	2013
Missional Allotment 2 and Church-Planting Project	12	2014
Missional Allotment 3 (Church Car Park)	10	2018
Missional Summer Children's Club	20	2009
Missional Youth Group	8	2015[14]
Fourteen House Groups	80	2009–18

I wondered how much overlap there was between the groups of people who supported various missional projects. Out of the sixty-four persons (53 percent) involved in missional projects (not including house groups), I was able to estimate that about ten (8 percent) of this number were involved with more than one of the missional projects. Hence, fifty-four (45 percent) members seemed to engage in missional projects regularly. With the inclusion of house groups, the number involved in missional activities increased. However, I did not want to include everyone involved in a house group in the category of "missional projects," but only those that seemed to be active in some form of missionary work.[15] Hence, I sought to identify house groups engaged in mission with

   13. Cf. Bryman, *Social Research Methods*, 151–54.
   14. The missional focus of the youth group seemed to emerge during 2015.
   15. This was a hard distinction to make. I wanted to err on the side of caution.

neighbors and friends. I found that five groups did this. For example, a young adults' group worked with people wanting to explore the Christian faith. There was a women's Bible study group that included three people exploring Christianity. Some of these people became Christians and were baptized at Phoenix.[16] Interestingly, the members involved in the five groups were not involved in other missional projects. Given that each group had about five members supporting it, there were about twenty-five (21 percent) members involved in mission activities. This meant that as many as seventy-nine (66 percent) congregants were involved in a missional project. Therefore, a majority of members were actively supporting missional projects.

There was a smaller but quite significant proportion of members who were not participating in missional projects (approximately 34 percent). As chapter 1 indicated, the missional change journey had led to some tensions and conflicts within the congregation (cf. ch. 1). Not every member was supportive of the new missional emphasis (cf. §5.2). There were complex reasons for some members not participating which this chapter will not investigate. Later chapters examine why some members resisted participating in mission (cf. chs. 5–7).

4.2 Indicators of *Missio Dei* Awareness

This section concentrates upon qualitative congregational data, which builds on the quantitative data. It indicates the degree to which a positive view of a Newbigin-like *Missio Dei* theology had impacted members. It analyzes congregants' testimonies for correspondences with one or more of the six characteristics of a Newbigin-like theology of *Missio Dei* (if any of them). This analysis makes it possible to obtain indicators of which of these characteristics seemed to influence congregants to become engaged in mission.

4.2.1 Characteristic 1: Theocentric Concentration on the Community

The first characteristic indicates:

---

16. About ten were baptized during my fieldwork.

(1) That a missional church views society at large as a mission field and concentrates its efforts on engaging in mission alongside God in its local community; it has a theocentric focus (cf. §3.1.1).

I observed that a movement had occurred in Phoenix from an inward concentration on supporting the church's program's, toward members becoming aware of what God might be calling them to do in the community (cf. §1.1.1–2). This reminded me of Niemandt's and Branson's research findings regarding the shift in churches from an ecclesiocentric to theocentric perspective because of the mediation of *Missio Dei* theology.[17] This seemed to be occurring with some of Phoenix's members. Three testimonies will be explored in what follows. The first (Caspian's testimony) indicates how things changed in the church from 2009 to 2018. The second (Lucy and Jake's testimonies) will indicate how members' interests in the church's local community were initially catalyzed (beginning in 2008). The third (Lynda's testimony) will provide a cameo of what happened in a missional project in the local community after several years of change.

Caspian's Testimony

Caspian's testimony was significant, as it described his perceptions of the impact of missional change on the congregation and what developed out of it:

> Over that period [2009–18] we've got much more involved with the community. So when the new minister came there was a change from an inner focus on the church towards a structure that focused on outreach. So we were considering at the time [before Bill's employment] whether to move from the church. The Lord resoundingly answered that by starting to get community involvement going [once Bill was employed]. (Appendix B:4)

Caspian also provided a relevant assessment of the impact of *Missio Dei* theology on the congregation:

> I think that a vast majority [of members] see it now, as it's like Bill would say, "It's not the church that's got a mission, it's God

---

17. Niemandt, "Five Years of Missional Church"; Niemandt, "Trends in Missional Ecclesiology"; Branson, "Missional Church Process."

who's got a plan." And we need to find out what that plan is and get involved in it. I think that's been thoroughly dealt with. (Appendix B:4)

The second extract from Caspian's testimony was given in the context of the church's later adoption of community-based missional projects. He indicated that by 2018 Phoenix's change journey had led to a significant proportion of members engaging in missional work. Missional projects had become intentionally structured parts of the church's outreach strategy. This corresponds well with the first characteristic of a Newbigin-like *Missio Dei* theology (cf. §3.1.1).[18] Importantly, Caspian's testimony was affirmed by other members who were engaging in missional work.

Lucy and Jake's Testimonies

Lucy's testimony concentrated on how the church first began to develop a missional outlook. She told me about an important catalyst which challenged members' perceptions about their role in the local neighborhood before, and then during, Bill's early ministry:

> We had a church fire [in 2008] which put us in a different realm missionally. Because it plonked us on the other side of the road [to the church], which is the estate side of the road. It made everyone really uncomfortable. It made us ask "Where is the church going?" It made all of the difference in people's thinking. (Appendix B:7)

There was not enough insurance money to rebuild the church. It left members without a building large enough in which to host worship services. On the opposite side of the road to Phoenix was a working men's club and bar. It was owned by a Hindu businessman. To the astonishment of congregants, the businessman approached the church and offered the club's large function room as a venue for worship. He refused payment for the use of it. The church worshipped in this bar until the early part of 2018. Lucy illustrated the impact that this had on members' development of an awareness of what God might be doing in their locality:

> And you know a lot of people were really hurt, the church was the place they had got married in, had been children in . . . and

---

18. Cf. Guder, *Missional Church*, 6–8.

they were plonked in a pub that challenged every single bit of their being. People started asking me and others, "What is this place and what is this area?" Wasn't it interesting that the bar staff was listening in on the sermon, and people started getting a bit more interested in what was going on locally? So that was a massive change of heart attitude really. It left us being less comfortable. (Appendix B:7)

Lucy explained to me that worshipping in the bar took members out of their old comfort zone. A key characteristic of their developing missional consciousness was discomfort. For example, discomfort about worshipping in a bar led to a few members leaving the church because it lacked the atmosphere of a church building. However, other members, although grieving for the loss of their building, recognized they had things to learn from the interest of the bar staff and locals who frequented it.

I wondered, had the church fire not happened, if there would have been enough interest for Bill and his team to bring about missional change. One member named Jake, a man in his forties, provided a clue that was held by other members like Caspian:

> I think that the people who were here before, well I think God burnt the building because they were such an inward-looking community before that point. I think with hindsight we can join up the dots. (Appendix B:18)

Jake's perspective seemed to imply a theology of divine intervention. In his view, God had been at work preparing for the church's change journey before the appointment of their new pastor, Bill. Caspian added an important insight. He believed God had used experiences like the church fire to help the congregation realize "we needed someone to reach out to the community."

Caspian, Lucy, and Jake seemingly believed God had used the fire to awaken interest to the needs of people in the church's neighborhood. It seems they believed that without it they would not have looked for a new minister who had Bill's abilities to help them engage in local mission.

Lynda's Testimony

Interestingly, about seven years after Phoenix began to worship at the bar, a missional café project was developed by a few of Phoenix's members (in 2016). I observed that missional projects, like this one, had taken time to develop despite the early interest in what God might be doing in the local neighborhood. Lynda and a small team of congregants established the café in one of four terraced shops in the middle of the estate near the pub where they worshipped. This estate was among the top 5 percent of most deprived city suburbs in Britain (cf. §1.1). Lynda, a member of Phoenix for more than twenty years, and a graduate of my college, coordinated the project and worked alongside other congregants there. During an interview, she shared her belief that God had guided the project to turn out differently from what she and others had initially planned. They had first conceived of the café providing an opportunity to launch a mothers and toddlers group to introduce locals to the Christian faith. Lynda commented:

> In the early days that didn't happen at all. We got quite a lot of lonely singles from the estate and the Mind Centers, so we started working a bit more with them. Since then we had an influx of some mums. (Appendix B:6)

Lynda explained that the café team believed God had other plans for their project than starting a mothers and toddlers group, which had led them to ask new questions from the ones they initially had when first planning it:

> It was talked about: "What shall we do?" "How can we get people to come to the church?" Whereas with the café it's been, "Okay, God, what do you want us to do?" "Where are you leading us?" We had ideas in the early days of what we thought it looked like, and it wasn't, and it's then that you start looking at what God wants you to do rather than what you want to do. (Appendix B:6)

Lynda elucidated the mission ethos of the café that emerged out of this process of questioning:

> It's taking Jesus into the estate. It's being an open place, being that oasis basically. It's a place where people can come out of the chaos of the world to a place where there's peace, calm, hope, and finding it through Christ. It doesn't have the best food and everything, although we pride ourselves on quality. But it's quality conversations, it's the quality of the people who are serving the Lord in that area. (Appendix B:6)

I visited the cafe a few times during my fieldwork. Local individuals and some families were regulars. I observed that some of them had built strong relationships with the missional team who served them. There was good-humored repartee between customers and staff. When staff served they would engage in conversations. They also took time to sit with customers to provide a listening ear and to offer them moral support when patrons were struggling with problems. I also heard conversations that included what staff termed "gospel gossiping." This "gossiping" involved members talking about their Christian beliefs and seeking to encourage customers to explore them for themselves. On several occasions, a client would ask for prayer and would be prayed for by a staff member in a discreet manner. Several men in their twenties became Christians apparently as a result of these interactions. I also noticed that three young men began to occasionally attend Phoenix's Sunday services.

Lynda shared that:

> The café wasn't ever about getting bums on seats. It was never about getting them [clients] to come to Phoenix, but it is amazing how people have drifted into the church. (Appendix B:6)

Like other missional projects, the café focused on what happened outside the church in the community. This was quite different from the practices of the past at Phoenix. As already discussed, the role of members had been to invite people to Sunday morning visitors' services to be converted by the professional pastor (cf. §1.1.1). The role of members had been to make visitors feel welcome, but not to convert or catechize them (cf. §1.1.1).

As I reflected on the journey that had led to the establishment of the first missional projects, I realized that before the intentional mediation of *Missio Dei* theology to the congregation the seeds of change seemed to have been implanted by the church fire. The theology of the *Missio Dei* assumes that discernment of divine guidance and agency precedes the work of mission.[19] Newbigin stressed that the "sovereign" Spirit fulfilled a preparatory and guiding role to enable the church to engage in mission.[20] I linked this aspect of Newbigin's theology to Jake and Caspian's ordinary theologies and their belief that God had been the agent of missional change at Phoenix. Lucy's testimony added the important insight

---

19. Newbigin, *Open Secret*, 56; Flett, *Witness of God*, 1–34; Goheen, *Church and Its Vocation*, 68; cf. Bosch, *Transforming Mission*, 389–93; Flett, *Witness of God*, 35–77.

20. Cf. Weston, "Ecclesiology in Eschatological Perspective," 79; Newbigin, *Open Secret*, 56; Cronshaw, "Australians Reenvisioning of Theological Education"; Tennent, *Invitation to World Missions*, 71.

that it took time for the church to "warm up" to the idea of doing local mission work. One example of this was the seven years it took to start the missional café. Arguably, any congregation that undergoes a missional change journey must be given time for its members to develop new missional beliefs and practices. Roxburgh and Romanuk concur with this finding.[21] They argue that congregants need to be enabled by leaders to develop at a pace of change they can sustain.[22] As the quantitative data indicates, by the end of my fieldwork a significant minority of members still had not adopted a view of themselves as missionaries (cf. Group 2's testimonies; §5.2). Like Lynda, some of them seemed to believe God was the one shaping and enabling their missional efforts in the community. Like Lynda, they were following what it seemed like God was influencing people they were working with to do in response to their efforts to influence them about Christ. In other words, they were developing a theocentric focus of discerning and participating in what God was doing through the Spirit with people in the neighborhood.

It was a case of following evidence of God's influence in faith-seeking peoples' lives in order to determine how congregants might cooperate with what God was doing in those peoples' lives. This might be termed as following the Holy Spirit's lead and collaborating with it. In other words, it was allowing God to lead mission rather than trying to do it themselves (at least to some extent). This was very Newbigin-like, as Newbigin insists that *Missio Dei* places the ownership and guidance of all mission in the sovereign Spirit's hands—it is the church's role to follow the Spirit's leadership if mission is really to belong to God.[23] This challenges every church to reconsider how it seeks to practically spiritually discern the Holy Spirit's guidance if it is really serious about letting God lead mission. Theocentricity is at the heart of Newbigin's theology of mission (cf. ch. 3). Some of Phoenix's members' ordinary theologies clearly had grasped something of this theocentric imperative. Later chapters will investigate the challenges the focus on mission in the community presented to the congregation.

---

21. Roxburgh and Romanuk, *Missional Leader*, 143–64; cf. Branson and Martinez, *Churches, Cultures and Leadership*, 210–31.

22. Cf. Roxburgh and Romanuk, *Missional Leader*, 37–60; Roxburgh, *Missional Map-Making*.

23. Newbigin, *Open Secret*, 56.

4.2.2 Characteristics 2 and 3:
Kingdom as Destination and Representation

This section investigates two linked Newbigin-like characteristics of the *Missio Dei*. They are topically based on a theology of the kingdom of God. Characteristics 2 and 3 may be summarized as follows:

(2) Proleptic theology of the coming kingdom concentrates the outlook of the missionary-sending church on the goal of the *Missio Dei* (i.e., the full arrival of the kingdom) (cf. §3.1.2);

(3) The church's missionary nature is redefined, placing it as a representative community of God's reign to wider society (cf. §3.1.3).

The early change journey in the congregation, from its former theology of clergy-centered ministry to a missionary one, may be characterized as an ongoing consciousness-development process. Bill had sought to place the Christian life in the bigger picture of every member perceiving themselves as part of God's eternal kingdom (2009–12). A theology of the eschatological[24] arrival of the kingdom of God is a common evangelical preoccupation.[25] Graham points out that at times it has not helped the church engage in efforts to transform the lives of people in the present world, because there has been too much focus on everything being transformed in the future kingdom.[26]

During 2009–12, Bill began a range of preaching series concentrated on the kingdom of God. The motto "Buy the Field"[27] was used for one of these sermon series. Members were encouraged to completely commit their whole lives to Christ as their Lord, which required them to act as witnesses to his lordship. Given the length of time concentrated upon this topic (eighteen months), I wondered to what extent members later linked it to *Missio Dei* theology. Lucy, Becky, and Desmond's testimonies provided some interesting insights related to my interest.[28]

---

24. Eschatology: the study of last things.

25. Cf. Bebbington, *Evangelicalism in Modern Britain*, 215; Webb, "Eschatology and Politics," 513, 514; Macchia, "Pentecostal and Charismatic Theology," 281, 282.

26. Graham, "Frailty and Flourishing," 336–37; cf. Webb, "Eschatology and Politics," 513.

27. "Buy the field" is based on Jesus' parable of the kingdom (Matt 13:44).

28. Social activism has particularly been a trait of progressive evangelicalism. It has been emphasized at Phoenix since missional changes began; cf. Warner, *Reinventing English Evangelicalism*, 138–46; Stanley, "Activism as Mission Spirituality," 67–82.

CONGREGATIONAL CHANGES 77

Lucy's testimony began with an account of her perceptions of the early stages of Bill's ministry, and went on to indicate developments of the kingdom theme that arose due to it:

> And then over the next eighteen months, with a new pastor [2009–10], all the teaching series focused on the kingdom. It has become a lot more normal to use missional language and to place everything into the plan of God. There is very much that focus in everything preached since then. So people got used to the idea it was more than just community work with poorer local people near the church. The church is quite white and middle class, and they felt uncomfortable with a working-class estate. They started to warm up to the idea that perhaps we should also be sharing our faith with our neighbors and our families, in the streets and our workplaces.[29] So that thinking has slowly developed. (Appendix B:7)

Becky's testimony illustrated how the theme of the kingdom of God was still important to some members in 2017:

> I think that everything we do is kingdom purposed, and our number one song that we've done the most since September is "Build your kingdom here." It says something about the way our church is. Because you're talking about bringing your kingdom here on the earth, we're not just talking about heaven—we're talking about the overall goal. (Appendix B:27)

Desmond's testimony also helped to indicate how members' expectations had gradually changed as they began to develop an understanding of what it meant for them to be part of the kingdom of God:

> I would say it's the difference between people brought up in the culture of the [old] church, which has given them unrealistic expectations that it's always going to be the same without changing. But the kingdom is bigger than that. It challenges because it's not about us, not a kind of club. It's about trying to be part of a change in the world around you, that is bringing the way the kingdom operates into how you live, rather than doing what's happening already in the world (Appendix B:10).

Starting with Lucy's testimony, she concentrated on Bill's initial strategy for congregational change (2009–12). It necessitated challenging members to reframe their lives by what she termed "the plan of God" and

---

29. Work-based mission was not a common theme during my research.

the "kingdom." She stressed to me that members started to comprehend that focusing on the community occasioned far more than just working with "poorer local people." It also encapsulated everything they did in life. In other words, it contributed to developing the consciousness of the congregation regarding God's "purpose," which made the coming of the kingdom of God the goal of mission.[30] This seemed very Newbigin-like to me, given that the research literature posits that the goal of the *Missio Dei* is the coming of the kingdom of God as a now-and-not-yet reality to look forward to.[31]

Newbigin was foremost a pastor. He was interested in the practical influence of his missional theology on the beliefs and practices of believers.[32] I observed that some members[33] seemed to feel encouraged by the idea that they were working alongside God in terms of the coming of God's kingdom in peoples' lives.[34] This outlook, mediated by Bill and his team to members, sought to expand members' understanding of the kingdom so it would not just focus on the future age to come, but also on it having an influence on peoples' lives in the present world.[35] Bill explained that this meant congregants needed to view themselves as involved in starting to bring about changes in peoples' lives in the present, rather than leaving it to the future eschatological world.[36] The later linking of participation in the *Missio Dei* with the coming of the kingdom as its goal seemed to help some members like Becky and Desmond to reconceive of themselves as sent to prepare others for its coming. This is one example of what Bill called "appropriate contextualization" of the church's already existing theology of the kingdom of God.

The need to represent the presence of the kingdom in the present world through members' Christian witness relates to Newbigin's representative theology of the reign of God.[37] Becky and Desmond's

---

30. Cf. Fergusson, "Ecumenism and the Doctrine of the Trinity Today," 553.

31. Cf. Newbigin, *Open Secret*, 64–65; Hunsberger, *Bearing the Witness of the Spirit*, 159–61, 279; Van Gelder and Zscheile, *Missional Church in Perspective*, 7.

32. Cf. Goheen, *Church and Its Vocation*, 8, 47.

33. Six out of thirty interviewees.

34. Cf. Fergusson, "Ecumenism and the Doctrine of the Trinity Today," 553.

35. Cf. Macchia, "Pentecostal and Charismatic Theology," 283, 284; Webb, "Eschatology and Politics," 412, 413.

36. Cf. Webb, "Eschatology and Politics," 413; Braaten, "Kingdom of God," 332–35; Newbigin, *Open Secret*, 56–65; Bosch, *Transforming Mission*, 389–93.

37. Newbigin, *Gospel in a Pluralist Society*, 222–33; cf. Weston, "Ecclesiology in

CONGREGATIONAL CHANGES 79

testimonies came the closest to an expression of a Newbigin-like representative theology (characteristic 3; cf. §3.1.3).[38] Desmond explained it was the church's role to be "part of a change" in the world.[39] He seemed to view himself as an agent of change in the world, acting as a representative of the new society of the kingdom of God through the way he behaved at work or in his neighborhood.

Becky's testimony provided evidence of how her view had changed as she obtained a deeper insight into the relationship of the coming kingdom to everything she did. She seemingly thought all her life practices needed to be informed by her understanding of what it meant to be part of God's kingdom. The worship song, "Build Your Kingdom Here," had seemingly helped her make the connection between her present life and God's reign in her own life.[40] She apparently understood the goal of the Christian life entailed more than going to a heavenly world that would be disconnected from life in this world. It meant God would transform the present world so that heaven would be on earth. I concluded from the excited tone of my conversation with Becky that she saw herself as a participant in the *Missio Dei*, which involved her pointing others toward a world to be transformed by God.[41] In her view, the kingdom's coming meant working alongside God to bring about the transformation of society.[42] I observed that, like Desmond, this perspective helped Becky to have a specific goal to aim for.

Lucy was the only other member who articulated a similar view to both Desmond and Becky's. For example, her ordinary theology of the kingdom influenced her ministry as the chaplain at a local school. She explained to me how her ministry there was influenced by a kingdom theology:

> I don't see them as a school, I see them as a community that I adore, and because I adore them I need them to know what the Good News[43] really means. (Appendix B:7)

Eschatological Perspective," 70, 71.

38. Weston, "Ecclesiology in Eschatological Perspective," 70, 71.

39. Cf. Newbigin, *Gospel in a Pluralist Society*, 222–33.

40. Cf. Guder, *Missional Church*, 5, 77, 78, 93–104; Hastings, *Missional God, Missional Church*, 140–41.

41. Cf. Weston, "Ecclesiology in Eschatological Perspective," 79.

42. Cf. Rae, "Congregation as Hermeneutic of the Gospel," 189–202.

43. Lucy seemingly associated good news with the kingdom of God.

Lucy illustrated how she sought to help students at the school to identify how God might be at work in their community. For example, she shared how she posed reflective questions to students:

> "How are you feeling right now?" "What's that telling us?" "What's that telling us as a community?" "What might God be saying about it?" (Appendix B:7)

Lucy engaged in what might be termed consciousness-development reflective exercises with students. She seemingly wanted students to represent a Christian lifestyle to peers. Her testimony indicated she was trying to enable pupils to view themselves as a kind of representative community (cf. §3.1.3).[44]

I observed that Lucy's theology of the kingdom, like Desmond and Becky's, seemed to have been modified by a Newbigin-like representative theology of the reign of God. It seemed to motivate her to participate in missional ministry as a chaplain. The extent to which other congregants viewed themselves as representatives was not as easy to determine, primarily because they did not speak about it.

Given that only six members discussed their understandings of the kingdom of God during interviews, I inferred that it had not made a significant impact on the majority of members. This surprised me, given that a common theme of evangelical theology emphasizes that Christians need to provide an example to society of what it means to be part of the kingdom by living Christlike lives.[45] Interestingly, an analysis of all of the congregational data did not even once report members using the phrase "Christlike" in a representative sense of imitating Christ's life.[46] The three testimonies discussed above were the only ones I was able to identify, which seemed to espouse something like Newbigin's representative theology of the kingdom. I concluded from this that it was likely not espoused by the majority of the congregation.

Furthermore, only a few members linked the coming of the kingdom to the goal of the *Missio Dei*. This was unexpected, given that GOCN scholars stress the importance of missional congregations adopting both

---

44. Cf. Guder, *Missional Church*, 5, 77, 78, 93–104.

45. Cf. Hancock et al. "Attempting Valid Assessment of Spiritual Growth," 129–53; Bouyer, *Spirit and Forms of Protestantism*, 29, 58, 70.

46. Cf. Boa, *Conformed to His Image*, 278; Bouyer, *Spirit and Forms of Protestantism*, 29, 58.

dimensions of Newbigin's kingdom of God theology (cf. §3.1.2; 3.1.3).[47] Perhaps it could be argued that congregants unconsciously made these links, given that Bill and his team had emphasized both dimensions in numerous sermons. It is of course inadvisable to argue from silence.

4.2.3 Characteristics 4 and 5: The Missio Dei and the Trinity

This section investigates two connected themes, characteristics 4 and 5:

(4) *Missio Dei* theology is understood to make God the sole agent and guide of all mission in the world (cf. §3.1.4).

(5) The sending nature of the triune God enables the missional church to conceive of itself in functional terms of being sent to participate in the triune mission (cf. §3.1.5).

By way of introduction to this section's testimonies, some background needs to be given to make sense of them. During 2015, there was a preaching series that concentrated on the Trinity and participation in the *Missio Dei* (it lasted for about nine months). The motto, "God's people on God's mission in the Spirit's power with the message of His Son," was used as the strapline for this series. After this series, this motto was adopted by the church to characterize the congregation. It was also displayed at the front of Phoenix's worship area. Jake explained that "this motto has stuck more than any other" because a majority of members were helped by it to understand what God was calling them to do as a church.

Interestingly, the church's official statement of faith did not articulate the actual word "Trinity," nor relate it to the *Missio Dei*. However, it implied a Trinitarian basis to its doctrine of God:

> Godhead: The unity of the Godhead and the divine co-equality of the Father, the Son, and the Holy Spirit. The sovereignty of God in creation, providence, and redemption.[48]

Bill explained that the leadership team had wanted to use a rhetoric that "contextualized appropriately" some of the new language of *Missio Dei* to the congregation, without using its theological jargon (like the

---

47. Cf. Hunsberger, *Bearing the Witness of the Spirit*, 159–61, 279; Guder, *Missional Church*, 5, 77, 78.
48. Reference not provided to anonymize Phoenix.

"Trinity" or "Trinitarian"). They did this to frame it in a "biblical language" which congregants were "used to hearing." Hence, they did not use Trinitarian rhetoric in the church's motto. Based on this intelligence, I listened carefully during interviews for an understanding of the sending nature of the Trinity related to the *Missio Dei*. I observed that congregants who espoused *Missio Dei* theology linked the Trinitarian language of "being sent" with the motto (almost every time).

For example, three congregants—Stacey (in her forties), Garth (in his forties), and Mark (in his sixties)—explained that they had been inspired by the rhetoric of *Missio Dei* to participate in missional projects.

Stacey's Testimony

Stacey had a fridge magnet with the church motto on it. She commented:

> To me, that's spot on. We are God's people on his mission, with the power of God, because we can't do it on our own, to spread, you know, the message of his Son. That is what we are trying to do. (Appendix B:25)

She added:

> It's not our mission, because churches think they've got a mission, but it's God's mission. (Appendix B:25)

Stacey, like other members, seemingly believed it was not the job of the church to tell them what to do in their missional projects, but it was rather for members to look to God to guide them (cf. chs. 5 and 6).

Garth's Testimony

Another member, Garth, was involved in one of the five missionally active house groups (cf. §4.1). His testimony provided another interesting perspective on the theme of the mission of God:

> It is something you take part in. We are called to this place and to witness as well. We are called to reveal God to those with whom we come into contact. We are expected to do that. It doesn't make us all evangelists, but we are all called to be missional in the sense that we are witnesses with a testimony. (Appendix B: Consultation Group 2)

Based on my conversation with Garth it seemed he believed God had called him to participate in the *Missio Dei*. He expressed it in terms of being "expected" to give his Christian "testimony" to others. I wondered if the language of being expected to do it meant Garth felt he was required to engage in giving his witness by God, whether he liked it or not. I did not get the impression from the tone of our conversation that he felt it was an onerous expectation. At a house group meeting in his home, I observed that he seemed to enjoy leading the group and offering support to attendees. This suggested he was comfortable in this missional role, and with what he believed God had called him to do.

Mark's Testimony

A third member, Mark, explained how the church's view of mission had changed:

> I think the church has changed from being focused in terms of supporting actual overseas missionaries to saying the mission is now on our doorstep. So it's much more locally focused. (Appendix B:9)

He explained that the new concentration on participation in mission had resulted in him, and his wife Debbie, feeling led by God to move to a new house in another district of the city. They felt called by God to support a missional project there which was not a Phoenix project. Hence, they moved house to engage in mission elsewhere in the city. This indicated to me that some members did not feel they only had to engage in Phoenix's missional projects. Mark and Debbie were the only members I spoke to who had left Phoenix for this reason (cf. Appendix B:8). This project involved Christians using their homes as bases from which they could seek to engage in missional work with local young people.[49] Mark commented on how *Missio Dei* theology had changed his view of the church:

> It's not like going to a Church. It's going to an area. Almost like saying "God, this isn't our house, we wouldn't have had this. This is your house now, we want you to use it for this area." In a sense, you're being planted. That's what we feel like we are planted. (Appendix B:9).

49. This is similar to missionary practices in the early church; cf. Gehring, *House Church and Mission*.

He later commented:

> You're placed exactly where you are. God has put you exactly where you are to do his work. So it doesn't matter where you are, you can still be a missionary—you don't have to go to far-flung fields. (Appendix B:9)

The testimonies of Stacey, Mark, and Garth regarding the impact of *Missio Dei* theology on them were similar to others which are analyzed in chapter 5.

I found it particularly interesting that members never used the word "Trinity" to describe what they felt sent to do, given that the church's motto was Trinitarian. It was used by one member to describe the Trinity as the basis to the relational life of the congregation, but not the *Missio Dei* (cf. Barbara's testimony; §5.2). Garth was the only member who explicitly asked me about the connection of the Trinity to the *Missio Dei* because of something he had heard during one of the church's Bible school meetings. He wanted to find out if the idea of *Missio Dei* was related to the nature of the Trinity as a sending deity—this was particularly surprising, as he did not link it to the church's motto. The link of *Missio Dei* to the Trinity for other members seemed to be implicit rather than explicit. For example, Stacey's testimony provided an example of how members implicitly expressed it (cf. above). I concluded that members understood the sending work of the Trinity at some level related to the motto. This, at least, indicated successful mediation of a Newbigin-like Trinitarian theology of the sending nature of God to congregants.

In terms of the use of "Mission of God" language, I observed that it was explicit in thirteen interviews, being used to describe what some members felt they were sent to do. It was implicit in all thirty interviews, as well as in congregational consultations. The language of mission was also expressed in typical evangelical terms of outreach,[50] witness,[51] evangelism,[52] and mission.[53] These words are not distinctive to formal *Missio Dei* theology, but were used by members when talking about local mission, probably because they were already part of their evangelical vocabulary.

---

50. "Outreach" used a total of thirty-two times in fourteen out of thirty interviews.
51. "Witness" used a total of eight times in five interviews.
52. "Evangelism" used a total of twenty-six times in nine interviews.
53. "Mission" used a total of 433 times in thirty interviews.

Stacey and Mark, like other members, seemed to understand that mission was not a possession of the church, but that all mission belonged to God (cf. §5.1; 6.2.3; 6.2.4). They seemingly had a basic understanding of divine agency related to the *Missio Dei* and to being sent.[54] This was very Newbigin-like (cf. §3.1.4).[55] Stacey and Mark indicated they had first developed an understanding of themselves as participants in God's mission during Bill's tenure.[56] They were among those members who had attended the church for twenty years or more. As chapter 1 highlighted, in Phoenix, before its missional change journey, missionary work was reserved for overseas mission work or mission that happened in other places not associated with what happened at Phoenix (cf. Beverley's testimony in §5.1). This was evidently different from the new situation in Phoenix.

Stacey had also been involved in organizing a missional summer children's club for several years with her husband Gary. A team of about twenty volunteers hosted this event in a local park. It involved playing games, worship music, crafts, and the telling of Bible stories, which aimed at influencing about 200 children who attended it. It had apparently been particularly inspired by the church's new missional focus. Gary indicated the level of organization it took to prepare for, and run, the event, "We've got monthly meetings twelve months of the year" (cf. Appendix B:26). I observed that these meetings entailed the raising of funds through the hosting of musical events, games evenings, and meals which people paid to attend throughout the year. It also required training a team of leaders for the event and placing them in the right roles.

Based on my interactions with members like Stacey, Garth, Gary, and Mark, I concluded that they had linked the sending nature of God (and perhaps the Trinity) with what they were doing in their missional projects. They were seemingly aware that they were participants in the *Missio Dei*, and seemed to believe they had been sent by God to do what they were involved in (at the very least).[57]

---

54. Cf. Goheen, *Church and Its Vocation*, 68–70.

55. Cf. Newbigin, *Open Secret*, 56; Goheen, *Church and Its Vocation*, 68–70.

56. Cf. Guder, *Missional Church*, 5; Grenz, *Rediscovering the Triune God*, 6–32; Fergusson, "Ecumenism and the Doctrine of the Trinity Today," 552.

57. Cf. Van Gelder and Zscheile, *Missional Church in Perspective*, 26–27, 109–10; Flett, *Witness of God*, 163–66.

4.2.4 Characteristic 6: A Missional Hermeneutic of the Bible

This last characteristic may be summarized thusly:

> (6) A missional interpretation of the Bible provides a framework to indicate how God works in mission in the world with and through believers (cf. §3.1.6).

Given that Bill and his team had primarily sought to communicate *Missio Dei* using biblical language, it might be expected that members would refer to the Bible to some degree to describe their views about mission. Surprisingly, there were not many examples of congregants referring to passages or texts from the Bible to discuss their views on mission, or the *Missio Dei*, except in the case of a phenomenon to be discussed in chapter 6 (cf. §6.2.1; 4.2.3). The lack of its use was noteworthy given the centrality of biblical usage in evangelicalism.[58] A reason for its absence might be because my research did not seek to ask members about their biblical understandings of mission.

Furthermore, I also noticed most members were seemingly accustomed to explaining their beliefs and practices without referring to the Bible (except in the case of telling Bible stories at the children's summer mission club, cf. §4.2.3). A good example of this was how Caspian had much to say about the importance of discipleship for mission during two interviews. He used the words "disciple" or "discipleship" seventeen times during one ninety-minute interview, but he never quoted from the Bible to illustrate his understanding of discipleship related to the theme of *Missio Dei*. Other interviewees were seemingly mature, experienced evangelical Christians who were well versed in the biblical text. They used their Bibles in church services and house groups I attended. Nevertheless, I did not hear examples of members referring to the Bible to talk about the *Missio Dei* or mission even once. Yet it was arguably assumed by them to be supported by the Bible, given that the church's biblical preaching was used to communicate it.

As I reflected on the lack of reference to the Bible in members' testimonies, I wondered if congregants had modified their use of the Bible in terms of how they expressed their beliefs and practices. A comment made by a church elder named Isaac suggested the new missional emphasis had led some members not to use biblical or doctrinal language so much:

---

58. Bielo, *Words upon the Word*; Foster, *Streams of Living Water*, 185–234.

> Yeah and you know I've been here forty years since I was a kid. I've come up through the church program, which was largely focused on teaching doctrine. If you knew the right doctrine then you could live the right way. And it was very inward-looking—that's the church I grew up in. . . . I feel like I've unlearned a lot of theoretical theology over the last ten . . . years. And to be able to work with various kids and youth stuff, trying to get them to understand the same theoretical theology, the emphasis is now totally different. I think we've moved into looking much more at how Jesus related to people, that relational sort of explanation, which means being in relationship to the triune God. It's quite different from learning the sixty-six books of the Bible so that you [can] recite them. . . . It's about how you reflect everything that God is to the society you're mixing with, on the front line, whether it's at home or whatever. (Appendix B; Consultation Group 1)

I observed that some members had seemingly become accustomed to explaining their understanding of the Bible in an everyday colloquial language.[59] It seems the focus had shifted from trying to show how much of the Bible congregants knew, to instead concentrating on living out their beliefs and values through what they did and said. This is arguably similar to a Newbigin-like theology of congregants' lives acting as a "hermeneutic of the gospel" (cf. §3.1.3). The lack of use of biblical language during interviews may, of course, be explained because members assumed they did not need to refer to the Bible to explain their beliefs, values, and practices to me.

4.3 Summary

This overview of the quantitative and qualitative data has provided indications of the extent to which members were influenced by a Newbigin-like theology of *Missio Dei*. It has also provided examples of missional projects that have arisen as a result of the mediation of *Missio Dei* theology. It has indicated that:

(1) Sixty-six percent of members had seemingly adopted a view of themselves as participants in community mission (at some level).

---

59. Cf. Bielo, *Words upon the Word*, 52–58; cf. Bevans, *Models of Contextual Theology*, 10–14; Moynagh and Harrold, *Church for Every Context*, 151–56; Moynagh, *Church in Life*.

Thirty-four percent did not seem to espouse a theology of mission in the community.

(2) A few members linked the climax of the *Missio Dei* to the eschatological coming of the kingdom of God. It was explicit in only six members' testimonies.

(3) A representative theology of the kingdom was not espoused by most members I interacted with.

(4) *Missio Dei*-like rhetoric was articulated, or was distinguishable, in the testimonies of the majority of members (whether they believed it or not).

(5) A Trinitarian understanding of the sending nature of God was evident in members' testimonies linked to the church's motto (but the terms "Trinity" or "Trinitarian" were rarely used). It seemed to motivate some respondents to view themselves as sent by God to engage in local mission.

(6) Members rarely referred to the Bible when talking about their ordinary theologies of *Missio Dei*, or their missional activities.

Out of the six characteristics, those that seemed to most facilitate a change in members' views of themselves were that they: (a) viewed themselves as participants in mission in society; (b) were personally sent by God; and (c) were participants in God's mission rather than their own (i.e., characteristics 1, 4, and 5). This indicates there had been a shift in some members' perspectives regarding their sense of personal calling to engage in mission.

The minimal articulation of a representative theology related to the kingdom of God, and to the coming of the kingdom as the goal of the *Missio Dei*, was particularly surprising given the emphasis placed on the kingdom by Bill and his team (i.e., characteristics 2 and 3). The fact that most members did not find it necessary to use this language might suggest they did not need it to explain what was motivating them to act as missionaries. This may suggest that kingdom of God discourse was less important to them than the idea that they were acting as missionaries engaged in the mission of God.

Referring to biblical texts and passages did not seem to be important to members who discussed their involvement in missional activities. This may raise questions about the relevance of the use of the Bible related to contemporary missional discourse. Has its use lessened due to the lack of biblical literacy in secular society, which in turn has impacted the degree of referral to it by those engaged in mission?

There seems to be enough evidence to suggest a majority of members of Phoenix had understood several key concepts of a Newbigin-like theology of participation in the *Missio Dei*, and were, as a result, active in some local mission work. More research is needed with other congregations influenced by GOCN/Newbigin-like theology to determine to what extent the characteristics of a Newbigin-like ordinary theology are articulated by members of other churches. This is where the reader may add to the need for more investigations of the ordinary *Missio Dei* theologies of Christians on the receiving end of a missional change process. I suggest that church leaders need to take time to listen to congregants' ordinary theologies, and based upon what they hear, to discern what God might be saying through them to guide the church in its local mission work.

I suggest that in order for a congregation to successfully become mission focused, it seems to require members learning to espouse their own ordinary theologies of mission so they can meaningfully learn to integrate it into their self-consciousness as people who are called and sent by God to engage in God's mission. I suggest this is urgent work if we are really serious about seeking to equip God's people for works of missional service.

Chapter 5

Experiences of Change

Introduction

THIS CHAPTER MOVES FROM an overview of evidence for missional change occurring at Phoenix, to a consideration of what congregants had to say about their experiences of change. Therefore, the chapter commences with an analysis of two out of three notional interest groups at Phoenix, which I term Groups 1, 2, and 3. I identified these groups based on what seemed to be three common perspectives held by congregants on the value of the church's missional change journey. They were, in brief: Group 1, consisting of members who were seemingly supportive of, and active in, the church's missional activities; Group 2, containing those who were apparently not supportive of the missional emphasis; and Group 3, comprising those who seemed to be seeking to help unite the congregation because of intergroup tensions.

These groupings are approximate because individuals will inevitably not share all interests in common.[1] Identification of overlaps in group interests will inevitably complexify analysis of group data.[2] It will help to nuance the range of views that people espouse when investigating congregational situations.[3] Where overlaps in individual interests with other groups are identified they will be attended to in the analysis of data.

---

1. Cf. Baroni et al., "Defining and Classifying Interest Groups," 141–51; Bryman, *Social Research Methods*, 544.

2. Baroni et al., "Defining and Classifying Interest Groups," 141–51; Swinton and Mowat, *Practical Theology and Qualitative Research*, 13–15; cf. Ward, *Introducing Practical Theology*, 10–12, 20, 103–4.

3. Swinton and Mowat, *Practical Theology and Qualitative Research*, 13–17.

This chapter aims to investigate two out of the three groups (Groups 1 and 2). The third group will be investigated in the next chapter. This is because Groups 1 and 2 had strong diverging views about the importance of engaging in local mission, which can be best characterized by first examining their distinctive differences in perspective,[4] whereas Group 3 seemed to play a complex mediatory function aimed at reducing tensions that existed between Groups 1 and 2 (cf. §6.2.1). A separate chapter is required to investigate the complex theological background to Group 3's data before it can be brought into critical conversation with the data of Groups 1 and 2 (cf. ch. 6).

This chapter is structured around four segments. It aims to: (1) examine Group 1's largely positive outlook on participating in the *Missio Dei*; (2) investigate what seemed to be influencing Group 2's apparent negative reactions to the church's focus on mission; (3) critically analyze the data of Groups 1 and 2; and (4) tentatively rescript the ordinary theologies of Groups 1 and 2 by reference to a mediating theology.

5.1 Group 1's Testimonies

This section seeks to characterize the experiences and responses of Group 1 to the mediation of *Missio Dei* theology. I identified Group 1 because of its common interest in engaging in missional activities. The examples that follow will illustrate what proved to be frequently repeated Group 1 themes. I will begin the discussion with Group 1's data because, in my judgment, it will help to place the data of Group 2 against the backdrop of what they were reacting to.[5]

Beverley's Testimony

Beverley, a woman in her forties, began her interview with an account of her early perceptions of the special status of missionaries before she learned about *Missio Dei*:

> Mission . . . I always thought that it was people doing amazing work abroad, and I definitely thought that wasn't for me. My only experience personally growing up was of two missionaries. They were amazing people. I saw in them something that

---

4. Cf. Baroni et al., "Defining and Classifying Interest Groups," 141–51.
5. Cf. Baroni et al., "Defining and Classifying Interest Groups," 141–51.

> we didn't have. I always thought, "That's not me, I'm not that person, I'm not good enough" or whatever. (Appendix B:15)

I noticed that Beverley seemed to have a low opinion of her abilities to be a missionary during her earlier Christian life. She appeared to think she had little aptitude to fulfill any kind of missionary service. However, she explained how she began to develop a more positive attitude in 2013:

> I just kind of figure[d] wherever I am, "That's my mission field." For example, last year I learned to make jam—for me that was massive. There were all sorts of things associated with it. I think God just showed me it doesn't matter what you do—there's a mission in it. There's a mission in jam. I learned to bake, there's a mission in that, you know? You can give away anything and it's all in the name of Jesus, and that's where I stand. (Appendix B:15)

I was intrigued that something as seemingly trivial as making jam and baking bread to help others became included in Beverley's understanding of mission. It is important to note that at Phoenix in the past practical activities of this sort were not associated with the work of missionaries. Beverley seemingly began to develop a view that God was intimately involved alongside her in every task of her life. I noticed that the contrast between once not believing she could be a missionary, to now seeing herself as a missionary, had apparently given her a greater sense of purpose regarding all of her activities. This new perception of herself seemed to lead her to believe she was working alongside God in her everyday-life activities.[6] She explained how this new understanding encouraged her to pioneer the first of Phoenix's missional allotment projects in the church's local neighborhood, and later to help advise in setting up two additional allotments. This resonated with a Newbigin-like theology that concentrates on joining with God's activities in a church's local context.[7] Beverley shared what she believed the purpose of these allotments were:

> I always thought with the allotments, "It is to feed the hungry." We are commanded to feed the hungry. That's my bottom line. I hope I do that in my life at home as well. You know, if you've got

---

6. Cf. Guder, *Missional Church*, 3–4, 81; Newbigin, *Open Secret,* 56; cf. Dehmlow Dreier, *Created and Led by the Spirit*, 3–26.

7. Guder, *Missional Church*, 3–8, 110–43; Newbigin, *Gospel in a Pluralist Society,* 222–41; Weston, *Lesslie Newbigin, Missionary Theologian,* 59, 117–20, 207–17.

people around you, you just feed them, don't you? (Appendix B:15)

She seemed particularly inspired by the idea of providing resources to help those who were in special need of food. For example, some of the food grown at the first allotment was used to support a city mission that provided a soup kitchen to feed the homeless. Other members who worked alongside Beverley also shared her vision to help those in need.

Jake's Testimony

At a second allotment, Jake, in his forties, worked with a team of eleven Phoenix members who had quite a different idea for their allotment compared to the one Beverley worked at. The team viewed it as a "church planting project" (cf. Appendix D2). Jake explained that the project was known in the neighborhood as a "church-run community allotment," which meant it was associated with a church. Two local ladies who did not espouse the Christian faith were included in the project's management committee, which Jake suggested helped them feel a part of what they were doing as a church:

> They run the bank account, they write the cheques. I wanted it to be one of them taking ownership of it, rather than it being a thing we do. (Appendix B:18)

He explained that this approach helped these women to feel an equal part of the project. Interestingly, both of these ladies had noticed that the atmosphere at the allotment had changed since the missional team had been managing it. They commented to Jake, "There is a strange presence here because you are in it." Jake seemed to believe these ladies' observations were evidence of God's presence with them in this project. He explained how this kind of interest had spurred the team on to find other ways to interact with local people, so they could become part of this rather novel form of church.

For instance, normally every Friday congregants and locals worked together at the allotment. A typical session would involve caring for plants, as well as a time of community socializing. Conversations would at times turn to the topic of the Christian faith. Sometimes a local school would bring children to engage in fieldwork at the allotment. The teachers allowed missional team members to have conversations with children about nature, creation, and God as Creator. One of the team members, Jessica, a teacher at this school, shared with me how her "relationship with teachers, children and their parents" meant that there was "someone they knew and trusted" at the allotment (cf. Appendix D1). I observed that this project seemed to be fostering a strong sense of community between congregants and local people. Jake explained that because the allotment had become associated with the church, local unchurched people began to support more overt Christian activities that the team offered on-site. For instance, he described one of the church services they had conducted at the allotment, and how some children associated with the local school came with their parents:

> We've done family events here. We've had seventy-six people in this ... space, not just children. Out of that seventy-six, eighteen were churched and the rest had no connection with the church. And when we do it that way, we do various things, like games in the field [opposite the allotment]. We get everyone together as families, and we do a five-to-ten-minute God slot. We did an event at Easter. We did the whole Easter story. You know, generally, the kids are sat here, taking part [on a covered, decked-out area in the allotment]. It's generally kids that engage with the stories across the age ranges. (Appendix B:18)

It was too early in the process to evaluate the impact of this approach to church planting on congregants or local people. However, based on my interactions with members it was evident they believed God was guiding them to plant a church there, or nearby.

Jessica's Testimony

Jessica explained what had first led her to join the allotment church. She described how she was looking for a new teaching job and applied for one at the school near the allotment:

> I said to God, "I really don't want to work at a school that's in special measures, you know." But I felt really led to go for this job. I thought, "This is going to be a right pain in the neck if I end up here, because it's going to be hard work." I didn't get the job. So I was sitting in the classroom after the interview saying to God, "Well, I don't know what all that was about, I didn't even get it." And then later they rang me up saying, "You didn't get that job but we would like to offer you a temporary one-year contract for

another job." And at that point I thought, "Well, this is definitely where I've got to be," because I was just literally at the point of shouting at God and saying, "What was all that about?" So when Jake was starting to pray for the allotment project I thought, "Oh I better go to this because I'm working in the area." It's called being dragged into something, ha ha. So once I started going to the prayer group I thought that "Drummond [her husband] ought to come to this as well." (Appendix B:11)

Jessica seemingly believed God had guided her to take part in the local school and allotment project. Her testimony related well to a fundamental Newbigin-like conviction that God was involved in guiding her to this missional project (cf. §3.1.4).[8] I noticed Jessica seemed to equate participation in what God was guiding her to do with "hard work." This was because she had to put a lot of effort into liaising with teachers, children, and parents who became associated with the missional work at the allotment. As in Beverley's case, Jessica seemed to believe missionary work was not for a special class of elite people who were specially endowed with extra divinely given capabilities. She spoke about her belief that all Christians were "called by God" to engage in some form of mission work, which resonated with a Newbigin-like theology of every Christian having a missionary function (cf. §3.1.5).[9]

As I reflected on the testimonies of members involved with this church planting project, I noticed that they believed it provided them with opportunities to interact with locals who would probably never come to Phoenix's worship services. This resonated with Newbigin's culture-critical theology, which challenged the church to critique its own culture if it was not helping it to publicly engage with local non-Christian people (cf. §7.2.1).[10] Jessica explained that trying to plant a church at an allotment felt quite alien to her whole experience of church life.[11] This had

8. Cf. Newbigin, *Open Secret*, 56; Dehmlow Dreier, *Created and Led by the Spirit*, xvii; Hughes, "Life in the Spirit," 95–105.

9. Cf. Guder, *Missional Church*, 4, 5, 142–82; cf. Stevens, *Abolition of the Laity*, 3–23.

10. Cf. Newbigin, *Open Secret*, 150–53, 159; Bevans, *Models of Contextual Theology*, 117; Goheen, *Church and Its Vocation*, 170–72; Kaiser, "From Biblical Secularity to Modern Secularism," 79–112; Karkkainen, *Holy Spirit*, 136–38.

11. My college's programs have encouraged students to be experimental in terms of their approach to planting churches, which may partly explain how this allotment project became associated with the idea for planting a church. In realistic terms, I found it hard to imagine an allotment becoming a church, and I think members of this

made her feel uncomfortable. For instance, after one missional session at the allotment she illustrated her sense of confusion and discomfort:

> I was digging away afterward thinking, "I don't know why we're here, and what I'm doing, because what am I doing? Digging, all I seem to do is dig and weed! Is that really what God wants me to do?"
>
> And we went to church on Sunday and Bill said at the start of his sermon, "Sometimes you might feel like you don't really know what you are doing, and you don't really know why God's led you to do what you do. But he just wants you to keep on." I just thought "This is hilarious," and you know, about a year ago, when we were starting to do a lot more work at the allotment, I heard so many messages about sowing the seeds, and planting. (Appendix B:11)

Jessica explained that the focus of several sermons at Phoenix on sowing seeds and planting had helped her think it was God's way of guiding the team to plant a very different kind of church related to the allotment. This seemingly helped her to cope with her unease about this church planting project.

Jessica, Jake, and other team members' evident commitment to this project led me to an important insight into what seemed to be a common trait of other Group 1 members. I noticed that overall they seemed to be motivated by what they could *do* as individuals outside the church, even if at times they did not feel comfortable about what they were *doing*. This individualistic theme is an important attribute of Group 1 data, and will be developed more fully in what follows later (cf. §6.2.1–6.2.2).

Three other important Group 1 themes need to be investigated next. They were, in brief: 1) participation in Phoenix's missional projects allowed members to be creative, which seemed to reinforce their passion for local mission; 2) the church offered members training through its Bible school, which gave them skills and confidence to engage in missional projects; and 3) the church's missional projects seemed to embody a common vision that encouraged some members to participate in mission activities.

---

project thought of it in terms of getting people interested in becoming part of a church to be planted near the allotment—although some like Jessica seemed to take it literally to mean a church at the allotment.

1) Reinforcing Passion for Mission through Creative Participation

Becky's Testimony

Becky, in her twenties, commented:

> I think Phoenix offers vision and excitement. I want something with a bit more challenge but with massive potential. Phoenix can grow and it's got people that are spiritually excited. It doesn't have programs that are all set, so you can be creative. (Appendix B:27)

As I reflected on Becky's testimony, I noticed it seemed to resonate with a Newbigin-like characteristic of an innovative missional church, which helps believers to embrace their calling to engage in mission.[12] She apparently felt a part of a church where some members were spiritually excited, because they could use their creative abilities to meaningfully take part in innovating new ideas through missional activities. Jake commented on the way Bill especially encouraged members to be innovative:

> No one is asking, "What are you doing? You have to tell us." They're free to experiment and be themselves. A lot of that is the pastor. He lets them be free. You know, he's very good at seeing people's gifting. (Appendix B:18)

Like Jake, Becky provided an example of the encouragement members were receiving. She appreciated the "opportunities" afforded her to "experiment" with "creative ideas" to work with a missional "young adult group," which she "helped to lead." She enjoyed being given the "freedom by church leaders" to run this group "without being told what to do." Indeed, Niemandt's research revealed a similar finding, that the missional churches he investigated had adopted a shared approach to leadership so that congregants could have greater freedom to be experimental in mission activities (cf. Appendix D3).[13] This sense of freedom to experiment and be creative was intrinsic to other accounts provided by Group 1 (cf. Appendix D4).

---

12. Cf. Newbigin, *Gospel in a Pluralist Society,* 222–45; cf. Guder, *Missional Church,* 77–109; Barrett et al., *Treasure in Clay Jars,* 33–58.

13. Niemandt, "Five Years of Missional Church," 406.

2) Skills Development and Confidence to Engage in Mission

Katerina's Testimony

Katerina, in her fifties, explained how the church's Bible training school had helped her to obtain the confidence to share her faith:

> I understand Scripture better now. I've risen to the challenge, if you like. I've surprised myself with what I could achieve. It's been really good for me. You'll remember those days, won't you, when I would be in a group and I would say nothing? And I would feel I was on the periphery all of the time? I didn't say anything because I didn't think I had anything really to offer. I didn't have an understanding and that foundation so I could share. Now I'm much happier to give my opinion. I've led house groups a few times. And it's like I'm a completely different person. It's amazing what God's doing, it really is. (Appendix B:20)

I noticed Katerina's evident enthusiasm, as she reflected on the impact that taking part in the church's Bible school had made on her. She smiled and laughed a lot during the interview and emphasized several times that she felt like a "completely different person." By "completely different" she seemed to be referring to her growing confidence for engaging in missional activities. She was now helping to integrate some newcomers into the congregation's missional way of life. She and her husband were also working with a teenage boy who had been convicted of some criminal offenses. His family (not Christians) had asked for their support to help him find new friends and interests. He regularly visited their home. This reminded me of what Van Gelder and Zscheile suggest, that equipping a congregation to engage in incarnational missional activity in the community helps members to make meaningful connections with local people, which can lead them to explore the Christian faith.[14]

Reanna's Testimony

The testimony of Reanna, in her fifties, captured well her sense of growing excitement and confidence about engaging in local mission. She commented:

---

14. Van Gelder and Zscheile, *Participating in God's Mission*, 38.

I'm excited, absolutely excited, for what the Lord's got next. . . . I feel we are just on the cusp of something. People are more open to mission and a lot of the sort of old-fashioned thinking has gone out the window. There's realization that we've got a heck of a mission field on our doorstep. And people are kind of more empowered because they've got more knowledge and confidence. I certainly have a lot more confidence. It's a big thing for me. People . . . are so enthusiastic about it, it kind of rubs off. (Appendix B:24)

During my interview with Reanna, she was evidently feeling very positive about what she believed God was doing at Phoenix. The preaching and teaching of Bill and his team had given her (and others) knowledge and confidence to engage in mission activities. For example, she mentored several new believers who had recently come to faith through the church's missional work. She explained that they needed help to make changes to their lifestyles because of their newly found Christian faith. During the interview, Reanna commented on how this kind of mentoring work was of particular interest to her and was suited to her background and life experiences. Reanna particularly helped me to appreciate the significant impact that graduate leaders' preaching had made on her and others. She directly attributed her view of the neighborhood as a mission field to what she had learned from graduate leaders. Reanna's comments regarding the church's old-fashioned way of thinking becoming less dominant and instead favoring missionary work in the neighborhood relates well to a key finding of Niemandt's research.[15] He found that members' attention generally tended to shift from supporting the church's programs[16] to "participating" in what congregants believed God was doing in society.[17]

Desmond's Testimony

Another member, Desmond, in his late thirties, described what had given both him and his wife motivation to engage in missional activities when they joined Phoenix:

---

15. Niemandt, "Five Years of Missional Church."

16. Activities intended for members within the church.

17. Niemandt, "Five Years of Missional Church," 408; cf. Guder, *Missional Church*, 3–4; Newbigin, *Open Secret*, 56.

> Yeah, I think it was a fresh kind of start for us, you know, not having to think of everything and do everything. It was like there was a community of people who were doing the same stuff. (Appendix B:28)

Desmond's family joined Phoenix soon after Bill became the senior pastor. He and his wife quickly took on roles in the church. I noticed what seemed to motivate them was that other members had mutual enthusiasm for participating in missional activities. They had seemingly got "tired" in their previous church, where they "had been the main people responsible for what the church did" (cf. Appendix D5). Apparently, the contrast between what had fatigued Desmond in the past compared to what now energized him at Phoenix had remotivated him.

I came across other expressions of members' anticipation, enthusiasm, and excitement because they were being equipped and motivated to engage in missional activities (cf. Appendix D6). This included longstanding members, as well as some of the sixty newcomers to the church.

3) An Embodied Vision that Encouraged Participation in Missional Activities

Jonathan's Testimony

Jonathan, a male in his forties, explained:

> Interestingly, I think I joined the church in about 2008, but I knew it in 1995/6 as a student. It's radically different from then. There is something positive, and I've personally seen the changes as very positive and moving forward into the sort of church that I want to be part of, and can be a participant within. I think you see more people doing things that I can get involved in, which is encouraging. You can sense stuff going on, including God's presence and stuff. (Appendix B; Consultation Group 4)

Like other members I interacted with, Jonathan seemingly sensed the Holy Spirit was at work in the church and its missional projects. What he saw other members doing seemed to give him a practical, embodied vision of what he could get involved in. The well-known saying that seeing is believing was illustrated by Jonathan's testimony. By being able to observe what he believed God might be doing in the missional practices of other members, Jonathan was able to imagine himself doing similar things. It seems a vision to participate in the *Missio Dei* was being communicated by more than words; it was also being mediated through participation by way of the practices of others.[18] Jonathan's comments reminded me of Newbigin's pneumatology, which bases the guidance of the Holy Spirit on looking for phenomenological evidence of God's work embodied in human life stories and practices (cf. §3.1.6).[19]

Reflections

Overall, Group 1 seemed to have a positive attitude regarding the church's missional change journey. There were, however, some members of Group 1 who seemingly thought engaging in missional work had been costly to them and their families (cf. §7.1.6).[20] For example, one family left the church during my fieldwork because of what they termed "exhaustion" due to ten years of supporting the church's change journey (cf. §7.1.6). Their testimonies will not be discussed here, as I dedicate chapter 7 to the theme of the cost of change. My aim at this stage is to keep the concentration on charting the tensions that seemed to exist between the ordinary theologies of Groups 1 and 2.

5.2 Group 2's Testimonies

The testimonies of Group 2 provided a counternarrative to the positive attitudes that most of Group 1 seemed to have about mission. This section aims to characterize Group 2's ordinary theology connected to the relational and communal life of the church. Group 2 seemed to believe the congregation was no longer a united community because of its focus on mission.

---

18. Cf. Ward, *Participation and Mediation*, 95–120.

19. Cf. Newbigin, *Gospel in a Pluralist Society*, 128–40; Goheen, "As the Father Has Sent Me," 355; Hughes, "Life in the Spirit," 95–105; Dehmlow Dreier, *Created and Led by the Spirit*, 3–26.

20. It is hard to quantify how many Group 1 members felt this way, but I noticed that about ten members expressed concerns that they were taking on too much in missional projects; cf. Jasmin's testimony, §7.1.6.

Belinda's Testimony

Belinda, in her twenties, explained:

> Yeah, I think there's always a danger in getting numbers and getting people in. I feel that I'm probably one of the few that feel we shouldn't be spreading the Word[21] and trying to get people to come to Christ. I ultimately feel that is not my job to do. If Jesus is going to move in their lives, he will find a way of doing it. Me shouting and screaming on a street corner is not going to do that.[22] So I'm far more concerned, I guess, for the people that are already in the door. People mostly don't leave the church because they don't believe in God anymore. It's because they feel that they no longer belong in that family. So, while I agree that the changes that have come have presented opportunities to reach out, I feel that we don't necessarily look after, and care for, the ones who are already here. (Appendix B:16)

Belinda seemingly had some understanding of what participation in the *Missio Dei* asked of her, although she did not embrace it. She seemed to believe it was not her role, but Christ's, to work in the lives of people who did not have a Christian faith. Like other Group 2 members I spoke to, Belinda apparently believed the primary purpose of the church was to care for those who were already Christians. Her testimony suggested the activist concentration on mission was detracting from the communal life of the congregation.

Another way concerns of this sort were expressed was provided by a member named Jasmin, in her fifties:

> What I see is, and I know I've had conversations with Bill about this, because I understand that it's [about] going out,[23] but I also see so many problems in people's lives within the church and within families, and how can I help with that? I don't feel led to going over the road to the [missional] café. There is so much going on in families in the church, they need building up. . . . I can't see us reaching out until some of us are right, you know? (Appendix B:1)

Jasmin seemed to feel strongly that the call to support missional projects, like the café, was taking away from the support that could be

---

21. Biblical message.
22. Some Reformed churches practice evangelistic street preaching.
23. Outside the church.

provided to the church's own families. Jasmin's comments helped me to identify a common concern of other members of Group 2, which suggested the church needed to be able to support its own members better before it sought to bring any more newcomers in through its missional activities. Evidently, at least some members of Group 2 seemed to be in favor of delaying more missional change in the church rather than stopping it all together.

Peter's Testimony

Peter, in his forties, added an important dimension to what he believed had affected Phoenix's communal life:

> I was in the church from 1986–95 and then left for a while for university, etc. There was a real sense of community [then]. Like lots of kids who went I felt part of the fabric. I felt accepted and part of the community. And now there isn't much community here. We don't go out on day trips anymore. We don't do church camps. I sense that people don't feel they belong. We're random particles in the building because it's all about mission out there. We don't gel together much as a community. So, it's like swinging from one extreme to another. I feel on the periphery of the church as well. I don't see some of the people that used to be here. I know the ones that have left, and I know part of that would be because they feel that community has gone. (Appendix B:17)

Peter seemingly believed the congregation had lost its sense of community because the focus on mission had led to members no longer concentrating their energy on the inner life of the church. Peter's use of the language of "random particles" seemed to imply the church's sense of community was being atomized. This characterization of Phoenix as a community of "random" individuals was quite different to Newbigin's vision of a missional congregation, which he portrayed as a community united by a common missional vocation.[24]

Peter also expressed concerns that the church was overextending itself by concentrating its efforts on mission with outsiders. He painted his picture of how he thought the church should function:

---

24. Newbigin, *Household of God*, 141; Weston, "Ecclesiology in Eschatological Perspective," 79–81; Barrett et al., *Treasure in Clay Jars*, 38–42.

> You know, it's about discipling, and I always think, "Well, people will do discipling if you're having that kind of community and having that support network." Then I think you will very naturally encourage people in from the outside anyway. Because I think the biggest mission field is if you imagine a . . . circle and that's the church, then it's those who are just on the edge of that circle, that's probably your more natural mission field. (Appendix B:17)

Apparently, Peter believed the church's primary mission field was not to outsiders in the neighborhood but to people who were the closest to it, such as its children and young people. From what I could gather from my conversation with him, his use of the term "discipling" did not imply an organized program of discipleship, but rather as something that would naturally occur as people concentrated on supporting each other. His perspective resonated with other members I spoke to, who wanted to help those already known to the congregation. This seemed to include members who had left because they felt they no longer had a place in the church (cf. §7.1.2–3).

Isaac's Testimony

Isaac, in his fifties, provided another insight during a congregational consultation for why members of Group 2 seemed to be finding it difficult to feel connected to the church's new missional way of life. It related to the sixty newcomers who had joined the church.[25] He commented:

> I think a lot of people feel that a barrier to being vulnerable in the church is because you don't know if you can trust these new people. You've got no shared history with them. I think we need to get to know each other, but to get to know each other is not sitting in a meeting—it's sharing life with each other. So that's one of the challenges I think that we face. It would help us to be more open if we do that more. (Appendix B; Consultation Group 1)

Isaac's testimony drew my attention to an important Group 2 theme, which concentrated on the congregation helping newcomers and long-standing members to build closer relationships of trust with each other. Their theology of the purpose of the church was, arguably, concentrated

---

25. Most newcomers joined Phoenix between the years of 2014 and 2018.

on increasing the church's relational and communal sense of well-being. Group 2's communal theology did not seem to support the activist theology of Group 1.[26] Group 1's discourse was mostly concentrated on what they were *doing* as individuals outside the church in its missional projects. They did not seem to value Group 2's desire to concentrate on supporting the inner life of the church. The kind of church Group 2 seemed to want arguably clashed with Group 1's desire to engage in mission outside the church.

Barbara's Testimony

During the same consultation, Barbara responded to Isaac's comments about the need for members to build stronger relationships with each other. Her testimony added a revealing insight regarding her belief that the church needed to model itself on the Trinity:

> Trinity is about a relational process of forming people through relationships. The pastoral support side is lacking in the church, which has to do with helping people to form a Christian identity. (Appendix B; Consultation Group 1)

Isaac affirmed Barbara's view, adding that the church was not doing well in modelling its "relational life on that of the Trinity." Neither was it helping members to make meaningful links with each other so they could learn from each other's Christian experiences regarding how to live more authentic Christian lives in society. Apparently, in his view, this was undermining the congregation's ability to support its members' various needs.

Reflections

Group 2 seemed to equate participation in the *Missio Dei* with individualistic activism that undermined the inner relational and communal life of the church. Peter's testimony seemed to capture a general sense of Group 2's dissatisfaction with the church's concentration on mission. Their outlook could be characterized as a sense of feeling *forced* to concentrate

---

26. Cf. Guder, *Missional Church*, 3–4, 81; Newbigin, *Open Secret*, 56; cf. Davies, "Mission and Spirituality for Life"; Kaggwa, "Mission and the Spirit"; and Dehmlow Dreier, *Created and Led by the Spirit*.

their efforts on missional work with people *they did not know*. It was not that they necessarily disagreed that believers should engage in some form of mission, but rather that they did not see it as a work requiring them to seek out people unknown to the church. Instead, they seemed to believe it was important to work with family members and friends who as yet did not have a Christian faith, and who were already known to the church. Their relational theology evidently prioritized working with people they knew rather than with unknown local people in the church's neighborhood.[27] Some of the members of Group 2 seemed to have developed a debilitating state of mind which affected all of their thoughts about engagement in church life. This led members like Belinda to leave the church. Other members I spoke to were also thinking about leaving (cf. §4.1).

5.3 Analysis of Group 1 and 2's Testimonies

Group 1 and 2's theological perspectives were evidently in tension. Lynda provided an excellent example of how Group 1's attitudes to missional projects differed from the perspectives of Group 2. Her team had often asked themselves, "How can we help those in need here in the café rather than by having them come to us at the church?" I observed that other Group 1 members also seemed to have an evident lack of interest in integrating faith-seekers into the congregation's spiritual and communal life. However, Lynda and some other Group 1 members I spoke to, like Jake, saw the value of providing a community to which non-Christians could belong (cf. §5.1). At the very least, this implied that some Group 1 members shared an interest in developing a sense of community in their projects. This might help to provide a partial solution to support those who were new to the Christian faith at the projects, but this would not necessarily help Group 1 to better support Phoenix's inner communal and relational life.

Graham discusses the importance of identifying differences in what she terms the "mental maps" of differing groups to understand what motivates them to act in the ways they do.[28] As I reflected on differences

---

27. A member named Terry added some key insights about the importance that longstanding members attached to the church's strong family-focused caring practices of the past; cf. Appendix B:3.

28. Cf. Graham, "Frailty and Flourishing," 337.

between the mental maps of Groups 1 and 2, I conjectured that Group 1's mental map caused them to concentrate on what they individually felt called to *do* in their missional projects.[29] Their map resonated with a fundamental Newbigin-like theology of engaging in mission in the local community outside of the church's walls,[30] whereas Group 2's map concentrated on supporting church members and families within the church. It was a theology that focused on the relational and communal *being* of the whole congregation. Tensions between two differing mental maps were apparent, which placed Groups 1 and 2 at a crossroads. This provisional finding suggested to me that if a means could not be identified to rescript and harmonize Group 1 and 2's differing ordinary theologies regarding the purpose of the church and its mission, then a schism might occur between these groups—as it already had with some members in 2015 (cf. §7.1.2).

5.3.1 *Potential Causes of an Activist Theology of Mission*

As I reflected on the differences between Group 1 and 2's theological values, I questioned what may have caused this rather individualistic activist theology of Group 1 to develop. It is important to recollect that fundamental to Bill and his team's theology of ministry and mission was that every member was to be equipped to view themselves as participants in missionary activities (cf. §1.1.2).[31] I surmised that *Missio Dei* theology was misunderstood to some degree by some congregants. The combination of claiming that all mission belonged to God, and that human participation in it was required, seemed to make some members of both groups believe mission required them to *do* things (whether they felt happy about *doing* them or not). *Missio Dei* was arguably interpreted by some members to require their *efforts* to make God's mission possible (cf. Jessica's testimony; §5.1).[32]

---

29. Cf. Graham, "Frailty and Flourishing," 337.

30. Cf. Weston, "Ecclesiology in Eschatological Perspective," 79; Newbigin, *Gospel in a Pluralist Society*, 222–33; Barrett et al., *Treasure in Clay Jars*, 33–58; Guder, *Missional Church*, 77–100.

31. Cf. Goheen, *Participating in God's Mission*, 206–9; Henderson Callahan, "Forming Lay Missional Leaders," 120–46; Barrett et al., *Treasure in Clay Jars*, 33–58.

32. For example, Jessica saw it as "hard work," but something of value that God had guided her to do.

Participation in the *Missio Dei* was seemingly equated with missionary activism, rather than on developing a strong relational and communal environment in the church.[33] Group 1 seemed to be particularly attracted to missionary activism itself, which I suggest probably resonated strongly with their evangelical instincts.[34] Works activism has often been a charge leveled at the door of evangelicalism because it can lead to works righteousness (cf. Glossary).[35] Works activism seems to be a common cause of evangelicals developing a strong sense of individual responsibility, which probably explains why some Group 1 members seemed to want to individually pursue work at missional projects. Group 2 had noticeably rejected Group 1's activist interpretation of the *Missio Dei* because it had not helped to support the church's communal life.

Reading Flett's complex discussion of opposing, and contradictory, interpretations of *Missio Dei*, which on the one hand focused too much attention on divine agency, and too much on human agency on the other, helped me to appreciate why some of Phoenix's members had found it so hard to understand. For example, if it was God's mission, then why should those who already believed that God would convert people, despite their human efforts, need to participate in the *Missio Dei* (cf. §3.1.4)?[36] The testimonies of Groups 1 and 2 revealed what might be termed a strange quirk of logic, where God's agency in mission became underemphasized in members' ordinary theologizing because of an overemphasis on engaging in missionary activism. Interestingly, the Reformed scholar Song theorizes that tensions especially arise in the participatory view of *Missio*

---

33. Cf. Guder, *Missional Church*, 3–4, 81; cf. Davies, "Mission and Spirituality for Life"; Kaggwa, "Mission and the Spirit"; and Dehmlow Dreier, *Created and Led by the Spirit*.

34. Cf. Bebbington, *Evangelicalism in Modern Britain*, 10–14.

35. Cf. Bebbington, *Evangelicalism in Modern Britain*, 10–12. It is to be noted that this conundrum is not known in other traditions, but it is a very real concern in Evangelicalism. Bird suggests confusion has arisen because of the Fresh Perspective regarding whether a believer is justified by imputed righteousness only, or by imputed and imparted righteousness together ("Incorporated Righteousness," 253–75; cf. Wright, *Paul*). During fieldwork I never found members who spoke about issues to do with the Fresh Perspective. Perhaps this might be a future topic for research with emerging churches which embrace insights from the Fresh Perspective; cf. Gibbs and Bolger, *Emerging Church*, 49.

36. Flett, *Witness of God*, 38, 39; cf. Goheen, *Church and Its Vocation*, 68–75; Van Gelder and Zscheile, *Missional Church in Perspective*, 110–11; Ward, *Participation and Mediation*, 26–29.

Dei because it is hard to posit mission as completely God's work.[37] He stresses that the participatory model leaves *Missio Dei* open to human agency.[38] This means it can easily lead to manipulation of divine will and purposes because mission can become associated with what the church plans to do to engage in mission.[39] In other words, the concentration on mission as an activity in the world of human performativity can lead the church to focus on what it *wants* to do, rather than concentrating on discovering what God might be *guiding* it to do.[40]

Song challenges churches that are engaged in mission to seek for the "transformation of the human soul."[41] He suggests this may be achieved by seeking to discern rightly what God is doing in peoples' lives, and then cooperating with God's influence on them so that the Spirit may be allowed to transform them.[42] In other words, those engaged in mission will need to learn to follow the Spirit's phenomenological activity in new believers' lives, rather than trying to lead people to do things the way they want them to do them. Song's theology prioritizes that new believers be helped to develop a relationship with God, which will provide them with the key to "free" their "human" spirits "from captivity to domination" by evil or injustice.[43] I found myself increasingly wondering if there might be a significant blindspot in what was being communicated about *Missio Dei* by graduate leaders to Phoenix's members. I believe the drive to enable every member to engage in some form of missionary activism led to it becoming a dominant understanding of the church's identity, which Group 2 did not want to accept because of its dehumanizing focus on individualism, and self-fulfillment, to the detriment of empowering others in a community of equals.

As graduate leaders had all been trained in missional leadership at the same college, I conjectured that its courses did not do enough to address the importance of the communal life of the church (cf. §8.3). Instead, perhaps, they had overly concentrated on missional work outside the church. The literature that my college's programs draws on has a

37. Song, "Freedom of the Human Spirit from Captivity," 18–20.
38. Song, "Freedom of the Human Spirit from Captivity," 25–33.
39. Song, "Freedom of the Human Spirit from Captivity," 25–33.
40. Cf. Song, "Freedom of the Human Spirit from Captivity," 25–33.
41. Song, "Freedom of the Human Spirit from Captivity," 15–34.
42. Song, "Freedom of the Human Spirit from Captivity," 15–34; cf. Benner, *Spirituality and the Awakening Self,* 173–90.
43. Song, "Freedom of the Human Spirit from Captivity," 25.

particular concentration on theories and praxis models that help to mobilize churches to engage in missional activism.[44] My research at Phoenix led me to wonder if college courses had not done enough to critically explore the vital role that pastoral and communal organizational structures play in sustaining the missional life of congregations (cf. §8.3). Hence, graduate leaders had perhaps not done enough to integrate a communal and relational theology into their *Missio Dei* theology.

5.3.2 Challenging Misunderstandings of Missional Ecclesiology

My research at Phoenix has led me to challenge the notion that all a church should do is reorientate itself to engage in local mission work.[45] For example, will it ever be possible for "everything a congregation does" to be shaped by its "missionary engagement" in society, as Van Gelder and Zscheile suggest is fundamental to GOCN's ecclesiology?[46] This is but one example of how totalizing mission-focused theologies can seemingly become somewhat myopic and idealistic. Other accounts, like that of Niemandt, seem to share similar myopia.[47] His research only concentrates on the positive benefits of a church becoming focused on mission.[48] Branson's research with churches undertaking a missional change journey also lacks sufficient reference to the perspectives of church members in terms of their reactions to their church's change journeys.[49] Arguably, other matters are of importance to churches, not just the missionary enterprise. As a result of my research at Phoenix, I have become quite suspicious of missional church rhetoric that does not give sufficient voice to members of churches who react against it.

Real life in any church is surely much messier than some of the literature suggests. A member of Phoenix named Sharon, in her fifties, captured this insight well. She commented that people often "have needs

---

44. Cf. Van Gelder, *Missional Church and Leadership Formation*; Van Gelder, *Missional Church in Context*; Roxburgh and Romanuk, *Missional Leader*; Branson and Martinez, *Churches, Cultures and Leadership*; Guder, *Missional Church*; Roxburgh, *Missional Map-Making*.

45. Van Gelder and Zscheile, *Missional Church in Perspective*, 4.

46. Van Gelder and Zscheile, *Missional Church in Perspective*, 4; Barrett et al., *Treasure in Clay Jars*, 38, 39.

47. Niemandt, "Five Years of Missional Church."

48. Niemandt, "Five Years of Missional Church."

49. Branson, "Missional Church Process."

that short-circuit their ability to fulfill a part in the mission of a church." For instance, she stressed that members' everyday lives were demanding and required hard work. They had to earn money, and to deal with the complex demands placed upon them by modern life. In her view, there was more to the Christian life than mission. The missiologist Bosch similarly stresses that mission is only "one of the expressions" of what the church does, not its sum total.[50]

As I reflected on the testimonies of Groups 1 and 2, I noticed they shared a common activist theological interpretation of what participation in the *Missio Dei* required of them. Most of Group 1 seemed to find particular satisfaction from engaging in missional work, whereas this kind of activist theology was evidently unpalatable to Group 2. This is a very important example of how the reader might seek to learn from the ordinary theologies of church members that arise in reaction to the mediation of a *Missio Dei* theology. Much can be learnt from a congregation's testimonies to ensure everything they do does not become about mission outside of the church in wider society to the detriment of its inner communal life.

Neither of the groups (i.e., Groups 1 and 2) had linked a Trinitarian relational theology to their interpretation of participation in the *Missio Dei*. Barbara and Isaac's testimonies seemed to be on the verge of making this connection (cf. §5.2). Their comments about the relational nature of the Trinity led me to consider how social Trinitarianism might offer a way to rescript an imbalance between Groups 1 and 2's differing activist- and relationship- focused ordinary theological values. A considerable amount of theological work has been undertaken regarding the importance of churches basing their communal theologies on aspects of Trinitarian theology, which helps to justify rescription of Group 1 and 2's ordinary theologies.[51]

5.4 Rescription

I conjecture that Newbigin's and GOCN's participatory *Missio Dei* theology unconsciously overemphasizes mission as *doing* rather than *being*

---

50. Bosch, *Transforming Mission*, 2, 3.

51. Karkkainen, *Trinity and Revelation*; Karkkainen, *Trinity and Religious Pluralism*; Wozniak and Maspero, *Rethinking Trinitarian Theology*; Mobsby, *God Unknown*; Holmes, *Trinity in Human Community*.

(cf. §8.1.2). In other words, there has been too much concentration on engaging in mission through activism (*doing*), and much less on the integration of a relational theology into participation in *Missio Dei* (i.e., a theology concentrated on relational *being*). Perhaps Phoenix's leaders might seek, in the future, to teach more on a communal theology of *Missio Dei* to address this deficit. Theological reference to social Trinitarianism may provide a resource to help leaders formulate a communal and relational theology of participation in the *Missio Dei* (cf. §8.1.1–2). Karkkainen stresses the importance of ontology to social Trinitarianism and to the church's communal life:

> ... there is no true being without communion; nothing exists as an "individual" in itself. Therefore, to be a "person" in contrast to an "individual," there needs to be communion, relation, and opening to the other.[52]

Zizioulas adds another important dimension, suggesting that social Trinitarianism links the participation of the church to the life of God and God's work in the world.[53] It may be inferred that participation in the *Missio Dei* can be informed by a theology of the relational being of the Trinity, which Zizioulas argues always reaches out to others beyond itself:

> ... a human being is a member of the church, he becomes an "image of God." He exists as God Himself exists, he takes on God's "way of being." ... It is a way of relationship with the world, with other people and with God, an event of communion, and that is why it cannot be realized as the achievement of an individual, but only as an ecclesial fact.[54]

Participation in the *Missio Dei* may be claimed to require deep communion between God and his people, and among his people. A church's deep, inner communal practices may also influence how believers seek to cultivate relationships with those outside their faith community.[55] If Zizioulas is right, then taking on "God's way of being" requires deep engagement in the communal life of the church, which he argues helps

---

52. Karkkainen, *Trinity Global Perspectives*, 90; cf. Holmes, *Trinity in Human Community*.

53. Zizioulas, *Eucharistic Communion and the World*, 24–33.

54. Zizioulas, *Eucharistic Communion and the World*, 15; cf. Zizioulas, *Being as Communion*, 1–82; Hastings, *Missional God, Missional Church*, 84–92, 140–46.

55. Cf. Van Gelder and Zscheile, *Missional Church in Perspective*, 101–24; Holmes, *Trinity in Human Community*, 46–60; 86–133.

to facilitate everyone's participation in the Trinity's communal "way of being."[56] For this kind of participatory way of life to be realized in churches like Phoenix, it would involve much more than a functional organizational structure concentrated upon enabling individuals to engage in mission work. It would need to prioritize members understanding themselves as interrelated to God and one another, as partakers in God's relational *being* and God's missional *doing* in the world. Communion with fellow believers, or non-Christians, would become about discovering God's presence in the mutual interactions that occur between people in fellowship (cf. §8.1.1).[57] It would also mean that building relationships with outsiders to the church could become more of a priority in terms of God's relational love that reaches out to everyone.[58] Based on these inward and outward relational movements of the triune Spirit, the whole church might be equipped to participate in something of the relational life of the God of mission.[59]

Critical reflection on Group 1 and 2's ordinary theologies suggested to me that a balance needed to be struck between what Phoenix was *doing* in mission and its communal way of life (i.e., its relational *being*). At the very least, theologies of relational *being* and missional *doing* will arguably need to be held in healthy tension in the future congregation if it is to become a more united community. If one continues to be prioritized over the other, then a schism might occur between Groups 1 and 2. Aspects of social Trinitarianism might help to rescript the espoused theologies of Groups 1 and 2, to help unite them.

My reflections on the ordinary theologies of Groups 1 and 2 have made me question whether much of academic missional ecclesiology has developed a kind of *blueprint missiology*. I use this phrase similarly to Healy's "Blueprint Ecclesiology."[60] Blueprint ecclesiology tends to stereotype how an idealized understanding of the church might function well, but fails to apply to the challenges faced by congregations at the grassroots level, making it hard to apply on the ground.[61] In similar terms, *blueprint missiology* could be characterized as an idealized understanding

---

56. Zizioulas, *Eucharistic Communion and the World*, 15.

57. Cf. Holmes, *Trinity in Human Community*, 134–93.

58. Cf. Zizioulas, *Eucharistic Communion and the World*, 12–16.

59. Cf. Van Gelder and Zscheile, *Missional Church in Persepctive*, 101–24; Fiddes, *Participating in God*, 3–61.

60. Healy, *Church, World and the Christian Life*, 25.

61. Healy, *Church, World and the Christian Life*, 25, 32–49, 54, 149.

of enabling churches to equip congregants to engage in mission, without taking into account the complex challenges they face in their real-life situations with respect to achieving this aim. A kind of *blueprint missiology* seemed to be identifiable at Phoenix. It seemed to overly concentrate on enabling all members to become active as missionaries, but did not develop the church's relational operant theology to sustain its inner communal life as this process of change took place. It was potentially idealistic in its aims for this reason. Group 2's ordinary theology of relational *being* drew attention to the need for a balance to be found with Group 1's theology of missional *doing*. In other words, by paying attention to differences in Phoenix's members' ordinary theologies, it may be possible for the church to avoid further imposition of an activist *blueprint missiology* on members to the detriment of supporting the communal needs of the church. Reference to social Trinitarianism may provide a means to rescript the theology of missional *doing* by a theology of relational *being* (cf. §8.1.1). I would suggest other congregations with similar experiences to Phoenix of missional change may have much to learn from engaging in rescription of diverging ordinary theologies of congregants by seeking to rescript them in conversation with some version of social Trinitarianism.

5.5 Summary

This chapter has indicated how Group 1 and 2's experiences of change in their congregation have led to tensions between two differing ordinary theologies of the purpose and work of the church. These tensions have been disclosed by analyses of members' theological responses. If a version of social Trinitarianism is used to rescript an activist, ordinary *Missio Dei* theology, then it may help Groups 1 and 2 to work more closely together. It is not the task of this chapter to conceptualize this kind of theological rescription. Chapter 8 will argue for an adapted version of social Trinitarianism, which will be necessary to make it suitable to Phoenix's Reformed theology of the sovereignty of God (cf. §8.1.1). Chapter 8 will also explain why an adapted version is required because of this kind of Reformed theology (cf. §8.1.1). Other congregations with similar stories to Phoenix's may also learn much from this analysis of Group 1 and 2's reactions to *Missio Dei* theology.

I would encourage readers involved in leadership to carefully consider how they might apply learning from the research of this chapter to their missional communities. I want to encourage those engaged in missional church research, in a variety of ecclesial traditions, to concentrate on how differing ecclesial traditions affect the ordinary *Missio Dei* theologies of congregants. For instance, how might a high Anglican congregation's ordinary theologies compare and contrast with a Pentecostal/charismatic theology of mission? This will help leaders in the future to predict what kinds of reactions they might need to be aware of within their ecclesial traditions when they take their congregations through missional change management processes. I would characterize this as urgent work for scholars and leaders involved in the missional church conversation and movement.

I believe Lesslie Newbigin, if he were still alive, would be at the vanguard of voices calling for this kind of learning to take place. He spent his life seeking to create opportunities for learning and collaboration within the worldwide Christian movement. Uniting the body of Christ was his sincere and passionate desire, which he realistically seemed to realize required unity within diversity to learn from each other's rich, nuanced ecclesial traditions. This resonates strongly with my own free church catholic ecclesiology. I would encourage organizations like GOCN, Fresh Expressions, and Emerging church groups (among others) to collaborate in work of this kind, as part of the one body of the living Jesus, who I believe calls all of us together to discern and participate in his ongoing mission. Comprehensive concentration (i.e., research) on ordinary *Missio Dei* theologies, and theological rescription of them, may well provide us with clues for how to equip all of God's people to integrate a self-consciousness of themselves as participants in the *Missio Dei*. *Missio Dei* theology is premised on its goal, i.e., the full and final climax of the universal kingdom of God being completely established on earth, as it is in heaven. Yet, in the between-times period of its in-breaking, each missional community has its part to play in its own local context, with the hopeful vision of this climax to motivate what they do.

Chapter 6

Discernment and Participation

Introduction

THIS CHAPTER MOVES ON to explore an interesting phenomenon that occurred at Phoenix due to the mediation of a participatory view of the *Missio Dei* to its members. This phenomenon is revealed by concentrating on the testimonies of Group 3, which consisted of a small number of women. These women claimed to be receiving *prophetic words*, through which they seemed to believe God was seeking to help the congregation discern God's guidance. The chapter will: (1) discuss the emergence of the phenomenon of *prophetic words* in the context of Phoenix as a Reformed congregation; (2) analyze Group 3's prophetic theology and practices in relation to the role of the prophetess, feminist liturgical scholarship, and ritual theory; and (3) use Group 3's testimonies to theologically rescript congregational discernment praxis.

6.1 Prophetic Words in Context

I identified Group 3 based on observing some of their prophetic practices, and because they claimed to be recipients of prophetic words, words, or prophetic pictures, or that they had been spoken to by God. A particular characteristic of this potential grouping was that these women seemed to be motivated by the desire to unite the church's members. Their testimonies provided valuable insights into their efforts to do this.

As Phoenix is a Reformed church, it was unexpected that the theme of prophecy had emerged. Karkkainen stresses that traditional Reformed churches generally do not engage in charismatic practices but limit divine revelation to the "Word" and the "Sacraments."[1] However, in the case of Phoenix, the occurrence of prophetic practices would seem to be evidence of a "charismatic phenomenon."[2] Its emergence may in part be explained by an observation made by the missional church scholar Dehmlow Dreier.[3] She argues that churches that develop a missional consciousness tend to become more open "to appearances of God's reality and power" and guidance.[4] Kim stresses that ideally the "first act of mission" is for a congregation to discern what the Spirit might be calling it to do.[5]

During a preaching series based on the book of Acts in 2015, Bill began to encourage members to share what they believed God was revealing to them about engaging in mission. This series ran alongside a Sunday evening series that explored the work of the Holy Spirit. Bill told me it gave members the freedom to explore charismatic practices like prophecy if they wanted to. Therefore, in essence, Bill gave congregants the official stamp of approval to explore potential manifestations of the Spirit like prophetic practices. This apparently encouraged a small group of eight women to begin to claim they were receiving messages from God.[6] Some of them started to share what they called *prophetic words* during Sunday morning church services (cf. §6.2.1–6.2.2). It was not a common practice for women to preach during services, but prophetic words seemed to be appreciated by some members. It is important to note that prophecy had not been practiced at Phoenix in the past.

I wondered if these prophetic words had been a cause of tension or conflict given that Phoenix as a Reformed congregation would probably have members who rejected charismatic phenomena. On one occasion a longstanding member named Duncan commented:

> Over the years I've always been very resistant to the works of the Spirit. I always equated that with raving Pentecostals. I remember going to a full gospel businessman's dinner and somebody

---

1. Karkkainen, *Pneumatology*, 83–87; Karkkainen, *Holy Spirit*, 45–56 cf. Bielo, *Words upon the Word*, 49–52.
2. Cf. Karkkainen, *Pneumatology*, 87–98; Karkkainen, *Introduction to Ecclesiology*, 68–78; Cartledge, *Testimony in the Spirit*, 81–104.
3. Dehmlow Dreier, *Created and Led by the Spirit*.
4. Dehmlow Dreier, *Created and Led by the Spirit*, 6, 7.
5. Kim, *Joining in with the Spirit*, 34–35.
6. Lisandra, Lucy, Tamsin, Jasmin, Kirsty, Jessica, Becky, Leah.

standing me up and praying for half an hour for me to speak in tongues. He gave up in the end (Appendix B:19)

At the surface level, it may appear Duncan was not in favor of charismatic phenomena. Importantly, Harris suggests that prophetic phenomena are generally not acceptable to Reformed evangelicals, particularly if they are put on the same level as the authority of the Bible.[7] However, she also points out that the Reformed scholar Grudem makes an accommodation to the practice of prophecy, as long as it is positioned in a second-order place of significance to the Bible as the primary source of divine revelation.[8] Interestingly, Duncan and other members were not hostile to these new prophetic practices. This was probably because when prophetic words were delivered to the church by Tamsin and Lisandra, they used biblical language to communicate them (cf. §6.2.1–6.2.2).[9] Their prophetic words seemed to be acceptable because the primacy of biblical authority was upheld. This is similar to the dynamic relationship thought to exist between the Bible as a revelation from God and prophecy in the Pentecostal tradition.

Interestingly, the openness to prophetic phenomena at Phoenix had evidently also become known in the local Christian community. During 2015–18, fifteen former Elim Pentecostal members began to attend the church. This provided evidence of how Phoenix had changed in terms of public perception about it. Intriguingly, none of these Elim newcomers openly practiced glossolalia or prophecy during Phoenix's public worship. From what I could glean from some of them, they felt encouraged by the congregation's openness to prophecy but also felt that as newcomers they did not know the congregation well enough to share their own words.

What is intriguing about Phoenix's missional change journey, as a Reformed church, is that the mediation of a participatory *Missio Dei* theology to its members may have led to the development of the charismatic practice of prophecy and Pentecostal believers joining the church. The following question may be legitimately raised: Does a Newbigin-like participatory theology of the *Missio Dei* somewhat naturally lead to

---

7. Harris, "Where Pentecostalism and Evangelicalism Part Ways," 41–56.

8. Harris, "Where Pentecostalism and Evangelicalism Part Ways," 41–56; cf. Pinnock, *Flame of Love*, 134, 135.

9. Cf. Suurmond, *Word and Spirit at Play*, 45–51.

manifestations of the work of the Holy Spirit? This is an open question, but it seems, in the context of Phoenix as a Reformed church, that it did.

6.2 Analysis of Testimonies

This section discusses the conversation partners I chose to use to analyze Group 3's testimonies. As I reflected on which of the testimonies of the women of Group 3 to include in this chapter (cf. §6.2.1–6.2.4), I was reminded of the important role the prophetess played in the mission and expansion of the early Pentecostal movement.[10] My attention partly turned to this topic because of the Elim people who had started to attend Phoenix, but also because I knew some African female students who called themselves prophetesses. The fact that only women claimed to be receiving prophetic words at Phoenix intrigued me. I wondered whether there might be some common characteristics of their practices that might relate to Pentecostal prophetesses (however modestly). Group 3 women did not refer to themselves as prophetesses, and neither did other congregants. However, as I started to analyze their testimonies, I found there were what seemed to be important links to the work of prophetesses. These links provided a valuable conversation partner to analyze Group 3's data.

I am not going to be claiming that a *this is exactly like that* comparison can be made between Pentecostal prophetesses and the modest efforts of the women of Group 3. Neither will I suggest that only women would receive and give prophetic words at Phoenix in the future. This is not the case in the Pentecostal tradition, and it is not the case in other kinds of charismatic churches.[11] However, as analysis of the data will indicate, these women made a modest but important impact on Phoenix's members' and leaders' missional beliefs, values, and practices—just as prophetesses have in the Pentecostal context (cf. §6.2.1–6.2.4).[12] I believe a useful conversation can be started between Pentecostal scholars and

---

10. Cf. Barfoot and Sheppard, "Prophetic vs. Priestly Religion"; Roebuck, "'Cause He's My Chief Employer,'" 42–46; Espinoza, "Shaping of Things to Come," 95, 96; Crumbley, "Sanctified Saints – Impure Prophetesses," 74, 75, 80; Alexander, "Introduction," 1, 2.

11. Cf. Alexander, "Introduction," 2; Barfoot and Sheppard, "Prophetic vs. Priestly Religion," 2, 3.

12. Cf. Roebuck, "'Cause He's My Chief Employer,'" 42–58; Espinoza, "Shaping of Things to Come," 95–104.

GOCN scholars regarding the prophetic role of women in discerning the *Missio Dei*. I hope the discussion that follows will encourage further conversations of this type to occur.

The prophetic practices of Group 3 will not only be analyzed related to the role of the prophetess but will also be investigated against the backdrop of feminist liturgical scholarship and ritual theory. I had suspicions during my research that there might be feminist issues driving the concerns of some of the women of Group 3. I am not claiming, one way or the other, that this was the case. Instead, in what follows, I make some connections to feminist liturgical scholarship where there seem to be overlaps with feminist concerns. The three approaches, noted above, will be utilized to analyze the data because they will: (a) help to reveal what might be a developing ordinary feminist theology of prophetic practices at Phoenix; and (b) provide yet another means to identify the causes of intergroup tensions because of changes in Phoenix's ritual practices. The insights provided by these approaches will also be utilized to rescript congregational discernment praxis, which might help to provide yet another means to address intergroup tensions. It is important to note the primary means of missional discernment at Phoenix up until 2015 had been based on graduate leaders' biblical preaching. The appearance of prophetic phenomena began to provide another means to discern God's guidance, which added to the spiritual ritual life of the congregation.

I am assuming the phenomenon of prophecy is a form of Christian ritual practice. The prophetic words of Group 3 were slowly becoming embedded into every layer of Phoenix's ritual life, not just Sunday worship services. Hence, it will be appropriate to use ritual theory to investigate the prophetic practices of Group 3, as they were used in different layers of the church's spiritual life (corporate worship, missional projects, and with individual congregants, etc.).

Group 3 provided four kinds of testimonies that will be analyzed in separate subsections in what follows:

- Prophetic words of comfort, disruption, and challenge (cf. §6.2.1);
- Prophetic words of caution (cf. §6.2.2);
- Prophetic words of encouragement (cf. §6.2.3);
- An individual's account of prophetic discernment (cf. §6.2.4).

My reason for choosing to analyze different dimensions of the data in four separate subsections is because: (a) analyzing one feature of data at a time will prevent confusing distinct facets of the data; (b) it will provide the context required to understand various prophetic messages in terms of the larger congregational story; and (c) each subsection will draw attention to a key facet of Group 3's data, which will later be factored into some suggestions for theological rescription of the church's theological discernment praxis (cf. §6.3).

6.2.1 Prophetic Words of Comfort, Disruption, and Challenge

This subsection begins with two testimonies regarding prophetic words given by one woman to the whole congregation, and by another to a team at work in one of the congregation's missional projects.

Tamsin's Testimony

The first account of prophetic practices came from a member named Tamsin, and a prophetic word which she believed she received from God:

> I remember the first one [prophetic word]. I remember Bill encouraging people to go missional. And I felt in my heart that they couldn't. And God gave me a word about a tree, about the roots, have to be strong and healthy for growth [she based it on a passage in Isaiah chapter 11]. It was a word of comfort for people not to be . . . upset or frustrated. The time would come when they would be ready, because I felt "You need to be ready." They wanted to do it in the flesh,[13] and that was kind of wrong, and God gave me this feeling to say "Don't worry, it will come." It was really the Father saying, "It's great, but don't be pressurized to do it." They actually clapped. They needed to hear it. (Appendix B:13)

Tamsin's testimony will be analyzed below alongside that of the testimony of Jake, which comes next.

Jake's Testimony

Jake's testimony relates to a prophetic word given to the missional allotment team he was involved with (cf. §5.1):

---

13. Cf. Eph 2:1-3—"in the flesh" has the meaning of human efforts directed at self-help instead of seeking divine help; cf. Wright, *Paul*, 35.

> There's a lady at Phoenix, Lisandra, . . . well she's actually got quite a prophetic edge and it's always very specific. It's not like someone saying at church, "I feel like somebody's hurting," I always struggle with that a bit, because that's 80 percent of the congregation. . . . She came up to me and said, "I feel that God's told me that you are just preparing the soil. Don't be discouraged because you are preparing the soil for things to grow." . . . And we were planting [stuff] that week [at the allotment], which was a coincidence as well. (Appendix B:18)

Lisandra's prophetic word helped the people of this allotment project to rethink their understanding of the church. This team had started to think of the allotment as a kind of church planting project (cf. §5.1). Lisandra's word, which focused on soil and growth, helped them to develop their understanding of the allotment as a rather novel form of church planting. Jake reflected with me on the questions Lisandra's message had led them to ask:

> We're all from a heavily churched background. It's hard to change what we do on Sundays. "Does a gathering still have to be on a Sunday?" It's those sorts of questions. "Can we do a community breakfast on a Saturday morning instead at the allotment?" and "Could that be our Sunday instead?" You know? So, we are thinking about that sort of thing as well. A couple of people are starting to get a bit nervous about that. (Appendix B:18)

Tamsin's word and Jake's testimony about Lisandra's message illustrated how women began to get more of a voice in worship services or other layers of congregational life. Generally speaking, women never preached except on one occasion when a visiting female speaker preached during a Sunday morning service. One of the reasons for this was because Phoenix adhered to FIEC's practice of not having women fulfill senior roles such as having a recognized preaching ministry.[14] Nicola Slee stresses that there is still resistance to female worship leadership in many congregational settings, although this has changed in many mainline churches.[15] The story of Phoenix's historic lack of female liturgical leadership supports Slee's thesis.[16] Importantly, as more prophetic words were shared at Phoenix, women began to be given more opportunities to have a voice in church services. For example, Lisandra became a regular

---

14. FIEC, "Women in Ministry."
15. Slee, *Women's Faith Development*, `.
16. Slee, *Women's Faith Development*, 178–80.

worship leader.[17] This was a significant development, given that this was not normative congregational practice. Indeed, Teresa Berger asserts that women's contributions to liturgy are often "a site of struggle over what shapes Christian women's lives."[18] She also stresses it can be very hard for them to have a significant influence on a congregation's liturgy. Berger goes on to comment:

> For the Christian tradition in which liturgical authority seemed to be the prerogative of a male priesthood, or more recently, a cast of (mostly male) liturgical experts, the fact that women themselves now actively construct and interpret their liturgical world is a primary mode of claiming power.[19]

Tamsin, Lisandra, and other women shared some prophetic words during services I attended (throughout 2016–18, cf. §6.2.2). Tamsin's message was in one sense aimed at comforting members who were struggling with the missional changes occurring in the church. Based on my conversation with her, I had the impression she had strong sympathies with members who were struggling with these changes, especially women. During the interview, she expressed concerns about the impact of mission on her family's life, and those of other members. She seemed to feel that too often women were having to support their families whilst men were following their desires to engage in missional work. I wondered if Tamsin and Lisandra's prophetic words revealed a "site of struggle" at Phoenix, because women had not been given a significant voice in worship services.[20] I also speculated whether prophetic words were giving women a medium through which to challenge male-dominated interpretations of *Missio Dei* theology.[21] After all, the claim that these words were given to them by God meant they might be considered to have some degree of authority, which is a claim made sometimes by prophetesses in the Pentecostal tradition.[22] Pentecostal prophetesses have tended to base

17. During sung worship Lisandra included *prophetic words*. I noticed that women would particularly ask to speak to her because a *word* seemed relevant to them after a service.

18. Berger, "Prayers and Practices of Women," 73; cf. Berger, "Feminist Ritual Practice."

19. Berger, "Prayers and Practices of Women," 73.

20. Cf. Berger, "Prayers and Practices of Women," 73.

21. Cf. Berger, "Prayers and Practices of Women," 70–74; Berger, "Feminist Ritual Practice."

22. Cf. Crumbley, "Sanctified Saints – Impure Prophetesses," 82; Stanley,

the authority for their calling to the prophetic ministry on the theology of the book of Acts, which records that women and men would "prophesy" after the coming of the Spirit on the day of Pentecost.[23] As I concentrated on the theme of authority, I conjectured whether Tamsin's prophetic word had sought to challenge the authority of what was being preached about *Missio Dei* at a subtle level. This seemed likely, because during my interview with her, she expressed concerns about the impact of mission on members. For example, she commented:

> I do not think everyone feels about mission the same way. . . . I think people may feel, not under pressure, but not able to enter into an area they are not able to function in. I don't think they are spiritually getting it. Maybe practically they do not know what to do. Would it be Spirit-led, would it be real? I believe . . . it's all about the work of the Holy Spirit, and what he does in our hearts, and only then will it be natural and what God really wants us to do. (Appendix B:13)

Tamsin seemed to believe too much emphasis had been placed on mission that required members to act (i.e., it focused on human agency). She apparently believed congregants did not understand that to engage in mission required them to be guided by the Spirit (i.e., to seek divine agency, as guidance and empowerment for mission work).[24] In other words, Tamsin was arguably challenging a works-centered interpretation of *Missio Dei*. Until members learned the importance of being led by the Spirit, Tasmin seemingly believed members would continue to feel inadequate to engage in missional activities. Her ordinary theology of *Missio Dei* went further than Newbigin's theology of discernment, because she believed God was still involved in guiding the church through prophetic practices (cf. §3.1.6).[25] Like Newbigin, her theology of mission was founded on a belief in divine rather than human agency (cf. §3.1.4).[26] The tone of our conversation indicated she was critical of a missional theology that concentrated on what was done, instead of what God might be guiding or empowering members to do.

"Wesleyan/Holiness and Pentecostal Women Preachers," 30.

23. Cf. Stanley, "Wesleyan/Holiness and Pentecostal Women Preachers," 30.
24. Cf. Newbigin, *Open Secret*, 56; Goheen, *Church and Its Vocation*, 51–54.
25. Cf. Hughes, "Life in the Spirit," 95–105.
26. Cf. Newbigin, *Open Secret*, 56; Hughes, "Life in the Spirit," 95–105.

As I reflected on Jake's testimony about Lisandra's prophetic word, I noticed another way that graduate leaders' theology of mission was possibly being challenged. Jake was a graduate of my college, and an elder of Phoenix. He was being encouraged by Bill to plant a missional church that was to be based in another ward of the city which would need to function along similar lines to Phoenix. Lisandra's word challenged the allotment team to rethink their understanding of church and church planting, which resonates with the experimental nature of emerging church ecclesiology.[27] For instance, the allotment team was questioning whether they needed to worship on a Sunday: Could a breakfast meeting at the allotment on a Saturday morning take its place? I recognized that Lisandra's message had seemingly caused them to question some rather hallowed norms of Phoenix's existing understanding of worship and the church.[28] Potentially Lisandra's message was questioning the authority of the congregation's version of the Reformed tradition, which was quite unexpected, and had the potential of being disruptive and challenging.

As I reflected on these dimensions of the data, I found Cartledge's work helped me to identify other potential levels of *Missio Dei* theology that were being challenged.[29] Cartledge draws on Caroline Franks Davis's important book, *The Evidential Force of Religious Experience*, to analyze data regarding experiences of Pentecostal baptism in the Spirit.[30] Davis theorizes that spiritual experiences provide an interpretive framework for their recipients.[31] I speculated that in the case of Tamsin's prophetic word, her spiritual experience had led her to challenge members' and leaders' prevailing activist interpretation of the *Missio Dei*. Arguably, her message provided an alternative interpretation.[32] It seemed to me that, like prophetesses in the Pentecostal tradition, Tamsin felt confident enough to challenge male leaders' hermeneutical authority because she believed God had given her an authoritative prophetic message.[33] It was

---

27. Cf. Moynagh and Harrold, *Church for Every Context*, 56, 57.

28. Cf. Bebbington, *Evangelicalism in Modern Britain*, 209; Bacchiocchi, *Divine Rest for Human Restlessness*, 11–15.

29. Cf. Cartledge, "Pentecostal Experience"; Cartledge, *Testimony in the Spirit*.

30. Cartledge, *Testimony in the Spirit*, 89; Davis, *Evidential Force of Religious Experience*.

31. Davis, *Evidential Force of Religious Experience*, 33–35; Cartledge, *Testimony in the Spirit*, 93.

32. Cf. Davis, *Evidential Force of Religious Experience*.

33. Cf. Crumbley, "Sanctified Saints – Impure Prophetesses," 74, 75.

subtly supportive of leaders' missional emphasis but also disruptive as it encouraged members not to give way to pressure to engage in missional projects before they felt led by God to do so. In other words, Tamsin's testimony challenged what was being preached at the fundamental level of hermeneutics, which went right to the root of the prevailing rhetoric preached by leaders.

As I further reflected on these prophetic words, I was reminded of an important finding that Rogers makes in the field of congregational hermeneutics.[34] He discusses the significance of paying attention to "affirmative" and "disruptive" interpretive congregational horizons voiced by members of a church.[35] Differing points of view can enable a congregation to discern or clarify what they believe, as well as influence what they want to do. Affirmative and disruptive dimensions in Group 3's prophetic words seemed to correspond with theological tensions that existed between Groups 1 and 2 (cf. §5.3.1–5.3.2). I noticed Tamsin's word seemed to relate to the concerns of Group 2, who were troubled about the lack of support of members and newcomers. This relates to Thiessen's findings that for congregations to grow they need to have stable communal support structures in place to facilitate growth.[36] It was particularly evident to me that Lisandra's message challenged the allotment team to reflect on separating from the church, which would be at odds with Group 2's communal theology. Matters like this suggested to me that the church might need to develop a more formal way for the whole congregation to reflect together on what God might be guiding them to do together, before action was taken on prophetic words (cf. §6.3).[37] Thiessen's research indicates that churches that unite around commonly accepted goals tend to be more stable and experience less conflict.[38]

6.2.2 Prophetic Words of Caution

This section concentrates on Lisandra's account of a significant message that she and a member named Lucy believed they had received.

---

34. Rogers, *Congregational Hermeneutics*.
35. Rogers, *Congregational Hermeneutics*, 39, 93, 181, 212.
36. Thiessen et al., "What Is a Flourishing Congregation?," 1–25.
37. Cf. Thatcher, "Theology, Happiness, and Public Policy," 252; Graham, "Frailty and Flourishing."
38. Thiessen et al., "What Is a Flourishing Congregation?," 1–25.

Lisandra's Testimony

> Lucy and I had the same word, not on a Sunday morning. I had a word, "Strengthen the nets," and Lucy had a word about, "Repairing the nets." It was really interesting—you know the picture of the disciples preparing the nets—and that happened at the same time for both of us. Lucy and I didn't speak about it for a couple of weeks [after having separately received them without knowing that each of them had]. We tracked back on it and we thought, "Oh, yeah, that was about the same time that we received these words." So we tried to bring them into the core leaders' meeting, to think of what they really meant. At our leaders' weekend away it came out again. It says in Revelation, "Strengthen what remains" (to the church of Laodicea). It was talking about "You've kind of gone to sleep a little bit, you need to wake up and strengthen what's left." That really resonated with everybody. So that is how the prophetic stuff gets into the leadership team. (Appendix B:29)

I asked Lisandra to explain what else she felt "mending the nets," etc., might mean to the church:

> Well, I think it's actually about building each other up. It's about getting to know each other more. To spend more time together. In the longer term, it would be about true discipleship. That is all part of it. It's about catching the fish and not letting any of them escape because someone isn't in a position to disciple them. It's again about equipping, really. For me, the next level of that was just about spending more time together. Quite often, when I look out on a Sunday morning, I think, "There are so many people here who I don't even know." I've seen them a couple of times and that's really it. (Appendix B:29)

At the leadership team's weekend away, the main topic of discussion was focused on finding ways to enrich the spiritual life of the congregation. Leaders were seemingly interested in Lisandra and Lucy's prophetic words and gave them serious attention. It was decided that more effort was required to ensure members who wanted to be involved in the missional life of the church be given more support and time to be trained to do so. For instance, one form of support was subsequently developed by Lucy. She was tasked with designing and coordinating an online prayer chain. Lucy explained that it aimed at enabling members "to make prayer requests of the" wider "congregation." It was hoped that it might make congregants feel "cared for and more connected to one another."

I observed that Lisandra and Lucy's prophetic words seemed to make an important contribution to the management of the spiritual life of Phoenix. Both women became included in the church's core leadership team, which played an advisory role to the pastor and elders and the leaders of the congregation's missional projects. Marjorie Proctor-Smith found that women are often not involved in congregational leadership hierarchies, but when they are, they can make essential contributions to the collaborative planning processes required to help faith communities thrive.[39] The voices of women began to make a positive impact on the leadership of Phoenix, which supports Proctor-Smith's finding.[40]

The inclusion of Lisandra and Lucy in the church's leadership team is reminiscent of the input of prophetically gifted women in the leadership of Pentecostal churches and their missionary work as these churches have continued to grow.[41] Barfoot and Sheppard argue that had it not been for the influence of prophetesses, the movement would not have made such an extensive impact.[42] Prophetesses performed/perform a vital role in working with all classes of society, and were/are known for their ethical concern for the vulnerable and marginalized.[43] Ma suggests they helped to establish and lead churches that accommodated the complex range of needs of those who came to them, which entailed the development of a range of supportive ministries.[44] It is important to note a similarity to what Tamsin, Lisandra, and Lucy's prophetic words concentrated upon. They sought to help leaders to strengthen the support structures of the church to enable it to care for its own vulnerable members, as well as those influenced by its missional projects.

Evaluation of the data reveals how prophetic practices were increasingly influencing the life of the congregation at all levels of ministry, not

---

39. Proctor-Smith, *In Her Own Right*.

40. Proctor-Smith, *In Her Own Right*; cf. Neu, "Women-Church Transforming Liturgy."

41. Barfoot and Sheppard, "Prophetic vs. Priestly Religion," 2–4.

42. Barfoot and Sheppard, "Prophetic vs. Priestly Religion," 2; Crumbley, "Sanctified Saints – Impure Prophetesses," 81; Cavaness, "Leadership Attitudes," 123.

43. Ma, "Changing Images," 210; Kossie-Chernyshev, "Looking Beyond the Pulpit," 67.

44. Ma, "Changing Images," 210; Kossie-Chernyshev, "Looking Beyond the Pulpit," 67.

just its concentration upon helping everyone to become missionaries. Prophecy impacted it at the levels of: (1) interpretation of *Missio Dei* theology (Tamsin's message); (2) discernment of divine guidance (Lisandra's message); (3) how the church structured its provision of ministry (Lisandra and Lucy's messages); and, (4) leadership decision-making (Lisandra and Lucy's messages). These emerging changes in the congregation's ritual practices make it important to discuss the role of ritual theory in the analysis of the prophetic activities of Group 3. This is because there were changes in congregational discernment rituals occurring at different levels of church life. Similarly, in the early part of the Pentecostal movement prophetesses helped lead and support many different kinds of ministries which sought to help people to hear from God, be healed, or have their spiritual and material needs met.[45] The emphasis on being guided by God plays an important ritual function in the Pentecostal tradition, and I noticed that, similarly, it was slowly becoming embedded into different layers of Phoenix's ritual life.

Ritual Theory and Data Analysis

Concentration on prophecy as a ritual turned my attention to ritual theory. Collins argues that ritual theory assumes "ritual has a function and that it is possible to reveal this function.[46] One of these functions is to enable participants in Christian rituals to discover and affirm their traditions, as well as their theological identity.[47] Ritual analysis was particularly developed by Van Gennep, and later Victor Turner.[48] It provided what has become a defining functionalist framework that remains important in the field of study.[49] Cartledge favors Turner's more developed ritual analysis approach, as do I, because its terminology is more suited to the examination of spiritual practices like charismatic prophecy.[50] Turner's

---

45. Cf. Ware, "Spiritual Egalitarianism," 216; Holmes, "Spirit, Nature, and Canadian Pentecostal Women," 201.

46. Collins, "Religion and Ritual," 673.

47. Cf. Collins, "Religion and Ritual," 673–75.

48. Cf. Collins, "Religion and Ritual," 678; Turner, *Forest of Symbols*; Turner, *Ritual Process*; Van Gennep, *Rites of Passage*.

49. Cf. Collins, "Religion and Ritual," 678; Turner, *Forest of Symbols*; Turner, *Ritual Process*; Van Gennep, *Rites of Passage*.

50. Cartledge, *Testimony in the Spirit*, 92, 93.

adaptation retained Van Gennep's three stages of ritual transformation, labeling each the:

1. *Preliminal stage*—which entails the beginning of the separation of a group from their old identity;

2. *Liminal stage*—transition that involves a period of perceived separation, where a group is suspended between their old and new identities; and

3. *Postliminal stage*—the emergence of a group which embraces its new identity, and hence takes on new roles pertinent to its new identity.[51]

Turner's methodological framework especially concentrated on the second liminal stage of ritual transformation.[52] During this second stage, he argued that some members of a community seek to hold on to their existing social structures, *societas*, whereas others seek to separate themselves from them.[53] Roxburgh helps to characterize Turner's concept of *societas* in the context of missional church studies.[54] *Societas* represents tensions that exist within a community between its older social structures and the need to respond to changes that require the development of new structures, which in turn seek to help a group to function in its new liminal situation.[55] When liminal changes begin to impact a community, some members of a group begin to feel threatened because they feel in imminent danger that they will be separated from their existing social identity, which is embedded in social structures.[56] At the same time, they also begin to realize their existing social structures no longer function to support them as well as they once did. Neither is it clear what will be needed in the future to sustain the needs of a group so they can survive in a changing environment.[57]

Not everyone experiencing uncertainties about the future of a community react negatively to liminality.[58] Instead, some group members embrace separation from their old identity, and thus take a journey of

---

51. Turner, *Ritual Process*; cf. Collins, "Religion and Ritual," 678.
52. Turner, *Forest of Symbols*, 95; Turner, *Ritual Process*.
53. Collins, "Religion and Ritual," 678.
54. Roxburgh, *Sky Is Falling*.
55. Roxburgh, *Sky Is Falling*, 102.
56. Roxburgh, *Sky Is Falling*, 103–9.
57. Roxburgh, *Sky Is Falling*, 100–12.
58. Roxburgh, *Sky Is Falling*, 101–4.

discovery to find a new group identity. A feature of this phase of ritual transformation is that those who accept the change journey can develop a sense of solidarity. Turner termed this "*Communitas*."[59] *Communitas* is theorized to give those who support the need for changing the strength to take a journey to discover a new identity and structures to support a group.[60] Turner termed this aspect of liminality "anti-structure," because during the second liminal stage old structures are abandoned, and new structures are only lightly held.[61] According to Roxburgh, it is when one group in a congregation seeks to hang on to their former social structures and another develops a sense of *communitas* that tensions can disrupt the life of a congregation.[62]

Applied to Phoenix's context, congregants who clung to the congregation's old *societas* were placed in tension with others who felt ready to support and embrace liminal change. Arguably, Group 2 resisted separation from their old identity, which had prioritized the relational and communal structures of the congregation of the past (pre-2009; §5.2).[63] Group 1 seemed to have largely embraced the liminal missional change journey of the congregation, and seemed quite positive about it (cf. §5.1).

Addressing Liminal Tensions and Changes through Ritual Praxis

It is against this backdrop of intergroup differences and tensions that Tamsin, Lisandra, and Lucy's prophetic words seemed to seek to develop a greater sense of congregational *communitas*.[64] They were, in essence, contributing to a ritual transformation process of the congregation to help Groups 1 and 2 unite around what God might be revealing to them.[65] Their prophetic rhetoric was evidently infused with the language of divine guidance, which concentrated attention on seeking to unite in what God was guiding the congregation to do. I noticed that this is consistent with feminist insights into ritual transformation. For example, Berger observes

---

59. Turner, *Ritual Process*, 94–130; cf. Collins, "Religion and Ritual," 678.
60. Roxburgh, *Sky Is Falling*, 102–4.
61. Turner, *Ritual Process*, 94–130; cf. Collins, "Religion and Ritual," 678.
62. Roxburgh, *Sky Is Falling*, 100–12.
63. Cf. Roxburgh, *Sky Is Falling*, 100–12.
64. Cf. Roxburgh, *Sky Is Falling*, 102–9.
65. Cf. Turner, *Ritual Process*, 131–65.

that "feminist rituals" are often "designed to be highly participatory."[66] She also stresses this "participatory" phenomenon has probably been stimulated against the backdrop "of centuries of women simply watching and hearing," without being given a voice within churches.[67] It most certainly resonates with and supports a participatory view of discerning the *Missio Dei*. It was the prophetic voices of women at Phoenix that stressed the need to mend the nets or strengthen what remained so that the church might not lose more members due to unresolved tensions (cf. §4.1; 7.1.2). I observed that their prophetic messages drew attention to a "holistic spirituality," which arguably sought to connect members as a work of the Spirit.[68] For instance, Lisandra indicated that practical steps needed to be taken so people could get "to know each other more." Ross speaks of the important prophetic role that the church as a "mother" represents to "nurture" a "hospitable" environment of communal connectivity.[69] I speculated that perhaps the language of mothering might help to characterize the kind of atmosphere Lisandra and Lucy were seeking to cultivate. At least it seems their prophetic words were seeking to address liminal intergroup tensions by encouraging congregants to find ways of supporting one another to build intergroup *communitas*. Their efforts might be characterized as seeking to unite the congregation so that it could become a more stable environment, which would strengthen rather than weaken members' relationships with each other.[70]

As I reflected on these testimonies and my observations of congregational practices, it became increasingly evident that the congregation did not have a clear strategy to enable the whole church to participate in spiritual discernment beyond Bill encouraging members to share their prophetic words. This, at least, provided an informal way to help the church discern divine guidance. However, there were no regular corporate prayer meetings, which could have provided an opportunity for a more formal discernment gathering to take place. Caspian, and some other members, suggested that in the Phoenix of the past (prior to its

---

66. Berger, "Feminist Ritual Practice," 537–39.

67. Berger, "Feminist Ritual Practice," 537–39; Berry, "Transforming Rites."

68. Cf. Woodhead, "Why so Many Women in Holistic Spirituality?," 115–26; Drane, *Do Christians Know How to Be Spiritual?*, 1–40.

69. Ross, "Hospitality," 67–84.

70. Cf. Weston, "Ecclesiology in Eschatological Perspective," 79; Newbigin, *Gospel in a Pluralist Society*, 222–33; Thiessen et al., "What Is a Flourishing Congregation?," 1–25.

change journey) the whole congregation had attended prayer meetings, and these had helped the church to unite as a group. This was a practice the church might want to revisit as it was valued by quite a number of Group 2 members I spoke to.

This led me to ponder whether the whole church might be encouraged to periodically meet for the purpose of praying for divine guidance, given the good memories that some longer-standing members had of the church's former corporate prayer meetings. It might function similarly to the leadership meeting with Lisandra and Lucy. Intentional corporate discernment meetings might help congregants feel they were working together in the shaping of their community's spiritual life. This realization led me to be more attentive to how other aspects of Group 3's data might provide insights to help construct a congregation-wide method of spiritual discernment.

In what follows, I will provide indicators of how other dimensions of Group 3's data might contribute to theological rescription of the congregation's discernment praxis (cf. §6.3). I hope that what has been discussed in this section will help other congregations going through a missional change process appreciate the importance of listening to the prophetic voice if this phenomenon starts to emerge as it did in Phoenix.

6.2.3 A Prophetic Word of Encouragement

Kirsty's Testimony

Kirsty's testimony added significant insights that identified key practices that helped to facilitate the missional youth team's approach to spiritual discernment. She commented:

> I think our approach was more reactive a few years ago, then a new lady came [Jasmin]. She had a picture of a barn and a harvest and it being filled—a really prophetic picture you know. We were sort of praying together, and over the next few years—whoosh—and we saw the youth group really grow! Now in the last year, we have seen a lot of harvest come in. At [youth] camp this year we are going to say [to the young people], "What are you going to do, how are you going to step out?"
>
> I think we [have] needed a few years to focus on discipling them, the winning and the building up of [the young people]. By the age of eighteen, they go off to university. We want them

to be able to read the Bible for themselves, have their own faith, stand on their own two feet, faith-wise. It's equipping them to go out into the world. We want them to make the decision for themselves, and we've seen them make that commitment to say, "I want to follow Christ for myself."

I think with having our more prophetic lady on board, it has led the youth team to become more relational, just getting alongside them and building those relationships. So rather than teaching them, we sit down next to them and say, "Let's bash this through from your life's point of view." That's changed from the past. And you know it's kind of humbling to be able to say to them "We don't have all of the answers, but let's sit down and try to figure this out together." So, if we are more open with them, then they will be more open with us. I say to them, "It is hard for me to share my faith with people at work." It's good to do this because it says to them, "That just because we are leaders, we haven't got all the answers."

There was one of the girls at camp this year who said, "I've been reminded of a lot of stuff I already knew, but it's now like God is asking me to go out and do something with it." That's brilliant, you know, She is actually now asking, "What can I do with it?" (Appendix B:2)

The youth team had apparently incorporated insights obtained from prophetic words into their work with the youth group. Kirsty underscored that the youth team was given the "picture" of the "harvest barn" to equip youth to become "committed disciples" (as well as "missionaries to their friends"). Her testimony also indicated the team wanted to be open to a voyage of discovery of divine guidance to help them discern how to support the youth. This relates well to Thiessen's findings that churches grow when members believe God is at work among them.[71] Kirsty explained the team had significantly benefitted from the ongoing support of the "prophetic lady" (Jasmin). It was largely due to her encouragement that they were observant of how God might be influencing the young people. This insight also relates to the kind of influence Pentecostals believe prophets or prophetesses have on the lives of believers.[72] Kirsty's testimony provided evidence of how a *Missio Dei* theology of divine prophetic guidance was having a transformative impact on this

---

71. Thiessen et al., "What Is a Flourishing Congregation?," 1–25.
72. Alexander, "Introduction," 2, 3.

team's missional practices.[73] Jasmin's prophecy of the harvest barn helped the youth team to identify, and then participate in, what they seemed to think of as a preparatory work of the Holy Spirit in the lives of the young people.[74] Youth group leaders were arguably trying to help young people go beyond their present frame of reference to explore what God might be guiding them toward.[75] I observed that the team had seemingly placed themselves in a liminal space of discovery alongside the youth, seeking to discover what the Spirit might be guiding them to do.[76] The adoption of this openness to liminality seemed to concentrate on facilitating a mutual spiritual journey of discovery, as well as a sense of group solidarity. It entailed leaders and the youth discerning together what God might be doing in their lives.

Kirsty's evidence also suggested to me that the attitude of the youth team was one of humility. They were striving to develop a learning community that adopted a conversational culture. The whole team had placed themselves alongside the youth as learners. They seemed to have adopted a learner-centered approach.[77] The aim was to bring out from young people's testimonies what God was guiding them to do, so that they might discover together God's future and their part in it. The team seemingly believed that if God were really at work preparing for a harvest of young people, then this required them to provide a facilitative conversational environment in which young people could spiritually mature. I suggest that Kirsty's testimony indicated that leaders and young people were developing some degree of mutual *communitas* rather than being distanced from each other by a more formal approach to leadership. I found myself wondering if the facilitative approach of the youth group might help to inform the development of the practices of a congregation-wide discernment group. A group of this kind is discussed below in terms of theological rescription of the church's discernment practices (cf. §6.3).

73. Thiessen et al., "What Is a Flourishing Congregation?"

74. Cf. Hughes, "Life in the Spirit," 95–105; Tennent, *Invitation to World Missions*, 71.

75. For a discussion of mysticism and transcendence, see Sheldrake, *Spaces for the Sacred*, 119–46.

76. Cf.. Roxburgh, *Sky Is Falling*, 102–8; Turner, *Ritual Process*, 94–130.

77. Cf. Heron, *Facilitator's Handbook*; Darsih, "Learner-Centered Teaching."

6.2.4 A Prophetic Impression

Leah's Testimony

Leah's testimony added another important dimension regarding the benefits of drawing on the experiences of others to help individuals discern divine guidance. She commented:

> I think the decision to step out into the mission field and serve a year with Youth For Christ caused me to understand the motto [i.e., "God's people on God's mission in the Spirit's power with the message of His Son"]. I asked God to "Break my heart for young people," which he did. But, then, I felt huge amounts of pressure when I thought that I was responsible to have them all converted. Through many conversations with godly people, and the big man himself, the Spirit revealed the motto to me in a new way. I realized that my role in the kingdom is not to "save" young people. I am just one tiny cog, whose job is to follow Jesus in God's great mission. (Appendix B:30)

I observed that Leah had seemingly learned from her earlier participation in the church's youth group about the benefits of prophetic discernment. Her testimony disclosed that she had received a prophetic impression which she claimed had been "revealed" to her by the "Spirit." To some extent, this fits with Newbigin's theology of the preecclesial work of the Holy Spirit.[78] This revelation provided her with a new perception of the church's motto. She obtained the insight that it was not her job to save young people. Instead, she needed to help them to rely on God to find salvation. This seemed to be an example of a Newbigin-like missional soteriology, which emphasized divine rather than human agency in the work of salvation and mission (cf. §3.1.4).[79] Leah seemingly found it liberating, because it changed her understanding of her role in mission work. She no longer seemed to feel under pressure, but free to trust that God was at work in the lives of others. She had evidently struggled in her own liminal space of uncertainty and was seemingly propelled by the discomfort to seek help from God and fellow congregants. It is an important insight that liminal uncertainty can prompt people to find resolutions to the discomfort it causes for them.[80] Testimonies like Leah's

---

78. Cf. Newbigin, *Open Secret*, 56; Goheen, *Church and Its Vocation*, 51–54.
79. Cf. Newbigin, *Open Secret*, 56; Flett, *Witness of God*, 38, 39.
80. Cf. Roxburgh, *Sky Is Falling*, 101–5.

could arguably help other church members learn how to resolve some of their liminal challenges by seeking to discern God's guidance together, rather than alone.

6.3 Summary and Rescription

Thus far, I have suggested that the all-female Group 3's affirmative and disruptive prophetic words have brought what could be feminist perspectives to prominence regarding the impact of *Missio Dei* on congregational life. Their testimonies were both supportive and disruptive of the church's missional emphasis. Tamsin and Lisandra's prophetic words also cautioned leaders and congregants alike not to make participation in mission the church's predominant outlook. For instance, the church needed to deal with intergroup theological differences if it was to become a more united community. Group 3 seemed to exercise their prophetic words to enrich congregational *communitas*. By inference, Group 3's testimonies indicated they were seeking to enable congregants to find fulfillment in what they did. They sought to do this by keeping members' and leaders' attention concentrated upon discerning what God might be guiding them to do together. This relates well to the important role of the prophetess in the Pentecostal tradition in terms of how encouraging varieties of ministries to support the needs of others can help a church to become more united.[81]

I suggest Group 3's version of a united congregation required that Phoenix's groups be enabled to discern together what God might be guiding them to do. This would involve listening to differing theological group perspectives. It also involved seeking to discern what God was revealing through each of these perspectives, even if it meant some disruption in the way of life of the congregation (cf. Tamsin and Lisandra's testimonies). This seemed very Newbigin-like to me. Newbigin believed that for a missional congregation to effectively function, it needed to enable members to be united with God and each other (cf. §3.1.3).[82] As a general observation, I noticed that Group 3 (especially Tamsin, Lisandra, and Lucy) sought to listen carefully to what God might be revealing through members' conflicting perspectives, and then brought them to

---

81. Cf. Alexander, "Introduction," 2–6.

82. Cf. Weston, "Ecclesiology in Eschatological Perspective," 79; Newbigin, *Gospel in a Pluralist Society*, 222–33.

the attention of leaders and members alike. This relates to a finding Collicutt makes that prophetic epiphanies particularly come during times of stress and conflict to help sustain individuals or a community by providing ways to resolve them.[83]

As I have already indicated, reflection on Group 3's data led me to identify potential clues to theologically rescript how the congregation might approach discernment of divine guidance in the future. As things stood in Phoenix at the end of my research, there was not an intentional forum at which the church could solely focus on prophetic discernment. Congregational business meetings or the Annual General Meeting provided some opportunities to discuss the future course of the church. However, they were not primarily designed to focus on spiritual discernment. It seemed what was missing was a means for the whole congregation to prophetically discern together what God might be guiding them to do. I suggest Group 3's efforts to develop *communitas* between different groups in the congregation provides a clue to rescript the discernment practices of the congregation. Perhaps a periodic congregation-wide corporate discernment meeting might be developed. It fitted to some extent with the positive memories some longstanding members had of the church's former corporate prayer meetings. Having a meeting of this type might send an important signal to members of Groups 1 and 2 that they could all pray for God's guidance to seek their future together.

It could aim to: (1) concentrate congregants' attention on seeking to prayerfully discern what God might be guiding the congregation to do; (2) encourage members of differing groups to engage in the mutual discussion of what they believe God is revealing to them; (3) pray for discernment of how to respond to new insights and ideas; and (4) make recommendations to help the church implement new ideas, or projects. Mutuality would be an important corporate aim of periodic gatherings if all groups in the congregation are to be helped to unite as a relationally cohesive community. An adapted form of social Trinitarianism could be used to portray a discernment gathering as a means to discern how God might be guiding the congregation to unite as a diverse relational community that seeks to live reconciled to one another in the love of Christ (cf. §5.4; 8.1.1).

---

83. Collicutt, *Psychology of Christian Character Formation*, 192.

Key Practices

In what follows, analyses of Group 3's data will be used to suggest some key practices that could be used to facilitate quarterly corporate discernment gatherings (comprised of leaders and members). These practices could entail developing:

1. *An approach aimed at facilitating conversations between peers:* Kirsty's testimony highlighted the importance of the development of a nonhierarchical community. This flat-level kind of communal environment meant that: 1) a facilitative approach was used with young people to encourage the sharing of different perspectives; 2) leaders' theological insights were put on the same level as everyone else's; and 3) a conversational culture was nurtured to empower the whole group to feel free to communicate as if they were talking with friends.

2. *A learning community:* Jake, Lisandra, Kirsty, and Leah's testimonies highlighted the importance of having a willingness to learn from God and others. If everyone at a corporate discernment gathering were to view themselves as learners, then this could help cultivate congregational solidarity (i.e., between leaders and members alike).

3. *Observational skills:* Kirsty spoke of the importance of planning responses to her missional community's needs based on observing indicators of what God might be doing in young peoples' lives. Similarly, observational practices like this could be learned at discernment gatherings based on members hearing peers' accounts of how they identify and then seek to participate in potential divine activity.

4. *A feedback approach:* Kirsty indicated the youth team and young people engaged in feedback on what was happening in their missional activities and lives. A discernment gathering might provide feedback opportunities for congregants to review the results of the implementation of new ideas for mission or other types of ministry in the church. Discernment of the validity of new missional projects could be based on seeking evidence of God's seeming activity in them. Recommendations could then be made for the church to experiment with or to implement.

Rescription Analysis

Reflection on the rhetoric of learning and discernment suggested to me that a corporate discernment gathering could be termed a "learning community of discernment." The language of learning related to ecclesial life is not an alien concept in the literature.[84] For instance, Astley theorizes that members learn their ordinary theologies arising from the "hidden curriculum" of their lives, engagement with Christian liturgy, and congregational life.[85] Alternatively, Lonsdale replaces the rhetoric of "learning" with that of "school" to describe communal spiritual discernment practices.[86] He utilizes Lash's notion of the church as a "school of discernment" to characterize the power the clergy and liturgy wield to influence congregations.[87] The language of school implies expert/professional inputs from trained teachers/leaders, whereas the language of learning community, with the emphasis being placed on all participants learning from God and one another, would seem more appropriate to Phoenix. This is because concentrating on learning from each other might enable members to feel they have a voice in discerning the future direction of the church, rather than feeling they are being told what it is through the church's formal Bible school or preaching (cf. §7.1.6).

After all, the prophetic practices of Group 3 had to some extent questioned the official teaching of *Missio Dei* provided by graduate leaders. Questioning relates well to the language of a facilitative learning environment.[88] The questions raised by some of Group 3's prophetic words arguably placed leaders and members on a mutual journey of seeking to better discern divine guidance. This is in keeping with Astley's view of ordinary theology, which he emphasizes facilitates a learning conversation that is as important to academic theology as it is to the members of a faith community.[89] The language of learning also fits well with Anselm of Canterbury's characterization of theology as "faith seeking understanding."[90]

---

84. Cf. Astley, "Ordinary Theology," 45–54.

85. Astley, *Ordinary Theology*, 4, 5, 19.

86. Lonsdale, "Church as Context for Christian Spirituality," 240.

87. Lonsdale, "Church as Context for Christian Spirituality," 239–53; cf. Lash, "Considering the Trinity," 258; Kenneson, "Nicholas Lash," 274–75.

88. Heron, *Facilitator's Handbook*, 85–86, 116, 119; Astley, *Ordinary Theology*, 17–19.

89. Astley, "Ordinary Theology," 45–54.

90. Anselm, "Proslogion," 82–104.

To seek is to engage in learning. Hence, the egalitarian language of learning community places everyone on the same level, undertaking together a pilgrimage of transformative divine guidance toward what comes next.[91] Participation in the discernment of divine activity as a form of learning might be said to entail seeking God's presence in the world of cultural experience.[92] God might be potentially revealed in every facet of life lived out in a variety of places where members interact with wider society.[93] In other words, life experiences, situated in places, might be thought of as theologically loaded with meaning, which requires discernment of the divine presence in specific locations as part of a learning journey.[94]

This emphasis resonates with a Newbigin-like theology of participation.[95] Newbigin considered that participation in the *Missio Dei* required that God always be placed ahead of the missional church as the agent and guide of all that it undertook (cf. §3.1.4).[96] Hence, the language of learning community of discernment places God as agent, guide, and facilitator of congregational beliefs and practices for leaders and members alike.[97] Perhaps this places ordinary theology in its proper domain as the intentional pursuit of every believer for communion and participation in the life of the triune God. After all, Group 3 was seemingly seeking to help Groups 1 and 2 mutually understand what God might be guiding them to do together.

I will argue in chapter 8 that Newbigin's/GOCN's theology of discernment could be helpfully rescripted by the ordinary prophetic and communal theology of Group 3 (cf. §8.1.3).

In terms of how the reader might apply the learning from this chapter to their own context, either in church leadership, missional community life, or academic research, it might be worth reflecting on how a congregation, or range of congregations across differing faith traditions, might be learning to prophetically discern the *Missio Dei* related to their context. I would suggest paying careful attention to the ordinary theologies of differing groups regarding divine guidance, can provide helpful

91. I suggest the language of learning community would be acceptable based on observations of how members and leaders related to each other.
92. Cf. Ward, *Participation and Mediation*, 95–105.
93. Sheldrake, *Spaces for the Sacred*, 33–63.
94. Cf. Inge, *Christian Theology of Place*, 123–44.
95. Cf. Guder, *Missional Church*, 4, 5; Goheen, *Church and Its Vocation*, 68–70.
96. Cf. Newbigin, *Open Secret*, 56.
97. Cf. Thiessen et al., "What Is a Flourishing Congregation?," 1–25.

indicators to help rescript the way groups seek to discern and participate in the ongoing mission of Jesus as something they share together. I would suggest it is very hard to conceive of how the church might seek to participate in mission, which belongs to God, if it does not first of all develop understanding of how to prophetically discern God's mission suited to a church's local context. This would seem to suggest the need for urgent research into the ordinary theologies of discernment, and resultant participation in the *Missio Dei,* that are experienced by ordinary believers. The triune God of revelation may be said to be at work in the people of God, rather than in an institutionalized hierarchical ecclesiastical structure. Hence, learning to locally discern God's guidance will provide a means to give attention to what God is revealing to his people about his mission for each context. After all, the people of God are all part of the body of Christ (i.e., they are part of Christ's universal church).

Chapter 7

Cost and Conflict

Introduction

THIS CHAPTER CONCENTRATES ON the cost of missional change for the members of Phoenix. The words "cost" and "costly" refer to members' accounts of the challenges, tensions, and conflicts that they seemed to believe impacted them because of their missional change journey. There does not seem to be any significant attention given in the missional church literature to the issue of the cost of a congregation becoming focused on mission in terms of negative impacts on congregants. This chapter will hopefully encourage others to engage in research on this important matter. I believe it is essential to draw attention to negative impacts on a congregation going through a missional change process, as it is my conviction that it will help useful conversations to occur in order to identify ways to reduce negative impacts on future change processes that occur in churches that take a similar journey to that of Phoenix.

The chapter: (1) discusses linked themes related to the cost of missional change; (2) analyzes these themes; and (3) rescripts the ordinary theological data. The rescription that is discussed in what follows seeks to provide an example of one way that a mediating theology can be used to address (rescript) the ordinary theological accounts of members who experienced negative impacts because of Phoenix's missional change journey.

7.1 Cost of Change Themes

This section concentrates on members' testimonies regarding the negative impacts of missional change on the congregation. The cost of change will not always be negative. Based on the coding process, I was able to determine the themes analyzed below. Paying attention to these themes helps to tell the story of the challenging change journey of the congregation. I will employ a narrative approach to explore the relationships between these themes so they can be further analyzed and then rescripted.

7.1.1 Differences in Theological Values

The telling of the congregation's story has already partly illustrated how differing intergroup theological perspectives have apparently caused tensions at Phoenix (cf. chs. 5 and 6). During a congregational consultation a conversation between two members named Theresa and Gerald illustrated what seemed to be a key cause of tensions at Phoenix. It related to differences in values.

> *Theresa:* There is stuff about values: What does this community gather around? What is this community about? We've had maybe fifteen or twenty from Elim join . . . people from different pathways. The question is, I wonder what God's doing in that, when you've got this melting pot? It is one of the things people have said, "This is quite a creative melting pot of things, what could come out of this?" And, we're wondering "What's God doing here?" In other words, it's not that normal sort of one defined thing this church is about, it's this melting pot. There's a sense of anticipation of "What's God doing here and what's possible?" (Appendix B; Congregational Consultation 4)

> *Gerald:* So you could also ask, "What are people doing in that melting pot?" You could ask, "What was the Devil doing by bringing them to us?" Because I get the impression that when someone leaves a church it's deemed as "They've got issues, they've got problems, they weren't committed." You could say that's what we're getting, we're getting flotsam and jetsam. So what is Satan up to in those other places? They've split, they've had divisiveness, they've got disgruntled, they've come to us. So I don't get too excited when I see an influx from a church, because I think "Well it's a split." (Appendix B; Congregational Consultation 4)

Theresa illustrated the optimism of some members who were excited by the arrival of newcomers, which she and they apparently believed to be evidence of God being at work in the church. These newcomers were among congregational groups that were part of Theresa's "melting pot" metaphor.[1] She partly shared in this optimism, but also expressed uncertainty about what might develop out of this melting process. Her uncertainty may be partly explained because earlier in the consultation she had expressed concerns that the church did not seem to have clearly defined values to gather around. Her comments reinforced my suspicion that the differences between Group 1 and 2's missional and communal values were causing some members uncertainty about what was expected of them as members of Phoenix.

Gerald's response to Theresa's reflections disclosed a more pessimistic point of view about newcomers. He did not place a high value on church growth that occurred due to members from another church joining them. His question about Satan's role in their arrival at Phoenix made him suspicious of their motives for coming to the church. Gerald's concerns about Satanic influence challenged an optimistic theology of divine activity in the church. There was an evident difference in the value-sets of Theresa and Gerald. I wondered if Gerald's perspective was actually a defense mechanism that had developed in reaction to a *Missio Dei* theology of divine agency. Gerald was not involved in the church's missional projects, and was apparently suspicious of the changes that could be attributed to the church's new openness to mission and the people who were coming to join it because of these changes.

Gerald's perspective illustrated yet another way of evaluating the impact of change on Phoenix's members. Differences in values had seemingly led to some members being confused about what the congregation actually stood for, or, in Gerald's case, resistant to building relationships with newcomers too speedily until he got to know them better.

7.1.2 Conflict and Coup Attempt

Serious conflict had already been experienced at Phoenix prior to my fieldwork starting because of the changes occurring in the congregation. This was between some longstanding members and Bill and his team

---

1. She seemed to use the language of "melting pot" colloquially rather than sociologically; cf. Giddens, *Sociology*, 643–47.

because these congregants did not value the missional changes that had taken place. Tensions erupted into conflict in 2015, when eight members and two elders sought to dismiss Bill from his role as senior pastor. They began congregational proceedings whilst Bill was on a short sabbatical. Upon his return, he learnt that a leadership team meeting had been called by one of these two elders in order to discuss his dismissal. Bill went to this meeting and confronted the leadership team. He explained, "I told them that they had to choose between me or him [the elder]."

The majority of the leadership team recommended that Bill should remain in office. At an extraordinary congregational meeting a majority of members voted in favor of keeping Bill. Ten coup group members chose to leave the church, as did about another ten in the months that followed this decision (cf. §4.1). I did not have the opportunity to interview coup members who had left, due to concerns that if I interviewed them it might stir up old animosities and lead them to contact members who had remained (thus stirring up yet more conflict). I was, however, able to interview members who had been especially impacted by the coup attempt. Isaac spoke about the tensions that existed in the years that led up to the coup (2009–15). He explained:

> The power that was wielded by these members actually strangled most of the new ministries in the church. And the overriding feeling out of this experience was that it had been a really hard time. But as I look back on that time, my overriding feeling is that in the midst of all the struggle, tragedy, and the heartache was relief. There was a palpable tension within our leadership meetings, and lots of other meetings—you were on tenterhooks all of the time. It was whether something was going to kick off or not. Once that came to a head and was largely resolved it was like the absence of toothache. (Appendix B; Leaders Consultation 5)

Isaac's data indicated three kinds of conflict that regularly arose between the coup members and leaders. First, the coup group sought to block leaders' and other members' attempts to develop missional projects. For example, Beverley indicated the resistance she encountered when she was developing the first missional allotment. She was told her efforts made no contribution to the life of the church and should therefore not be supported. Due to this resistance she had to work on her own for about a year to develop the first missional allotment before others joined her (during 2013; cf. Appendix D7). Second, elders who were part of the coup group sought to block Bill's efforts to train members to engage in mission. For example, Bill discussed how resistance had led to the delay of the development of the church's Bible training school (cf. Appendix D8). And finally, at congregational business meetings, as well as in worship services, members of this group objected to the missional emphasis of Bill's preaching. For instance, Desmond highlighted how members stood up during worship services and objected to the idea that everyone had responsibility to engage in mission (cf. Appendix D9).

As I reflected on these testimonies, I realized that I was largely hearing the history of the cost of change from the perspective of those who had remained in the congregation. In other words, I was hearing the accounts of the winners. I wanted to avoid listening just to their accounts. Hence, I spoke to members who still had sympathies with the coup group. Belinda provided some useful insights into what the coup group valued, and had fought to preserve in the congregation. Interestingly, her parents were part of the group that had left Phoenix after the coup. She helped to characterize the family-life model of church that existed in old Phoenix by sharing memories of family camps that had once been a common feature of the church's annual calendar. Apparently, this family atmosphere was one of the things the coup group had fought to keep. To Belinda's evident sadness she was the only one out of her family who still attended Phoenix:

> I feel like I have to keep the family name in Phoenix. It's my duty maybe. I think the church has definitely changed, but then, it was bound to change. . . . I attended my first church camp when I was five weeks old, and those camps were huge. I remember when I went to camp the entire church would come on it. . . . So you'd have the golden oldies turn up in their tent. Jess Overton looked after us when we were toddlers. We all went to her tent for toast in the morning. . . . [T]hinking of my family, I've had my grandparents do the camp, my mum and dad did the camp, I've done the camp. It can be that kind of foundation of watching either your family or peers who you look up to, thinking, "That's what I want my faith to look like." So I think the church is about a foundation for those things. . . . When I think of Phoenix before, I feel that we were better at nurturing the people that came already. We were a type of family. I think with the new motto ["God's people on God's mission in the Spirit's power with the message of His Son"] it takes away from what happened in the past. It's this constant need for new things and for change. I don't

think we necessarily need to change. So, I think without the foundations being strong and solid . . . no amount of outreach is ever going to work. (Appendix B:16)

Belinda apparently believed the church needed to be a strong, close-knit, family-like community in order for it to be effective in its outreach. It was this kind of church her parents had fought to maintain. As I listened to her memories of the past, I recognized she seemed to be grieving because of the changes that had occurred more recently in the church. It seemed like she no longer felt at home in the congregation. Indeed, Belinda also left Phoenix. She, therefore, sacrificed her desire to keep her family name in the church when she left.

As I reflected on these testimonies, I concluded that a cost of missional change was that members who had strongly identified with Phoenix's older model of family church could not accept that it needed to change. Isaac's testimony indicated that coup group members had fought to halt the development of new ministries in the church, which had caused unhappiness for them and the church. Apparently, it was only after these members had left that there was greater freedom to really develop the church's missional work. Belinda's testimony provided some background to the tensions that led up to the coup attempt because of the erosion of the church's close-knit community. It seems that coup group members felt they could not compromise: either Phoenix needed to preserve a family model of church life, or they could no longer belong to the church. This led them to sacrifice their membership at Phoenix. In an important sense, an implicit theme of sacrifice may be inferred as a common thread that runs throughout the data in this chapter. Jerry, in his late twenties, captured something of the strong feelings of the coup members:

> I think a lot of people said "Screw this, I'm off." A lot of people have gone. They have said, "Actually this isn't for me, this isn't for people like me. It isn't comfortable, we're going too far." (Appendix B:12)

Apparently, in the view of the members who left the church, the congregation was going too far by becoming a missional church that was constantly changing, and because it was welcoming untrusted newcomers into its community. It was going too far to concentrate the church's efforts on developing the missionary abilities of all of its members. The coup group, like Belinda, seemed to believe concentrating on mission outside the church detracted from its communal life (similar to Group 2; cf. §5.2).

7.1.3 Discouragement

I wondered if the departure of the coup group had been perceived as helping to improve how congregants and leaders related to each other. As already illustrated, from Isaac's point of view things had improved because their deliberate strategy of openly contesting the missional work of the congregation had ceased (cf. §7.1.2). However, there was a strong theme of discouragement among some members because of their departure. Libby and Jasmin expressed their concerns during a congregational consultation:

> *Libby:* I struggle with that, I struggle . . . that people . . . are not here anymore. It's actually harder than it should be, it's because they haven't lost their faith, you know? They've chosen somewhere else to worship, because it suits them for their own personal reasons. But sometimes you just don't connect with them anymore. So you just never see them again. (Appendix B; Consultation Group 2)

> *Jasmin:* And you know we poured into some of those people . . . and then you kind of think, "Why have they gone and we're here? Is there something wrong with me staying? There's something wrong here with people leaving." You know, "Have they got it right and I've got it wrong?" You have to kind of work that out, because there's so much to do at church. There's so many needy people here. You think, "How can we say there is nothing for us here?" You know, that's what I find is hard to get my head around. They just don't see that, do they? They just see their need, I suppose. (Appendix B; Consultation Group 2)

Libby seemed to be grieving because she no longer connected with members she had personally known as friends. Jasmin questioned whether the coup group had been right to leave. However, what seemed to motivate Jasmin and her family to remain at Phoenix was caring for the needs of others who, like them, had remained in the church despite their doubts of whether they should stay.

Interestingly, most of those who seemed to be discouraged aligned themselves with the concerns of Group 2 (cf. §5.2). However, Jasmin also had sympathies with Group 3 (cf. §6.2.3). Based on these conversations,

I realized these congregants valued the strong relational family model of the past. I had the strong impression from the tone of my conversation with these two women that they would have preferred the church to concentrate much more effort on ministry with its families, and less on mission. Feelings of discouragement seemed to be associated with a grieving process for the church's former way of life. It seems part of this grieving process related to whether members like Jasmin could accept the sacrifice of the congregation's former family-life model of church. This was illustrated by how members like Jasmin were still questioning whether they too should leave as the coup group had done.

7.1.4 Churches-Within-a-Church

I first became conscious of the theme of "churches-within-a-church" as I reflected on Theresa's observations about the lack of clear commonly held congregational values (cf. §7.1.1). I realized that because the coup group had valued the older family focus of the church, they had become a kind of church-within-a-church. They were seemingly living out a different set of theological values that concentrated on nurturing others within the church, whereas the new missional outlook was apparently perceived to focus on supporting outsiders to the congregation (i.e., in the community). These value-sets were fundamentally representative of two differing kinds of ecclesial frameworks (cf. §7.2.2). This provided the insight that if other groups in the congregation did not have their values affirmed and integrated into the way of life of Phoenix, then yet other churches-within-a-church might emerge in the future.

Barrett et al. argue that in order for missional churches to function successfully, congregants need to unite around a commonly espoused missional vocation.[2] Phoenix of 2018 was still not united around a commonly espoused vocation. Differences between interest groups' values meant there was still the potential for different models of church to be valued by congregants (cf. §7.2.2). It seems a cost of transforming a congregation from one model of church to another is that different models of church might become desirable which may conflict with each other.[3]

---

2. Barrett et al., *Treasure in Clay Jars*, 33–58.
3. Cf. Croft, *Transforming Communities*.

7.1.5 Deficits in Pastoral Care and Isolation

Ben, a member for fifty years, discussed the changes in the congregation that had particularly impacted elderly members. He seemed to be in favor of some of the missional changes that had occurred, especially those that aimed at training members to support the running of the church. However, he was concerned about alterations that made the leaders of the church less responsible to provide pastoral care. He seemed to be confused:

> What about us older ones? Cos I've been here years, been a Christian for years... who do I speak to? That's one of the problems I've had for some time now. (Appendix B:21)

Ben, like other members of Group 2, was concerned that pastoral care was not being provided for members in the church. In his view, this was because leaders were concentrating their efforts on supporting mission in the neighborhood (cf. §5.1). It seems the deconstruction of the former family-life model of church had the effect of also dismantling its previous normative pastoral care structures for which the pastor and elders had once been solely responsible (cf. §1.1.1). Evidently, a cost of missional change was that some elderly members felt isolated. They expected the pastor and elders to be responsible for their spiritual care.

In a conversation I had with Bill, he emphasized that some long-standing members did not consider a visit from anyone else but the pastor to count as pastoral support (cf. Appendix D10). It was hard to change older members' expectations regarding the pastor's role because they were deeply ingrained. The new every-member ministry model had in effect made it hard for elderly members to know who to turn to for professional pastoral support of the kind they trusted.

7.1.6 Sacrifice and Burnout

A related theme to deficits in pastoral care was highlighted in my conversation with a member, and former elder, named Adrian. He and his family had experienced what he termed "burnout" and "exhaustion" due to their efforts to support Bill and his team. He commented:

> It will take some time to recover. Eleven years—that's a lot of service. That's eleven years of radical change. I don't entirely know if the church has the answer. Phoenix is great at service,

> but it's not great at helping its worn-out and wounded troops to recover. There are times when Debbie [his wife] and I have felt so lonely. There was a time when an outgoing elder said to me, "People will be suspicious of you." I've had this conversation with Morgan [a new elder].[4] I've sat down with him, and he's said to me that he has started to see how people behave differently towards him, which is human nature. But I think that has had an impact on me. (Appendix B:14)

Adrian seemingly had become discouraged and exhausted. Both he and Debbie had been treated with suspicion and, at times, hostility by some members because of their support of the missional change process. Debbie wanted to leave Phoenix to find a place to recover. Adrian explained that he felt he needed to find a way to do this as well. He apparently felt there was inadequate capacity in the leadership team to support their recovery from the sacrifices they had made. Adrian seemed to be personally conflicted about leaving. He had forged strong relationships in the leadership team which he did not want to lose. Yet at the same time he did not seem to believe the church could pastorally support him, or his family, in their recovery. Indeed, Adrian and his family left the congregation.

Based on the tone of my conversation with Adrian, I observed how conflicted he felt about leaving the church. He did not want to make this sacrifice, but it seems he felt it was much more important to find somewhere for his family to recover than to remain at Phoenix.

The themes of sacrifice, exhaustion, and burnout were evident in the testimonies of other highly active members. For example, Jasmin explained her situation to me thusly:

> I work three days a week in a school and it's intensive and it's tiring, really tiring. I'm not as young as I used to be. I also have elderly parents. I am also aware that by Thursday and Friday [the days she did not work at school] that these are the times that I can catch up with people over a coffee [i.e., other people involved in missional projects]. So this week my husband and I planned all these things. He asked me, "Have you thought about when we're going to see John [a family member]? Have you

---

4. Morgan and his wife Venessa talked about the personal challenges they were facing, as they had only been Christians for just over two years and they had found it hard to adjust to the demands that becoming a church elder placed on them as a family; cf. Appendices B:22 and B:23.

thought about when we're going to see [another friend]?" And oh, then, "We've got no weekends left!" (Appendix B:1)

Thus, it became evident that it was not just church elders like Adrian who were under strain, but also other members like Jasmin. Exhaustion and burnout may be considered a serious cost of missional change, when members become excessively busy because of it. It threatens mental, spiritual, and physical well-being. For example, the spouse of one member was suffering from severe depression, which was attributed by her husband to helping support the church's missional work. Apparently, due to deficits in Phoenix's support structures, there was a risk that yet more members might become unwell. An implicit theme of sacrifice particularly seemed to underlie the themes of burnout and exhaustion.

7.2 Analysis of Key Themes

This section is divided in two. The first concentrates on potential causes that led to costly sacrifices, tensions, and conflicts within the congregation. The second analyzes how the phenomenon of churches-within-a-church seemed to lead to conflict because a new model of leading the church was developing.

7.2.1 Potential Causes of Tension and Conflict

I suggest that the mediation of a Newbigin-like theology of *Missio Dei* was a key cause of strain, tension, and conflict at Phoenix. As discussed at an earlier stage, Bevans stresses that a culture-critical tension lies at the heart of Newbigin's theology of the missionary gospel, because it seeks to challenge Christians to reconfigure their lives around public missionary witness that is countercultural (cf. §3.1.4).[5] This has been costly in terms of the sacrifices of time and effort it has required in order for some members to maintain ongoing engagement in mission. Barns highlights that Newbigin believed Christians needed to engage in public missionary work to challenge secular ideology that made all claims to truth relative.[6] This was because Newbigin wanted secular society to adopt a Christian

---

5. Bevans, *Models of Contextual Theology*, 117–19.
6. Barns, "Reimagining the Gospel as Public Truth," 155–57; Newbigin, *Proper Confidence*.

faith in order to bring *hope* back to its peoples.[7] Ironically, the theme of cost reveals how some of Phoenix's members were not using the language of hope to describe their reactions to the church's missional focus. The congregational data reveals that some congregants felt strained, unsupported, isolated, confused and exhausted.

Kaiser makes an important observation that helped me obtain a deeper insight into what potentially made a Newbigin-like theology of the missionary gospel so challenging to some at Phoenix.[8] It challenges congregants to make their faith public rather than a matter of private opinion, which means it is much harder for them to remain missionally inactive when faced with sustained pressure of this kind.[9] Goheen stresses that Newbigin's public theology challenges Christians to make disciples of new converts, rather than hiding their Christian identity in the private ecclesial sphere.[10] Public Christian witness arguably exposes believers to having their faith challenged, and also to being impacted by a society that does not share their theological worldview. Some Newbigin scholars add that his culture-critical theology deliberately seeks to de-secularize the church, thus in effect propelling members into society as public missionary witnesses.[11] The deliberate deconstruction of Phoenix's former family-focused church had essentially forced congregants out of their comfort zone, to make their faith public rather than keep it private (cf. §5.3.1–5.3.2). It also seemed to disrupt the operant pastoral theology of the congregation of the past, which had emphasized a theology of God as protector, because it placed members in need of care and support from leaders, whereas in the contemporary congregation, God was arguably portrayed as enabler and challenger, propelling congregants into the world to engage in mission. I observed that two divergent operant theologies of God seemed to be clashing, which is demonstrated by what happened when the coup group challenged Bill's leadership. It was also

---

7. Jackson, "'And the Truth Shall Set You Free,'" 102–21.

8. Kaiser, "From Biblical Secularity to Modern Secularism."

9. Kaiser, "From Biblical Secularity to Modern Secularism," 79–112; cf. Newbigin, "Can the West be Converted?," 181–82; Newbigin, *Gospel in a Pluralist Society*, 222–33; Newbigin, "Gospel as Public Truth"; Newbigin, *Truth to Tell*.

10. Goheen, "*As the Father Has Sent Me*," 247; cf. Goheen, *Church and Its Vocation*, 20–22; Rae, "Congregation as Hermeneutic of the Gospel," 189–92.

11. Newbigin, "Evangelism in the Context of Secularization"; Jackson, "'And the Truth Shall Set you Free,'" 104–6; Cf. Hunsberger, *Bearing the Witness of the Spirit*, 3–7; Weston, *Lesslie Newbigin, Missionary Theologian*, 46–47, 142.

observable in the tensions that still existed between Group 1 and 2's activist and communal theological values.

I was surprised Phoenix was still experiencing significant tensions after nine years of missional change. It might be expected that things would have stabilized more than they had. Missional change processes seemingly had led to sustained stress.

No attention is given to the theological voices of church members in the published GOCN research literature regarding the themes of exhaustion, sacrifice, and burnout when churches become focused on mission.[12] There is copious literature in the field of ministerial studies that concentrates on burnout among the clergy.[13] Much can be learnt from the existing literature, but I suggest there is a need to engage in more research with members who act as volunteers in missional work. It will arguably provide invaluable insights regarding what helps or hinders congregants from getting exhausted.

It is not surprising that Newbigin's/GOCN's version of missional ecclesiology has been critiqued by those who appreciate other models of ecclesial culture.[14] During Newbigin's lifetime, Graham and Walton challenged his culture-critical theology for being "repressive" of alternative beliefs and practices.[15] Newbigin responded to their critique by claiming GOCN theology was only critical of cultural ideologies that obfuscated "the truth" claims of the gospel.[16] However, I suggest it is not just critical of nongospel-centered belief systems. A version of it was seemingly used to critique Phoenix's former practices of pastoral ministry, and probably repressed them. I think the term "constrain" is better than "repress" to describe what happened at Phoenix, as constrain does not have such a pejorative tone. The GOCN research literature gives no attention to the constraint of church's preexisting normative, espoused, or operant theologies, due to them adopting a theology of participation in the *Missio Dei*. My research suggests that when churches take a missional change journey, they will inevitably face a degree of constraint concerning their existing theologies of ministry and mission when these theologies do

---

12. Cf. Barrett et al., *Treasure in Clay Jars*.

13. Cf. Jackson-Jordan, "Clergy Burnout and Resilience"; Coate, *Clergy Stress*; Davey, *Burnout*; Francis, "Caring for Clergy in Crisis"; Gill, "Burnout"; Sanford, *Ministry Burnout*.

14. Cf. Graham and Walton, "Walk on the Wild Side."

15. Graham and Walton, "Walk on the Wild Side," 1–7.

16. Newbigin, "Gospel and Our Culture," 9.

not equip members to engage in missional practices in their own right. I suggest this will especially be the case if a church's approach to ministry is similar to that which existed prior to change at Phoenix. This is a significant finding to take into account for any church contemplating a missional change journey.

As I reflected on the constraint of Phoenix's older model of church, I recognized it was contradicted by Newbigin's sacramental theology. Newbigin was a passionate proponent of Christian unity, and lamented the ecclesiastical divisions within the worldwide Christian movement.[17] Much of Newbigin's desire for Christian unity derived from his reflections on John's Gospel.[18] He believed the lack of ecumenical communion did not present the Christian faith in a favorable light to the onlooking world.[19] It seemed particularly ironic to me that Phoenix provided an example of constraint of the church's former Reformed model of pastoral support, given Newbigin's ecumenical convictions which had been taught as part of college programs.[20] I reasoned that there need not be a false dichotomy made between equipping members for mission and the church offering pastoral support to its own community. Newbigin's theology envisaged mutual respect for differing traditions rather than their deliberate deconstruction by some kind of "blueprint missiology" (cf. 5.5).[21]

At Phoenix the will of the majority meant a minority (i.e., the coup group) were forced to accept changes they did not want to embrace. There was also a significant minority that was still not convinced about the value of being part of a missional church (i.e., Group 2). I wonder if it is, perhaps, too costly to bring about missional change in congregations which are overly ecclesiocentric to begin with, such as was the

---

17. Cf. Wainwright, "Contemporary Ecumenical Challenges," 277–89.

18. Cf. Newbigin, *Light Has Come*.

19. Cf. Newbigin, "Missionary Dimension of the Ecumenical Movement"; Newbigin, "Missions in Ecumenical Perspective"; Wainwright, "Contemporary Ecumenical Challenges," 277–89.

20. Cf. Newbigin, *Open Secret*, 150–52; Newbigin, "What Is 'A Local Church Truly United?'"

21. Cf. Weston, *Lesslie Newbigin, Missionary Theologian*, 70–80. It is to be noted that Newbigin argued for a version of ecumenism which allowed each ecclesial tradition to trace its unity with other traditions based on their confession of Christ, thus uniting them in one Lord, whilst at the same time allowing them to engage in critical respectful conversations with other traditions with which they were at variance; cf. Weston, *Lesslie Newbigin, Missionary Theologian*, 70–80.

case at Phoenix. A question for future research could be, "How might a constraining dimension of Newbigin's culture-critical ecclesiology be resolved with recourse to his ecumenical theology?" This may offer one avenue to help resolve how highly pastorally supportive congregations might rescript their operant theologies of ministry to equip members for pastoral and missional ministry.

7.2.2 Competing Ecclesial Frames

Another dimension of the cost of missional change for Phoenix is potentially disclosed with reference to Becker's research on congregational conflict.[22] Becker theorizes that conflict especially occurs in churches when there are significant differences between more than one congregational frame.[23] She characterizes four kinds of congregational frames, which are:

1. *House of Worship congregations:* which concentrate "on the core tasks of worship and religious education. Their primary goals are to provide an intimate and uplifting worship experience and to train members . . . in the denomination's heritage, doctrine, and rituals." The presence of the church as a place of worship in the local community is considered to be its witness.[24]

2. *Family congregations:* offer "a place where worship, religious education, and providing close-knit and supportive relationships for members are the core tasks." The presence of the church in the community is considered as a witness as it lives out these values in the church, which visitors might also choose to embrace by joining them.[25]

3. *Community congregations:* seek to offer a similar environment of congregational life like family churches, but they go further. They seek to support their local neighborhoods: "Their chief form of

---

22. Becker, *Congregations in Conflict*; cf. Becker et al., "Straining at the Tie that Binds."
23. Becker, *Congregations in Conflict*; cf. Chou, "Impact of Congregational Characteristics." It is to be noted that Chou's research builds on Becker's work, adding that the chance for conflict to occur in a congregation is increased when they are led by inexperienced leaders; cf. Chou, "Impact of Congregational Characteristics."
24. Becker, *Congregations in Conflict*, 13.
25. Becker, *Congregations in Conflict*, 13.

witness is in living their values, institutionalizing them in local congregational life" and in the way they treat others within and outside the congregation.[26]

4. *Leader congregations:* like the other models these provide opportunities for worship and religious education. They differ considerably from community and family congregations. They adopt the pastor's or denomination's theological perspectives. "Their view of witness is more activist, having less to do with living their values and more to do with changing the world beyond the congregation.... Providing members with intimate connections or a feeling of belonging are low priorities" compared to what is done outside the church.[27]

Becker's congregational models are obviously ideal types. They are useful to help characterize the degree to which congregations function like one or more of them. I found them useful to illustrate the kinds of church structures that differing groups in Phoenix seemed most predisposed toward. In a similar vein to Becker's approach, critical analysis of the data led me to identify three competing congregational frames which seemed to be implied to some extent among different groups at Phoenix.[28] The coup group had arguably fought to retain the values of a family model of church,[29] whereas Group 1 seemed to have adopted something that was most like a leader model because they had seemingly embraced the missional activist focus of graduate leaders. They also seemed to deprioritize developing an intimate congregational environment of belonging, and instead put their time and effort into their missional projects (§5.3.1).[30] Groups 2 and 3 seemed to have values that resonated with a community congregation, either through seeking to develop the communal life of the church, or by encouraging intergroup *communitas*. These three frames seemed to sufficiently characterize the kinds of congregations each group might value the most. Some of Group 2 also had sympathies with the coup group (cf. §7.1.3). Hence, a family model was also appreciated by some of them.

26. Becker, *Congregations in Conflict,* 13, 14.
27. Becker, *Congregations in Conflict,* 14.
28. Becker, *Congregations in Conflict*; cf. Chou, "Impact of Congregational Characteristics."
29. Becker, *Congregations in Conflict,* 13.
30. Becker, *Congregations in Conflict,* 13.

Identification of the inherent tensions that lay between these congregational frames might explain another cause of conflict that had occurred, or might surface again, between groups within Phoenix. However, I am cautious of making a broad generalization. Qualitative group data is hard (if not impossible) to generalize, because members of a group will inevitably share sympathies with more than one group.[31] I am very much aware of this caution related to tensions that existed between these potential congregational frames.[32] It is therefore not possible to do more than suggest the potential for future conflict because of this caution. Nevertheless, it seems likely that a "between-frames conflict" occurred when the emerging leader model clashed with the family model during the time of the coup attempt.[33] It probably arose because the two models concentrated on differing expectations of what the church existed to fulfill. The family model valued developing intimate connections between members in the congregation's communal environment, and the leader model deprioritized the family model.[34] Hence, conflict arose because some members wanted the church to remain more like a family model, and others valued the priorities of engaging in mission in the world outside the church.

I observed that a leader model of church had apparently become increasingly dominant during Phoenix's change journey. This is probably because graduate leaders espoused a theology of missional leadership that presupposed it was their role to bring about the missional transformation of Phoenix.[35] Their *modus operandi* was arguably preconditioned by an assumption found in the GOCN academic literature that missional change is necessary and requires the deliberate deconstruction of models of church that do not support change.[36] For example, Guder stresses that missional leaders must intentionally bring about missional change in congregations, which would seem to prioritize the development of a

---

31. Cf. Bryman, *Social Research Methods*, 187–88.

32. Cf. Becker, *Congregations in Conflict*, 12–15.

33. Cf. Becker, *Congregations in Conflict*, 12–15; Chou, "Impact of Congregational Characteristics."

34. Cf. Becker, *Congregations in Conflict*, 13, 14.

35. Cf. Guder, *Missional Church*, 183–220; Roxburgh and Romanuk, *Missional Leader*.

36. Guder, *Missional Church*, 183–220; Roxburgh and Romanuk, *Missional Leader*; cf. Bliese, "Developing Evangelical Public Leadership," 72–96.

leader model of church.[37] Other congregational types may be argued to be subject to repression because of this seeming preference for leader models of church.[38] This implies inflexibility, and might partly explain why tensions and conflicts have characterized Phoenix's change journey.

A key finding of my research is that changes in Phoenix's leadership and ministry practices had not transformed the deeply held convictions of some members who valued a family or community focus for the church. Conflict, schism, and tension were characteristics of the church's continuing change journey. This affirms McClendon's theory that challenging the deeply held affective-level convictions of a group will tend to lead them to fight to maintain them.[39] It seems Phoenix's leader model was put in conflict with other group values because it was not prioritizing the needs of the congregation but rather its mission work outside the church. It is this finding that provides a good rationale for the rescripting of the church's predominant leader model. A rescripted model would need to develop a balance between the inner communal pastoral needs of the congregation, as well as the church's outer focus on mission, if it is to address the deep convictions of Groups 1, 2, and 3.

Another key finding is the amount of tension and conflict experienced by a congregation undertaking a missional change process will probably depend on what model of church it practices when embarking upon a change journey. Churches which already practice a leader model will be the most likely to respond better to the kind of missional leadership approach used at Phoenix. House of worship, family, and community models will probably be less responsive to missional change if a leader model is adopted to bring about missional change. The discussion of theological rescription that follows may provide clues for how to facilitate change in churches planning to undertake a missional change journey.

---

37. Guder, *Missional Church*, 183–220; Roxburgh and Romanuk, *Missional Leader*; Cf. Daubert, "Vision-Discerning vs. Vision-Casting," 147–72; Stache, "Leadership and the Missional Church Conversation," 209–38; Henderson Callahan, "Forming Lay Missional Leaders," 120–46.

38. Cf. Guder, *Missional Church*, 183–220; Frederickson, "Missional Congregation in Context," 44–64; Cormode, "Cultivating Missional Leaders," 99–119.

39. McClendon, *Biography as Theology*; cf. McClendon and Smith, *Convictions*.

7.3 Rescription

Rescription methodology allows for some reinterpretation of espoused and operant theologies of leadership (cf. §2.3).[40] A survey of potential missional leadership models that might be used to rescript Phoenix's predominant theology of leadership did not reveal a plethora of candidates. I surmise it would be most relevant to seek a model of leadership and ministry that is based on *Missio Dei* theology, and has the capacity to address Phoenix's context the best. There are three models of missional leadership which may be considered: (1) Roxburgh and Romanuk's Missional Change Management model;[41] (2) Branson and Martinez's intercultural leadership model;[42] and (3) Frost and Hirsch's version of "fivefold ministries."[43]

Based on my conversations with Bill, I noticed the first two models had already influenced graduate leaders' approaches to change at Phoenix. They are the missional change models which my college's programs[44] particularly concentrate upon.[45] Both of these change management models particularly seem to favor a leader model of church, because they concentrate on leaders helping to change nonmissional structures within a church.[46] The application of them to Phoenix's context seemed to indicate they had already contributed to intergroup tensions and conflicts because they had seemingly constrained other models of church. Furthermore, a significant weakness shared by the first two models of leadership was revealed by the congregational data. They both lack a sufficiently robust pastoral approach, which the family and community models of church value. I also observed, based on interviews with leaders like Bill (during 2018), that the leadership team were exploring ways to mitigate the strains that existed between groups at the congregation. This openness to explore ways to enhance the provision of ministry at

---

40. Cf. Cartledge, "Pentecostal Experience"; Cartledge, *Testimony in the Spirit*, 17–20.
41. Roxburgh and Romanuk, *Missional Leader*.
42. Branson and Martinez, *Churches, Cultures and Leadership*.
43. Frost and Hirsch, *Shaping of Things to Come*, 205–24.
44. Or derivatives of these models are used.
45. Cf. Roxburgh and Romanuk, *Missional Leader*, 100–105; Branson and Martinez, *Churches, Cultures and Leadership*, 213–26.
46. Cf. Roxburgh and Romanuk, *Missional Leader*; Branson and Martinez, *Churches, Cultures and Leadership*.

the church was indicative of an opportunity to rescript their approach to missional leadership.

Significantly, Frost and Hirsch's version of the "fivefold ministries" model concentrates on leaders equipping and supporting a congregation's inner communal life, as well as its missional life.[47] This model had not been adopted by leaders at Phoenix. This suggested to me that it might be used to rescript the predominant approach to leadership at Phoenix. I discussed this with Bill, and he indicated the church was considering adopting this model.

The fivefold ministries model of Frost and Hirsch are made up of apostles, prophets, evangelists, pastors, and teachers.[48] These ministries are well known within the Pentecostal and charismatic traditions (cf. §8.1.2). According to Frost and Hirsch, the first three ministry types concentrate on the outward missional life of the church, and the last two focus on supporting the inner life of the church.[49] Taken together, all five leadership types seek to equip congregations to discover their spiritual gifts, and to use them in the church's inward and outward expressions of ministry and mission.[50] The strengths of Frost and Hirsch's model for Phoenix would be to identify leaders who can: (1) facilitate the ongoing development of members' missional work in the broader community (i.e., the apostolic function); (2) encourage the church's emerging charismatic identity (i.e., the prophetic function); (3) develop the congregation's relational and communal support structures (the pastoral function); (4) focus on the mediation of coherent theological values through teaching and preaching (i.e., the teaching function); and (5) concentrate on evangelism within and outside the church (i.e., the evangelistic function).[51]

An overall weakness in Frost and Hirsch's model is that it portrays the fivefold ministries as functions to be carried out by leaders (i.e., it bases leadership on a theology of *doing*).[52] This concentration on function arguably needs to be enriched with reference to a theology that concentrates on a church's existential *being* (cf. §5.4) I suggest it is required to address profounder dimensions of Christian ministry, so as to tackle

---

47. Frost and Hirsch, *Shaping of Things to Come*, 205–24; cf. Hirsch and Catchim, *Permanent Revolution*, 3–27.

    48. Frost and Hirsch, *Shaping of Things to Come*, 205–24.

    49. Frost and Hirsch, *Shaping of Things to Come*, 205–24.

    50. Frost and Hirsch, *Shaping of Things to Come*, 205–24.

    51. Cf. Frost and Hirsch, *Shaping of Things to Come*, 205–24.

    52. Frost and Hirsch, *Shaping of Things to Come*, 214–16.

the underlying existential needs of congregations (cf. §8.1.2).[53] In other words, Frost and Hirsch's theology needs a stronger theology of existential *being* (cf. §8.1.2). For instance, this kind of existential theology is identifiable in Paul's[54] theology of ministry, which is based on a theology of co-suffering with the crucified Christ.[55] It is also reflected in his existential theology, which he used to encourage churches facing suffering to find strength through Christ.[56] The underlying theme of sacrifice was arguably an existential need of Phoenix's members, which could be partly addressed by an espoused and operant theology of sacrificial ministry (cf. §7.1.6). According to Moltmann, theologies of Christlike sacrificial ministry go to the very heart of the ancient Christian tradition, and inform the way the church seeks to address the existential needs of believers.[57] I suggest Frost and Hirsch's theology of Christian leadership could benefit from being rescripted by a cruciform theology of sacrifice in order to contextualize it to the needs of Groups 1, 2, and 3. Therefore, in chapter 8, a rescription of Frost and Hirsch's incarnational theology will be suggested, which might help it to address the existential needs of Phoenix better (cf. §8.1.2). Other churches facing similar challenges to those at Phoenix may also benefit from this kind of modified theology of incarnational ministry.

7.4 Summary

This chapter has indicated that Phoenix's missional change journey has been costly, particularly because valued members have left the church and because of the sacrifices, tensions, and conflicts members have been making or experiencing. I have suggested the church's espoused theology of leadership be rescripted with reference to Frost and Hirsch's model in order to help address the needs of the congregation. So as to make this model existentially relevant to the experiences of church members, it will itself be rescripted in chapter 8 (cf. §8.1.2).

---

53. Frost and Hirsch, *Shaping of Things to Come*, 214–16.
54. Paul's writings are found in the New Testament.
55. Cf. Col, 1:24–29; Gal 2:20.
56. Cf. Col, 1:24–29; Gal 2:20; Phil 1:12—2:18; 2 Cor 1:3, 4.
57. Moltmann, *Crucified God*, 276–303.

Chapter 8

Conclusions and Recommendations

Introduction

THIS RESEARCH HAS INVESTIGATED the impact of the communication of a Newbigin-like theology of *Missio Dei* on Phoenix's church members. The account of my investigation has primarily used a qualitative research methodology to obtain emic data which arises from the ordinary theologizing of church members. Cartledge's approach to rescripting has been employed to engage theologically with verbatim transcripts of members' testimonies.[1] It has also drawn on an adaptation of the "four voices" concept, which enabled me to be attentive to the theological insights that arose from the interactions between these voices, particularly the espoused and operant theologies of congregants.[2]

I engaged in etic reflection on these testimonies using theological sources to suggest rescriptions of congregants' ordinary theologies. The aim was to suggest how member's ordinary theologies that were in tension might be rescripted. Each of the data chapters (i.e., chs. 4–7) have also suggested theological rescriptions that might help Phoenix to address tensions, conflicts, and challenges the congregation has faced.

A larger aim of the book has also been to provide a working example of how ordinary theology and rescripting methodology might be utilized by researchers, and practitioners in missional churches, to conceive of ways to positively address challenges that churches going through a missional change journey might encounter. Insights obtained from

---

1. Cartledge, *Testimony in the Spirit*; Cartledge, "Pentecostal Experience"; cf. Martin, "Undermining the Old Paradigms."

2. Cf. Cameron et al., *Talking about God in Practice*; Watkins, *Disclosing Church*.

members' ordinary theologies will also be used in this chapter to suggest modifications to aspects of missional church theology (cf. §5.3.1; 5.3.2). This is important to do, because as I have argued earlier in the book, I believe idealized views of the ease with which churches might become focused on mission seem to be predominant in many of the formal works in the field of missional ecclesiology. I write this with deep humility and respect for writers who have blazed the trail in encouraging churches to become focused on equipping their congregations for mission. My hope is that this book will provide some more tools to the field of study to help churches from varying ecclesial traditions to successfully negotiate missional change within their congregations.

This chapter: (1) synthesizes key themes arising from members' ordinary theologizing and recommends potential rescriptions of the academic literature; (2) makes recommendations for future congregational praxis and for future research; (3) discusses potential transformations in my own professional praxis that may impact college courses and other aspects of my work (I suggested in chapter 1 that this is something readers can learn from to help them develop personal praxis based on what research can reveal to them about their contexts); and (4) indicates the primary contributions made to the field of missional church studies.

8.1 Rescripting Missional Ecclesiology

The overall aim of this section is to synthesize the rescriptions of members' ordinary theologies suggested in earlier chapters so as to modify aspects of missional church theology (cf. §5.4; 6.3; 7.3). It contains four subsections.

8.1.1 Rescripting a Social Trinitarian Version of Participation

In chapter 5 I suggested a social Trinitarian rescription of Group 1 and 2's understanding of *Missio Dei* theology (cf. §5.4). I posited that it might help them to reinterpret participation in the *Missio Dei* by drawing on a relational and communal view of the nature of God. This would make participation in the *Missio Dei* about bringing people into a relationship with God and God's people (cf. §5.4). This could help Phoenix's members develop a strong communal environment, with the capacity to relationally support believers and those exploring faith. I also suggested that for social Trinitarianism to be acceptable to Phoenix it would need to be rescripted. The need for rescription arises because Phoenix traces its theology of God to the classical Reformed view of the sovereignty of God. This view challenges the notion that humans can participate in the triune perichoresis[3] because of a theology of divine transcendence.[4]

This raises the legitimate question of whether going to the effort of modifying social Trinitarianism to suit it to a Reformed theology of God is worth it. I suggest it is, because, as discussed earlier (cf. §5.4), Zizioulas argues that a church shaped (or influenced to some degree by it) by a social Trinitarian theology can become a community that meaningfully integrates people into a life of communion with God and one another (cf. §5.4).[5] It arguably provides a theological vision for a missional church to be motivated to enter into deep relationships with Christians and not-yet-Christians alike. It is this dimension of social Trinitarianism that particularly provides a rich theological source to mine in order to help churches like Phoenix shape their communal and missional ecclesiology.

I provide the following background to remind readers of some key facets of GOCN's/Newbigin's Trinitarian theology that has seemingly influenced Phoenix's members.[6] GOCN theology concentrates on the church as an instrument of God, sent to fulfill the function of engaging in God's work of mission in the world.[7] Van Gelder and Zscheile stress that Western theology tends to separate the work of the Father, Son, and Spirit to maintain the Father's transcendence in the divine economy.[8] The aim of doing this is to explain how humans can participate in the *Missio Dei* without compromising God's transcendence.[9] Concentrating on God's

---

3. Perichoresis refers to the interdependent mutual relational communion that is believed to exist between the persons of the Trinity; cf. Louth, *Introducing Eastern Orthodox Theology*, 30, 31.

4. Canlis, *Calvin's Ladder*, 67–70; Holmes, *Holy Trinity*, 21–31; cf. Volf, *After Our Likeness*, 208–13; Cf. Van Gelder and Zscheile, *Missional Church in Perspective*; Van Gelder and Zscheile, *Participating in God's Mission*.

5. Zizioulas, *Being as Communion*, 12–16; cf. Karkkainen, *Trinity Global Perspectives*, 90–94.

6. Cf. Guder, *Missional Church*, 4–7; cf. Franklin, "Missionaries in Our Own Back Yard," 176.

7. Van Gelder and Zscheile, *Missional Church in Perspective*, 102–8; cf. Sarisky, "Meaning of the *Missio Dei*," 262; Guder, *Missional Church*, 6–12.

8. Van Gelder and Zscheile, *Missional Church in Perspective*, 105–10.

9. Van Gelder and Zscheile, *Missional Church in Perspective*, 105–10; cf. Tavast, "Challenging the Modalism of the West," 355–68.

transcendence can have the effect of accentuating an individualistic, rather than communal, understanding of how the persons of the Trinity communally interact (cf. §5.3.1; 5.4). If the roles of the persons of the Trinity are understood as individual functions in the divine economy of mission, then Christians may adopt an individualistic theology that devalues relational and communal life (cf. §5.3.1; 5.4). This seemed to have happened in the context of Phoenix. The data of Group 1 indicated individual believers enjoyed engaging in missionary work to the detriment of their participation in the communal life of the church (cf. §5.3.1–5.3.2). This is why I posited that social Trinitarianism has the virtue of deemphasizing individualism of this kind, and instead emphasizes the integration of individuals into a relationally united community (cf. §5.4).[10] For this relational and communal dimension to influence Phoenix it will be important to avoid any suggestion that believers can participate in the actual divine life of the Trinity (i.e., the perichoresis).

I found that Volf's theology provided a relevant means to modify the notion that humans can participate in the perichoresis.[11] His work draws on aspects of social Trinitarianism, and modifies it to develop a participatory ecclesiology modeled on the communal life of the Trinity.[12] He challenges social Trinitarian notions that suggest believers can participate in the actual life of the Trinity, as indeed does a Reformed theology of the sovereignty of God.[13] He argues humans cannot relate to God, or one another, in the same manner as the persons of the Trinity.[14] This is because humans lack the infinite capacities of God due to both the limitations of their finite natures and sin, making it impossible to participate in the perichoresis.[15] Yet Volf's theology helpfully implies believers can benefit by modeling something of the relationship of the Trinity through the motivating work of the Holy Spirit in each of them.[16]

---

10. Cf. Karkkainen, *Trinity Global Perspectives*, 90; Zizioulas, *Being as Communion*, 15; cf. Zizioulas, *Eucharistic Communion and the World*, 1–82.

11. Volf, *Exclusion and Embrace*; Volf, *After Our Likeness*.

12. Volf, *Exclusion and Embrace*; Volf, *After Our Likeness*.

13. Volf, *Exclusion and Embrace*, 180; Volf, *After Our Likeness*, 208–13; cf. Kim, *Joining in with the Spirit*, 20–39.

14. Cf. Volf, *After Our Likeness*, 180.

15. Volf, *After Our Likeness*; Volf, *Exclusion and Embrace*, 208–13; Gaines, "Politics, Participation, and the *Missio Dei*," 72–89.

16. Volf, *After Our Likeness*, 207–13; cf. Gaines, "Politics, Participation, and the *Missio Dei*," 76.

As I contemplated the important contribution that Volf's theology might make in order to adapt to social Trinitarianism, I found Timothy Gaines's reflections on Volf's theology particularly helpful.[17] Gaines conceives of how to apply Volf's pneumatology to a version of social Trinitarianism that avoids the notion that humans can participate in the divine perichoresis. His work helped me to reframe Volf's theology of the Spirit by providing clues for a motivating theology of *imitation* of the communal life of the Trinity.[18] Gaines, like Volf, positions the communal life of the church in the activity of the Spirit of God, which he suggests motivates believers to unite in Christ and the love of God.[19] I suggest there is a category difference between assuming that interecclesial unity can be based on the perichoresis compared to a theology of *imitation* of the mutual selfless love that is thought to animate the life of the Trinity.[20] *Imitation* is not full participation in the life of God, but it may motivate congregants to aspire toward the kind of mutual communion that the persons of the Trinity experience. Volf's Trinitarian theology has the merit of emphasizing the sovereignty and otherness of God, as well as grounding its communal theology of participation in the unity of believers as a work of the Spirit.[21] Hence, a degree of meaningful *imitation* of participation in God's communal life is made possible by Volf's version of Trinitarian theology.[22]

Phoenix's rather individualistic and activist understanding of *Missio Dei* could be rescripted by an *imitative* theology of this kind.[23] If leaders of the church want to avoid reference to social Trinitarianism, then they could draw on insights from it and then seek to communicate it using biblical language.[24] For example, Johannine theology would seem well suited to do this because of its strong relational and communal language.[25] I have

---

17. Gaines, "Politics, Participation, and the *Missio Dei*."
18. Gaines, "Politics, Participation, and the *Missio Dei*," 72–77.
19. Gaines, "Politics, Participation, and the *Missio Dei*," 72–77.
20. Cf. Gaines, "Politics, Participation, and the *Missio Dei*," 72–77; Volf, *After Our Likeness*, 213–17; cf. Karkkainen, *Trinity Global Perspectives*, 90.
21. Volf, *After Our Likeness*, 207; cf. Gaines, "Politics, Participation, and the *Missio Dei*," 76.
22. Volf, *After Our Likeness*; cf. Gaines, "Politics, Participation, and the *Missio Dei*," 76.
23. Cf. Yarnell, "Imitation of Christ and Pauline Discipleship," 75–91.
24. This might suit their evangelical bibliocentric instincts.
25. Cf. Witherington III, *Jesus the Seer*, 69–79; Hurtado, *Lord Jesus Christ*, 374.

written elsewhere about the model John's Gospel provides concerning participation in the triune life.[26] Johannine theology is premised on portraying the communal life of believers as becoming "one" with Christ and his Father in their shared love for the whole cosmos.[27] The gospel's pneumatology indicates that the Holy Spirit enables believers to discern and participate in the ongoing mission of Jesus.[28] This resonates with key aspects of social Trinitarianism and *Missio Dei* theology.[29] It will arguably provide a way to help Phoenix's members understand God's social and communal life related to divine activity in the church and world (i.e., as communal arenas).

GOCN academic theology might benefit from an adapted social Trinitarian rescription by Volf's view, or by developing a Johannine communal theology informed by a social Trinitarian hermeneutic.[30] My research provides a working example of how Reformed churches might conceive of rescripting members' ordinary theologies so that congregations can relationally and communally unite as missional communities after the likeness of the imminent life of the Trinity.

A practical communal theology would need to emphasize congregants *imitating* the communal and relational nature of the triune God. This theology could build on a Newbigin-like understanding of a united missional congregation.[31] Newbigin conceived of the church's most fundamental witness being centered on God's uniting love (cf. §3.1.3).[32] He believed this kind of church would provide an interpretive lens through which people might obtain a compelling vision of the difference that God's reconciling love might make to secular society.[33] Theology of reconciliation strongly implies God's relational and communal nature

---

26. Hardy, "John's Gospel and Discipleship," 46–74; Hardy, *Pictures of God*, 98–126.

27. John 3:16; 17:1–26; cf. Hardy, "John's Gospel and Discipleship," 46–74; Witherington III, *Jesus the Seer*, 70, 71; Hurtado, *Lord Jesus Christ*, 374.

28. John 14:12–20; 16:12–16; Mercer, "Jesus the Apostle," 457–60; cf. Hardy, "John's Gospel and Discipleship," 46–74.

29. Cf. Horrell, "Toward a Biblical Model of the Social Trinity," 407.

30. For instance, the GOCN scholars Van Gelder and Zscheile could perhaps draw more fully on Volf's theology than they have to modify their theology of participation in the *Missio Dei*; cf. *Missional Church in Perspective*, 102–8.

31. Cf. Newbigin, *Open Secret*, 141; Weston, "Ecclesiology in Eschatological Perspective," 79–81.

32. Cf. Newbigin, *Light Has Come*, 227–33.

33. Newbigin, *Gospel in a Pluralist Society*, 222–33.

because it concentrates on bringing human beings into communion with God and one another.[34] If Christians seriously believe the Trinity's communal and relational nature causes God to engage in mission, then *imitation* of it might lead them to do the same. If this understanding of God becomes deeply internalized in members' consciousness, then it may lead to churches not needing to put so much effort into motivating them to engage in missionary work. It is this outcome that probably would be most beneficial for churches like Phoenix because it provides a means to rescript individualistic and activist-espoused theologies of participation in the *Missio Dei*.

8.1.2 Rescripting Theologies of Being and Doing

In what follows, I will discuss how Phoenix's members' accounts of their sacrifices helped me to identify how Frost and Hirsch's fivefold ministries model of leadership might be partly rescripted.[35] In chapter 7, I suggested their model could be used to rescript the church's theology of leadership to at least partly help to adjust for an imbalance between the church's pastoral support needs and missional work (cf. §7.3). So far, I have only suggested the need to modify their theology with reference to an existential theology of sacrifice (cf. §7.3). In what follows, I will discuss how a crucicentric theology might help to modify Frost and Hirsch's incarnational Christology. I suggest it is needed to address the costly sacrifices being made by congregants (cf. §7.3). My aim is to indicate how the rescripting of Frost and Hirsch's functional theology of leadership by a crucicentric theology of sacrifice might help make up for deficits in Phoenix's existential theology of communal *being*. This may also prove helpful to other churches with similar experiences to that of Phoenix. These deficits seemed to arise because of an overemphasis of mission as *doing*. I suggest a balance needs to be found between theologies of *being* and *doing* if the church is to ground what it *does* on a meaningful existential theology of communal *being*.

It is important to recall Group 1 was seemingly motivated by an activist theology of *doing*, whereas Group 2 was stirred by a theology concentrated on relational and communal *being* (cf. §5.2; 6.2.2; 6.3). Apparently an activist theology of mission concentrated more attention

---

34. Cf. Hills, "Theology of Restitution as Embodied Reconciliation," 2.
35. Frost and Hirsch, *Shaping of Things to Come*, 214–16.

on how Phoenix should function in its mission work outside the church than on its inner communal life (cf. §5.4).³⁶ Hence, an imbalance seemed to exist between the church's theology of *doing* and *being* (§5.4). I posited in chapter 7 that Frost and Hirsch's model could partly help to rescript Phoenix's emerging leader model of church by the way it addresses imbalances between a church's communal and missional support structures (§7.3).³⁷ However, for it to address the existential needs of Phoenix's suffering members, I suggested their functional theology of leadership would need to be modified by a crucicentric theology (§7.3). After all, Phoenix seemingly lacked a practical theology of leadership with the capacity to help members cope with the costly existential demands of missional change (cf. ch. 7).

Theological adaptation of Frost and Hirsch's model seems justified, as it has been critiqued for theological and methodological weaknesses, especially because it downplays "the significance of serious theological reflection."³⁸ For example, they do not reflect on how differing ecclesial traditions' theologies of God cause them to interpret Trinitarian theology in different ways.³⁹ According to Espinoza, some of these theologies reject the notion that God is a missionary by nature.⁴⁰ The lack of a reflexive theological dimension to their work might explain why they have not paid enough attention to the development of existential theology. They assume incarnational Christology will help a church to engage with people in mission in their communities, but do not give attention to the cost of this kind of living on a church's existential needs.

I began to wonder whether a crucicentric theology might be used to modify their incarnational model of missional ministry.⁴¹ I speculated that their model could be rescripted to include a deep theology of incarnation, which might help leaders develop an understanding of ministry

---

36. Cf. Van Gelder, *Missional Church in Context*; Van Gelder, *Missional Church and Leadership Formation*; Branson and Martinez, *Churches, Cultures and Leadership*; Barrett et al., *Treasure in Clay Jars*.

37. Frost and Hirsch, *Shaping of Things to Come*; cf. Hirsch and Catchim, *Permanent Revolution*.

38. Cf. Espinoza, "Shaping of Things to Come," 466.

39. Cf. Espinoza, "Shaping of Things to Come."

40. Espinoza, "Shaping of Things to Come," 464–67.

41. Cf. Moltmann, "Is God Incarnate in All That Is?," 119–31; Karkkainen, *Christology*, 147–54.

as shared co-suffering with the God of the cross.[42] This would arguably suit the context of some of Phoenix's members, who were experiencing suffering because they felt isolated, conflicted, confused, grief-stricken, uncared for, and discouraged (cf. §7.1.1–7.1.6). Crucicentric theology is not a foreign language but an integral part of evangelicalism, and relates to Phoenix's members' struggles, making it relevant to their context.[43]

Frost and Hirsch's incarnational Christology places a priority on believers visibly living closely alongside people in their neighborhoods.[44] They suggest it will be through this kind of close living that nonbelievers will have the opportunity to witness the impact of Christian life on believers, and be potentially influenced by it.[45] The theology of Christ's incarnation is intimately connected to his suffering on the cross.[46] It involves "being with" people in the world of human suffering from which they seek liberation.[47] This is arguably relevant to the cost of members engaging in challenging incarnational mission.

As I reflected on the need to rescript Frost and Hirsch's incarnational Christology with a relevant crucicentric theology, my attention turned to Moltmann's theopathic[48] theology,[49] which seems to provide a compelling vision of the sacrificial nature of the triune God.[50] I suggest it might help to motivate Phoenix's members to understand the deep roots of sacrificial incarnational living as a fundamental defining attribute of God's nature and the work of the *Missio Dei*. It could also help Phoenix's leaders to develop a theology of sacrifice modeled on participating in God's sacrificial nature as a means to empathically engage in mission with

---

42. Cf. Gregersen, "Introduction," 1–21; Moltmann, *Crucified God*; Moltmann, *Trinity and the Kingdom of God*, 23–30.

43. Bebbington, *Evangelicalism in Modern Britain*, 14–17; Warner, *Reinventing English Evangelicalism*, 17, 18.

44. Frost and Hirsch, *Shaping of Things to Come*, 62–66.

45. Frost and Hirsch, *Shaping of Things to Come*, 62–64.

46. Moltmann, *Crucified God*, 206–303; cf. Tanner, "Incarnation, Cross, and Sacrifice," 35–56.

47. Cf. Wells, *Incarnational Mission*, 9–24; Bohache, *Christology from the Margins*, 81–102.

48. I.e., God's suffering.

49. Cf. Moltmann, *Crucified God*; Moltmann, *Trinity and the Kingdom of God*, 23–30.

50. Cf. Moltmann, *Crucified God*; Moltmann, *Trinity and the Kingdom of God*, 23–30.

people in a suffering world.[51] Moltmann's work has the virtue of utilizing an adapted form of social Trinitarianism, making it relatable to rescription of Phoenix's ordinary theologies (cf. §8.1.1).[52] Moltmann argues that God's sacrificial nature motivates the interior life of the Trinity, as well as its exterior works in creation and redemption.[53] Theopathic *being* and *doing* are intimately interwoven into his theology of the life cycle of the Trinity.[54] In Moltmann's view, human suffering is taken up into the life of the Trinity, meaning a suffering God of the cross shares with humans in their afflictions—as believers also share in Christ's.[55] Moltmann's theology allows for a two-way connection between the believer and the suffering God, and God and the suffering believer. In this sense the God of the cross incarnationally enters into the depths of human suffering.[56]

Yet this must not mean that everything the church does becomes colored by an unbalanced concentration on the suffering of the God of the cross. Importantly, Moltmann's thinking also builds on a theology of hope, by which he encourages Christians to share in ushering in God's new creation.[57] Theologies of suffering and the inbreaking of the new creation are important balances Moltmann's theology provides.[58] Both of these theological dimensions may work together to help bring theological balance to Phoenix's way of life. Arguably, the congregation will need to invest resources to support and supervise members so they do not overextend themselves because of unhealthy theological imbalances in their theologies of *being* and *doing* (cf. §7.1.6).

I surmise Phoenix can take its theology of Christian mission beyond helping members to only engage in missionary activism. They could also help the congregation cultivate an environment that can empathically

---

51. Cf. Moltmann, *Crucified God*; Moltmann, *Trinity and the Kingdom of God*, 23–30. It is to be noted that Smith critiques Moltmann's theopathy for making God passable and, therefore, subject to human suffering; cf. Smith, "Protest of Christ," 15–26.

52. Cf. Moltmann, *Crucified God*; Moltmann, *Trinity and the Kingdom of God*.

53. Moltmann, *Trinity and the Kingdom of God*, 23–60; Moltmann, *Crucified God*.

54. Cf. Moltmann, *Trinity and the Kingdom of God*, 23–60.

55. Moltmann, *Trinity and the Kingdom of God*, 23–60. Which is controversial, but itself could be modified by Volf's theology.

56. Moltmann, *Trinity and the Kingdom of God*, 21–60; Moltmann, *Crucified God*; cf. Mobsby, *God Unknown*, 55–70.

57. Moltmann, *Theology of Hope*; Moltmann, *God in Creation*.

58. Moltmann, *Theology of Hope*; Moltmann, *God in Creation*.

support its various communities (the church and its projects; cf. §5.4).[59] Moltmann's theopathic theology paints a picture of the persons of God empathically sharing in the joys and sorrows of its creation.[60] This kind of empathic mutuality could be *imitated* by members and leaders alike in the way they seek to support each other. This might motivate a deeper relational life of fellowship within the church, as well as in its mission work.

A theology of sharing in Christ's sufferings may provide missionary-active churches with a more profound way of engaging in mission with suffering people in society. A theopathic rescription of Frost and Hirsch's functional incarnational Christology could also help motivate believers to conceive of participation in ministry as a form of *imitation* of the divine way of life. The divine way of life might be characterized as a form of reaching out to deeply connect with the joys and sorrows of the world. After all, Christ celebrated a wedding just as much as he empathized with those in need of healing.[61] Concentrating on *imitating* theopathy draws attention to deeply engaging in quality relationships with others. It may deepen a missional community's existential approach to ministry and mission.[62]

I suggest this kind of rescripting approach may provide clues for how other theologies of *being* and *doing* might be rescripted by paying critical attention to the ordinary theological stories of believers.

8.1.3 Rescripting Theologies of Discernment and Participation

This section is divided into two parts, investigating how (1) a charismatic prophetic theology like that of Group 3 might help to rescript Newbigin's noncharismatic theology of discernment; and (2) the gifts of the Spirit might be used to rescript Phoenix's theology of every-member ministry.

---

59. Cf. Moltmann, *Trinity and the Kingdom of God*, 23–60; Moltmann, *Crucified God*.

60. Moltmann, *Crucified God*; Moltmann, *Trinity and the Kingdom of God*.

61. John 2:1–12; Mark 8:22–26.

62. Some Reformed churches may not want to use the language of fivefold ministries because they believe the gifts of apostles and prophets have ceased; cf. White, "Missional Study of Ghanaian Pentecostal Churches"; Grudem, *Systematic Theology*, 1031, 1046, 1078; cf. Thiselton, *Systematic Theology*, 280; Ruthven, "On the Cessation of the Charismata," 14–31.

Rescripting Newbigin's Theology of Discernment

I begin by contrasting a Pentecostal-charismatic view of prophetic discernment with Newbigin's rational nonmystical approach (cf. §3.1.6).[63] I will then examine how an ordinary prophetic theology might be used to suggest a rescription of Newbigin's theology of discernment. I do this with the hope that Newbigin's version of *Missio Dei* theology might be given more attention within Pentecostal and charismatic scholarly circles.

Unlike Newbigin, Pinnock argues the exercise of the gift of prophecy is "the most important" spiritual "gift in a congregation."[64] This is because it acts as a means of "revelation" by which God can speak "through someone, giving a word needed at that moment."[65] Pinnock stresses that prophecy is a normative practice for the contemporary church as it was for the early New Testament church:

> The picture Paul paints for us is that of a people waiting on God and listening to the Spirit. The potential can be glimpsed in the fact that world missions began by means of prophecy. The church in Antioch was fasting, praying and listening to its prophets when the call came to commission Paul and Barnabas as missionaries.[66] Prophecy is one way the Spirit leads God's people forward in mission.[67]

In a similar vein, Harris's research concentrates on the Pentecostal phenomenon of "hearing God's voice," and the important part it plays in guiding contemporary believers to engage in a variety of missionary activities.[68] Similar to my research findings, her investigation indicates how a theology of divine agency in mission seems to lead to examples of divine prophetic guidance.[69] Apparently, *Missio Dei* theology particularly resonates with a Pentecostal-charismatic theology of divine agency and prophetic revelation.[70]

---

63. Cf. Pinnock, *Flame of Love*; Harris, "Hearing God's Voice"; Turner, *Holy Spirit and Spiritual Gifts*; Hughes, "1995–1996 Newbigin Sermons."

64. Hughes, "1995–1996 Newbigin Sermons," 134.

65. Pinnock, *Flame of Love*, 134.

66. Acts 13:1–4.

67. Pinnock, *Flame of Love*, 134; cf. Turner, *Holy Spirit and Spiritual Gifts*.

68. Harris, "Where Pentecostalism and Evangelicalism Part Ways," 31, 32, 35; Harris, "Hearing God's Voice."

69. Harris, "Hearing God's Voice."

70. Cf. Harris, "Hearing God's Voice"; Cartledge, *Testimony in the Spirit*; Alexander,

By way of contrast, Newbigin's theology of discernment relied on a rational rather than mystical process of discerning the Spirit's guiding work (cf. §3.1.6; 6.2.1).[71] He did this by using biblical narratives, which he believed could provide indicators of how God might be at work in contemporary society (cf. §3.1.6).[72]

Newbigin, like some Calvinistic Reformed Christians, was cautious about theologies that relied on charismatic gifts of the Spirit.[73] Because of this, if his theology of discernment is to be rescripted, there will be a need to navigate the tensions that exist between Newbigin's countercultural theology and other models.[74] Bevans highlights how Newbigin's countercultural model prioritizes divine revelation by pointing to the authority of Scripture and tradition, and by downplaying experience as a source of revelation.[75] Whereas the anthropological model[76] gives equal authority to revelation through human and biblical sources alike.[77] This provides a useful working example of the role of the Bible in Newbigin's theology compared to another approach. Newbigin's theology of revelation gives authority to the Bible, making other sources of potential revelation subservient to it.[78]

Based on my reflections upon Group 3's ordinary prophetic theology, I identified a clue to help bridge the gap between Newbigin's rational biblical theology of discernment and a Pentecostal-charismatic prophetic theology (cf. §6.3). Interestingly, Group 3 espoused a theology of biblical authority to frame and inform their prophetic words (cf. §6.2.2). Their prophetic words needed to resonate with biblical testimony for them to be accepted by church members (cf. §6.2.2). Similar to Newbigin, their theology of revelation placed the Bible in the prime position of

---

"Introduction."

71. Cf. Hughes, "Life in the Spirit."

72. Cf. Newbigin, *Open Secret*, 56, 60–61; Newbigin, *Gospel in a Pluralist Society*, 119; Hughes, "Life in the Spirit"; Goheen, *Church and Its Vocation*, 159–60.

73. Hughes, "Life in the Spirit"; cf. Harris, "Where Pentecostalism and Evangelicalism Part Ways."

74. Cf. Bevans, *Models of Contextual Theology*.

75. Bevans, *Models of Contextual Theology*, 124.

76. Not anthropology.

77. Cf. Bevans, *Models of Contextual Theology*, 54–69, 117–38.

78. Goheen, *Church and Its Vocation*, 159–62; cf. Hilber, "Diversity of OT Prophetic Phenomena," 243–58; Turner, *Holy Spirit and Spiritual Gifts*; Johnston, *Mystical Theology*, 15–28; Karkkainen, *Trinity and Revelation*, 215–50.

authority.[79] Group 3's testimonies led me to identify aspects of Newbigin's theology of discernment that could be rescripted. It would require that, (a) prophetic words always be evaluated in the light of biblical testimony; (b) prophetic words which are accepted as relevant might be acted upon; and (c) once prophetic words are acted upon, the evidence for potential divine activity in what has resulted from acting upon them be evaluated in the light of biblical testimony.

There is room for this kind of rescription of a Newbigin-like theology of discernment because nowhere in his writings did he suggest the gift of prophecy ceased with the close of the apostolic age. Newbigin's pneumatology allows for the Spirit to guide the church, and he was not unsympathetic to the exercise of the gifts of the Spirit in Pentecostal churches.[80] For example, Goheen indicates Newbigin preached in Pentecostal churches, and was persuaded that the Spirit was active in mission through them.[81] He remained cautious about avowing charismatic spirituality but did not reject it, rather claiming it had enriched his own life.[82] The evidence suggests there is room in Newbigin's theology of discernment for a charismatic prophetic theology, given his emphasis on divine guidance by the Spirit, as long as it places Scripture in the first-order position of authority. Theologies of this type have helped, and are progressively being developed to help, frame them in useful biblical, theological, and philosophical frameworks.[83]

It is not my aim at this stage to offer more than this characterization of what a charismatic rescription of Newbigin's theology of discernment might entail. It will have to be the work of a future piece of research to develop a theology of this kind.

---

79. Newbigin, *Gospel in a Pluralist Society,* 66–79; 89–102.

80. Newbigin, *Open Secret,* 56; Goheen, "As the Father Has Sent Me," 100. It is to be noted that I have colleagues who knew Newbigin. They suggest he became particularly interested in charismatic contributions to mission in Britain towards the end of his life. For example, he engaged in giving some sermons at Holy Trinity Brompton in London, whose Alpha course was based on a charismatic trinitarian pneumatology; Hughes, "1995–1996 Newbigin Sermons." Apparently, he was interested in the development of the Alpha course and its potential for missionary work in society at large.

81. Cf. Goheen, "As the Father Has Sent Me," 99–100.

82. Goheen, "As the Father Has Sent Me," 100.

83. Cf. Witherington III, *Jesus the Seer,* 293–328; Hull, *Towards the Prophetic Church,* 29–64; Koet, "Dreams and Revelations," 7–9.

Rescripting a Theology of Every-Member Missional Ministry

I will now reflect on the theme of the work of the Spirit related to other gifts of the Spirit (i.e., other than prophecy). I will seek to illustrate how a theology of the gifts of the Spirit might enable members to discover their particular ministry gifts. This builds on what I posited in chapter 7, that Frost and Hirsch's fivefold ministries model might help leaders equip members to develop their spiritual gifts to support the communal and missional life of the church (cf. §7.3). Phoenix's leaders might learn much from how the Pentecostal tradition emphasizes the key role of the fivefold ministries to equip congregants to discover and exercise all of the gifts of the Spirit.[84] Hence, the reference to this tradition's theology may also help missional churches like Phoenix modify their approaches to equipping members for ministry in the church and wider world.[85]

Given that Groups 1 and 2 seemingly accepted Group 3's gift of prophecy, it suggested they might also be willing to explore other gifts of the Spirit.[86] For example, they could explore discernment, healing, service, wisdom, and/or teaching.[87] This line of thinking reminded me of Turner's biblical theology of the gifts of the Spirit.[88] He stresses that all the gifts are equally important in the church, whether they lead to ministries focused on the communal life of the church or its apostolic witness.[89] Turner's biblical theology might also provide a useful means to rescript Phoenix's understanding of every-member ministry, by the equal status it suggests for every gift of the Spirit.[90] Group 2 may particularly benefit from identifying, and then being given opportunities to exercise, their spiritual gifts to support the communal and missional life of the congregation. It may enable them to feel less isolated from the church because they will have recognized ministries to exercise.

I have made the case in this section that Group 3's prophetic charismatic practices provide clues to rescript Newbigin's theology of discernment. I have also suggested that other spiritual gifts may be incorporated

---

84. Cf. Kelebogile, "Critical Analysis," 177.

85. Cf. Harris, "Hearing God's Voice"; Kelebogile, "Critical Analysis."

86. "Gifts of the Spirit" language was not used by members I spoke to.

87. Cf. Rom 16:1–16; 1 Cor 12–14; cf. Kelebogile, "Critical Analysis."

88. Turner, *Holy Spirit and Spiritual Gifts*; cf. Pinnock, *Flame of Love*, 131–42; Harris, "Where Pentecostalism and Evangelicalism Part Ways."

89. Turner, *Holy Spirit and Spiritual Gifts*, 262–64.

90. Turner, *Holy Spirit and Spiritual Gifts*, 262–64.

into the church's theology of every-member ministry alongside the prophetic gift. Churches that have a similar story to Phoenix's may also benefit from exploring *all* of the gifts of the Spirit (if they have not).

8.1.4 Rescripting Constraining Missional Ecclesiologies

My research has highlighted the seeming constraint of Phoenix's former theological tradition of ministry because of the mediation of a participatory *Missio Dei* theology to the congregation (cf. §7.2.1). This is not a matter that has been empirically investigated in published GOCN research literature.[91] It is important to give it attention, as the optimistic tone of GOCN missional ecclesiology could be misunderstood to suggest that becoming a missional church can harmlessly be realized in a variety of faith traditions.[92] Yet my research suggests it can have a costly impact on some congregants (cf. ch. 7). I suggest more research is required regarding the constraining dimensions of all types of missional ecclesiology, not just the GOCN version.

Chapters 5–7 have highlighted rescriptions of members' ordinary theologies to integrate differing groups' values into the church's espoused theology, which may help to lessen repression of their deeply held convictions. These rescriptions could be viewed as threads that might be weaved together to help unite the church by placing equal value on its communal and missional life. It is unlikely any single rescription will address the complex tensions that existed at Phoenix. The metaphor of a weaving process is, therefore, relevant. This is because it represents the need for members to jointly imagine the shape of church life that meets its complex spiritual needs and values. A weaving together of rescripted ordinary theologies may also inform missional church studies on how to apply rescription methodology to other ecclesial contexts or research projects.

---

91. Cf. Guder, *Missional Church*; Barrett et al., *Treasure in Clay Jars*; Van Gelder and Zscheile, *Missional Church in Perspective*; Van Gelder and Zscheile, *Participating in God's Mission*. It is to be noted that Barrett et al.'s research hints that some constraint may have been felt by some members of Reformed churches, though it does not sufficiently develop this as a line of argument; *Treasure in Clay Jars*, 12–17.

92. Guder, *Missional Church*; Barrett et al., *Treasure in Clay Jars*; Van Gelder and Zscheile, *Missional Church in Perspective*; Van Gelder and Zscheile, *Participating in God's Mission*; cf. Niemandt, "Five Years of Missional Church"; Branson, "Missional Church Process."

I suggest every congregation experiences a weaving process of its members' ordinary theologies, whether they are becoming missional churches or not. Congregants' ordinary theologies take time to develop and they will need help to rescript them if a new missional ecclesiology is to be successfully mediated to them. Based on my reflections on Phoenix's story, I have identified three principles that may help to mitigate some strains from unnecessarily impacting churches during a change process. I suggest that

1. Significant attention needs to be concentrated on congregants' motivating affective-level theologies. McClendon indicates the affective-level of group convictions needs to be given attention to understand what motivates them to act and react in the ways they do when they are faced with new challenges.[93] The constraint of deeply held theological convictions will almost certainly lead to tension, conflict, or even schisms (the coup group; cf. §7.1.2; 7.3). Hence, for a new missional church theology to be successfully mediated to a congregation, it will probably require leaders to concentrate on contextualizing it so it resonates with deeply held congregational convictions.

2. A church's support structures will need to be strengthened by giving particular attention to enabling leaders, members, and newcomers to develop trust between one another (cf. §5.2).[94] Hence, congregational fellowship gatherings will need to become regular features of a church's social calendar to help members develop strong bonds of friendship. It will take time for deep relationships to be forged, as Phoenix's change journey seems to indicate (cf. chs. 5–7).

3. Christian leaders need to identify reactive ordinary theologies that develop during a change process, and then seek to theologically rescript them through their preaching and teaching. Rescriptions will need to focus on addressing the affective-level convictions of reactive ordinary theologies. By doing this it may become possible to develop appropriate theologies of *being* and *doing* so members might better engage in the communal and missionary dimensions of congregational life (cf. §5.4, 8.1.2).[95]

---

93. McClendon, *Biography as Theology*; McClendon and Smith, *Convictions*.

94. Unless they are already very good.

95. Cf. Clark, *Breaking the Mould of Christendom*, 3–12.

I would stress that some constraint of preexisting theological beliefs, values, and practices seems inevitable if a church is to equip members to participate in the *Missio Dei* (cf. §7.2–7.3). Reflection on Phoenix's story made me question whether missional change might be too costly for some congregations because of the inevitable constraint of some of their highly regarded values and practices. Hopefully this research narrative will help congregations carefully evaluate the costs of missional change before they take such a journey. This will inevitably require a process of careful and prayerful seeking after discerning God's guidance for what our churches need to become.

8.2 Recommendations

This section makes recommendations for: (1) enhanced missional congregational praxis; and (2) future research projects.

8.2.1 Enriching Congregational Praxis

The goal of my research has been to investigate the impact of a Newbigin-like *Missio Dei* theology on Phoenix's members. Each of my recommendations for rescription is based on responding to the ordinary theological data provided by Phoenix's members. Practical theology aims to make an impact on praxis development, so it is relevant to indicate how this investigation might contribute to enhancing congregational life, as well as the discussion of enhancing missional church praxis.[96] It will also potentially relate to other congregations that have been on similar journeys of missional change. It may also enable others to rescript aspects of their congregations' ordinary theologies. The recommendations that follow largely suggest rescriptions of congregational espoused theologies, which in turn may lead to changes in their practices (i.e., operant theologies).

Developing a Language of Participation

The tensions that existed between the activist and relationship-focused theologies of Groups 1 and 2 suggested to me the need to rescript their theology of participation in the *Missio Dei* (cf. §8.1.1). Phoenix, or

---

96. Cf. Lawler, "Faith, Praxis, and Practical Theology," 199–224.

congregations like it, may wish to concentrate significant attention on the rescription of their Trinitarian theological language by considering a version of participatory social Trinitarianism (cf. §8.1.1).[97] One positive outcome of doing this could be to enable divergent groups within the congregation to work more closely together based on a common understanding that links their theologies of *being* and *doing* (§8.1.2). The phronesis of church life often reveals members who are the *doers*, as well as those who are *the relational glue* who help to keep a congregation communicating. It is this kind of practical theology of *being* and *doing* that might provide a better congregational language to help members mutually understand the need for a balance of this type.

For other Reformed congregations undertaking a missional change journey, I have discussed the merits of adapting social Trinitarianism with reference to Volf's seminal work on participation (cf. §8.1.1). I recommend considering an *imitative* theology of participation in the triune life. This kind of theology might enable churches to reconceive of participation in the *Missio Dei* as enabling believers to enter into relational communion with God and one another. Importantly, John's Gospel portrays the unity of believers with God, and one another, as the highest kind of missional witness a church can provide (cf. John 13:34, 35).[98] Johannine theology of this kind may provide bibliocentric Reformed churches with a helpful relational Trinitarian language.

Modifying the Theology of Leadership

I have explored how differences between intergroup theological values at Phoenix have led to groups valuing differing things, for example: (a) engaging in missional work outside the church (Group 1); (b) supporting families in the church as opposed to outsiders (Group 2); (c) developing the communal and relational life of the church (Group 2); and (d) helping congregants to develop communion with a God of prophetic revelation (Group 3). These differing ordinary theological values have concentrated on mission outside the church, as well as ministry within it. There was an imbalance at Phoenix which favored mission outside the congregation. This had already led to a coup attempt and a schism (cf. §7.1.2). It was

---

97. Cf. Zizioulas, *Being as Communion*; Papanikolaou, "Contemporary Orthodoxy Currents on the Trinity," 334–36.

98. Cf. John 13:34, 35.

also causing tensions between different interest groups in the congregation because a leader model of church was apparently not addressing the relational[99] and communal theology of Group 2 (cf. §5.4; 7.3).

Hence, I posited that the predominant theology of leadership needed to be rescripted through Frost and Hirsch's fivefold ministries model. A modified cruciform theology of their model may make it especially relevant to meet the needs of Groups 1, 2, and 3 (cf. §8.1.2). It may be prudent to also reflect on how to equip the church to explore how a theology of sacrifice might be *imitated* in all of the ministries of the church. I recommend leaders with the capacity to equip members for the church's pastoral and missionary work collaborate to ensure a balance is struck between the existential, communal, and missionary dimensions of congregational life.

Developing Discernment Praxis

In chapter 6, I discussed the merits of developing a congregation-wide learning community of discernment. Hence, I recommend that Phoenix, or churches similar to it, consider developing a periodic gathering to engage them in a process of prophetic discernment to decide what God may be calling them to do together.

Additionally, there would seem to be merit in recommending that prophetically experienced leaders engage in a process of helping the whole congregation learn about and explore hearing God's voice, or discerning God's guidance.[100] This chapter has discussed the importance of rescripting congregational theological praxis related to a theology of divine revelation (8.1.3). There is precedence in Group 3's testimonies for this kind of theology to be explored within the Reformed evangelical context, which draws on biblical authority and presupposes God still communicates directly with human beings (cf. §6.1). A biblical theology of prophetic discernment could be developed by suiting it to congregational tradition. Furthermore, the discussion of Pentecostal-charismatic theology also draws attention to the topic of the gifts of the Spirit. I suggest Phoenix's theology of every-member ministry be rescripted by a theology of the gifts of the Spirit. This may enable all members to develop

---

99. Cf. Wright, *Relational Leadership*.

100. Cf. Harris, "Hearing God's Voice"; Harris, "Where Pentecostalism and Evangelicalism Part Ways."

meaningful ministries to support the communal and missional ways of life in the church.

Furthermore, perhaps discernment task groups might be developed. Small groups of members could be tasked to investigate potential evidence of what God might be: (a) inspiring fellow members of the church to do; or (b) doing in the lives of people in the neighborhood. Groups of this kind could utilize a discernment process that might be based on an adaptation of the pastoral cycle (cf. §3.1.6).[101] A task group might engage in an interrogative reflective process which: (a) explores potential evidence of what God might be doing in a neighborhood; (b) seeks to understand why people are showing interest in spiritual matters; and (c) proposes an action plan for the larger congregation to prayerfully reflect upon.

8.2.2 Future Research

I make the following recommendations for future research, other than those discussed previously:

- To examine a wide range of ordinary missional church theologies espoused within differing ecclesial traditions.
- To investigate how church leaders have experienced changes in their interpretations of the *Missio Dei* through the ordinary theologizing of members in their churches.
- To examine the theological challenges that students engaged in the academic study of missional theology experience as they seek to rescript their ordinary theologies.

8.3 Personal and Professional Development

As I suggested in chapter 1, I chose to include how my own personal and professional development as a reflexive practitioner have been affected by my research journey at Phoenix church. I believe this is very important to do as every reader will hopefully benefit greatly from applying what they learn from research to their own practice contexts as well. When I began

---

101. Cf. Ballard and Pritchard, *Practical Theology*; Trokan, "Models of Theological Reflection," 144–58.

CONCLUSIONS AND RECOMMENDATIONS 185

this research five years ago, I was much less aware of the impact of my college's, FCC's, and Newbigin's hermeneutical and epistemological horizons on my theological perspective. I had become increasingly absorbed in focusing on educating leaders to equip their congregations to engage in mission. This absorption meant I did not take time to understand some very real challenges congregants on the receiving end of missional change processes faced. I was overly focused upon missional leadership, and the restructuring of churches to participate in the *Missio Dei*.

Having taken this research journey, I have become much more conscious of the significant impacts of missional change on congregants. I am particularly concerned that participatory *Missio Dei* theology can lead to constraining (or perhaps repressing) a congregation's preexisting model of church (and theology). I am also concerned it may unnecessarily marginalize longstanding members of congregations, which at times may lead to their departure. I suspect other churches led by college graduates, or leaders who draw on a Newbigin-like theology of *Missio Dei*, may also be facing similar challenges to those of Phoenix. A Newbigin-like theology of *Missio Dei* seemingly set up graduate leaders in Phoenix to overly concentrate on the missionary life of members. Hence, less attention was seemingly given to the congregation's communal and relational life. Now, being more aware of impacts like this, I want to engage in more research with other congregations undertaking missional change journeys. I hope to work alongside some of them, to enable them to discover ways of addressing challenges that occur when they seek to become mission-focused.

Because of this research, I have come to the view that theological rescription is not only required of members' ordinary theologies, but also of some assumptions made in the field of missional church studies. I also believe ordinary theology used in conjunction with rescripting methodology will enable me to enhance how I go about designing future leadership education programs. For example, in the short term I recommend the rescription of four areas in my college's curriculum based upon learning derived from my research. They are:

1. Members' accounts of deficits in Phoenix's pastoral care and support structures seemed to correspond with the absence of pastoral studies modules in my college's programs. I will recommend that programs be modified to include modules in pastoral theology and

ministerial studies. At present they are dominated by missional leadership theory and praxis.

2. Another theme that arose from the congregational data was the impact of deconstructing Phoenix's older normative tradition of ministry. Graduate leaders could have been better enabled to understand how to innovate missional changes in Phoenix's tradition had they engaged in modules concentrated on the history of Christian traditions. No comprehensive courses of this type are currently offered by my college. I recommend courses be developed that will aim to meet four key learning outcomes: (a) to explore how variances in theological traditions arose in the history of the Christian church; (b) to focus on new movements that have been birthed out of preexisting traditions; (c) to investigate how schisms occurred between birthing traditions and new traditions (or vice versa); and (d) to develop hermeneutical approaches that have the utility to integrate new theological innovations into preexisting traditions.

3. Tensions seemed to arise in Phoenix due to strains between family, community, and leader models of the church (cf. §7.2.2). This may be related to a deficit in my college's programs. They include neither courses in congregational studies, nor congregational organizational theory and praxis, although courses exist that concentrate on reorganizing churches to become missional. I would recommend college courses be modified by the development of congregational studies, which will need to focus on common ways congregations organize themselves to develop understanding of these kinds of structures.

4. The constraint of Phoenix's former congregational structure arguably revealed ethical issues that perhaps needed to be given more attention. For example, a minority of members seemed to be forced by a majority to either accept missional changes in the congregation, to tolerate them, or to leave the church. The college's programs do not have specific ethics modules, and, in my view, lack a robust ethics concentration. I would recommend ethics courses be developed that seek to fulfill at least three aims: (a) to explore ethical issues related to bringing about change in churches; (b) to investigate human rights issues such as marginalization and exclusion; (c) to examine ethical issues as an integral part of theological reflection, related to the use, misuse, and abuse of power.

In the medium, to longer terms, I will seek to develop a team of peers and students to engage in further research in the field of practical and ordinary missional ecclesiology. Indeed, I hope some readers will join me in this venture, or develop ways of doing this with others in their particular contexts. I would most certainly value conversations with interested parties. I believe rescripting methodology has the flexibility to facilitate critical conversations with congregants' ordinary theologies, and the intellectual capital that can be developed to enhance academic programs, as well as the way churches seek to go about facilitating missional change within them. Given that I also act as External Examiner for five undergraduate and three postgraduate programs offered by other colleges, I will seek to encourage them to engage in more empirical research with missional communities. The aim of doing this would be to help them base their program designs on insights provided by practical and ordinary theology. I would also like to develop an intercollegial research team in the field of ordinary missional ecclesiology.

The largest impact of this research on me has come from spending many hours over the past few years engaged in critical reflexive learning from church members, graduates, the literature, peers, supervisors, analysis of data, and the writing and rewriting of chapters included in this book, among other things. This process of learning has made me much more attentive to the ordinary theologies of congregants, which in turn has translated into me taking time to conceive of ways to modify college courses—not just my own college's, but also other colleges with which I engage in consultancy work. One important way my thinking has changed is I now believe it is vital for students to learn more of their theology from the ordinary theology of Christians, who are engaged in mission in their everyday lives. In the future, I will aim to design (and enhance) academic programs based on insights that are derived from practical and empirical theology. In other words, less attention will be given to theoretical missional ecclesiology which divorces itself from engagement in research with grassroots missional movements. This is an important change in my professional practice as a program designer and educator.

8.4 Research Contributions

My research makes the following contributions: (1) it has found a majority of members seemed to be fulfilled and encouraged by seeing themselves as participants in the *Missio Dei*, and by engagement in missional projects; (2) it draws on the insights provided by ordinary theology and utilizes these to rescript facets of a Newbigin-like theology of participation in the *Missio Dei*; (3) it develops Cartledge's innovation of theological rescription, taking the additional step of suggesting theological rescriptions of some aspects of academic missional theology, as well as college programs; (4) it investigates the impact of the communication of a Newbigin-like theology of *Missio Dei* on British Reformed church members by graduates of my college; (5) it provides evidence that a participatory activist theology of *Missio Dei* seems to have had positive and negative impacts on different groups in a congregation; (6) it provides indicators of congregants' ordinary theologies of the *Missio Dei*; and (7) it offers somewhat of a template that, with appropriate modifications, might be used to help others engage in research with other ecclesial traditions, or missional change processes occurring in their congregations.

8.5 Concluding Remarks

Phoenix church, like the mythical bird of legend, seems to have gone through a fiery ordeal. Its old church was burnt down, and then it faced the costly experience of having its preexisting theology of professional clerical ministry and family church life consumed by the flames of change. The church that has emerged has developed a multicolored plumage which is nuanced by tension, strain, conflict, sacrifice, and a sense of fulfillment, for some, because of its missional change journey. The Phoenix has to pass through fire in order to emerge as the fiery colorful resurrection bird of legend. It seems this will be the case, to differing extents, for any congregation taking this kind of journey.

When I asked members of Phoenix how they felt about all of the changes in the church, I heard varied responses, including: "I feel exhausted by it"; "I feel more comfortable about it now"; "It's not for me"; "We're thinking about leaving"; "I love it"; "The journey has been hard but worth it"; "It's had a good impact on the church"; "It's discouraging"; "It's harder than it should be"; "I can't understand why we needed to change"; "Change inevitably had to happen"; or "It's stirred something good up

CONCLUSIONS AND RECOMMENDATIONS   189

in quite a few of us." Based on these testimonies, I conclude that missional change has led to complex reactions among members. They need to be evaluated against the criteria of whether all of the changes have been worth it or not for congregants. Much will depend on the theological perspectives of each member regarding the value of the congregation equipping them for participation in the *Missio Dei*. And here we come back to a primary assertion of my book. I suggest if missional church research literature concentrates on investigating ordinary theologies of this type, it will have to be much more attentive to complex reactions to *Missio Dei* theology.[102] It will make it much harder to maintain idealistic theoretical rhetoric that paints overly glossy portrayals of the benefits of churches developing a missional ecclesiology.

Missional change seems to have been a rather messy experience for Phoenix. A different kind of congregation is emerging. Indeed, a Newbigin-like theology of participation in the *Missio Dei* assumes the God of creation will keep on equipping the church to explore and imagine fresh ways of reinventing its life practices so it can engage in mission.[103]

During the time of my research at Phoenix, I had an incredibly vivid dream one night. I was in a room in which a huge, beautiful, colorful, fiery phoenix was to be found. All of Phoenix's members were in this room as well. Each of them held strings attached to the bird, as if they were trying to make it dance and move in the ways they wanted it to. In fact the reverse was occurring. The Phoenix was much stronger than they, and it instead was teaching them how to dance and move to its music and its way of being.

Near the end of my research, I shared this dream with members during one Sunday morning service. I said to them that perhaps God was seeking to help us follow the lead of the Spirit, so we could learn to discern and participate in what Jesus was calling the church to be, and sending the church to do.

This dream may be a useful metaphor of what we all may need to do—to learn from the missional Spirit of God how to participate in the *Missio Dei*. It seems to me that a God who calls each of us to be ambassadors for God, and ministers of reconciliation,[104] requires each of us to be shaped by the challenges of change God calls us to face. To become

102. Cf. Swinton and Mowat, *Practical Theology and Qualitative Research*, 13, 72.

103. Smith portrays imagination used in worship as a form of participation in the coming of God's kingdom (*Desiring the Kingdom*; Smith, *Imagining the Kingdom*).

104. 2 Cor 5:11–21.

like Christ might be thought of as becoming able to only see and do what we see the Father doing.[105] This seems to provide a clue for how the people of God might join together with the triune God, to do what God is doing—after all, all mission belongs to God. This would seem to be a fundamental starting point of an ordinary *Missio Dei* theology. It is to discern and share in what God is calling us to participate in as part of his divine strategy for the whole of creation. May God bless us all as we seek to do this together.

---

105. Cf. John 1:19, 20.

Appendix A

Ethics Consent Confirmation

Dear Andy,

Ethics Application (Amendment 10.17)

Applicant: Andy Hardy

Title: Investigating the efforts of graduate church leaders to communicate a '*Missio Dei*' missiology and its impact on congregational life

Reference: HUM 17/027

Department: Humanities

Original Approval Date: 21.08.17

Many thanks for your response and the amended documents. Under the procedures agreed by the University Ethics Committee I am pleased to advise you that your Department has approved the minor amendment to your above application dated 26.10.17 and confirmed that all conditions have been met. We do not require anything further in relation to this amendment.

Please Note:

This email confirms that any conditions have been met and thus confirms final ethics approval for this amendment (it is assumed that you will adhere to any minor conditions still outstanding, therefore we do not require a response to these).

University of Roehampton ethics approval will always be subject to compliance with the University policies and procedures applying at the time when the work takes place. It is your responsibility to ensure that you are familiar and compliant with all such policies and procedures when undertaking your research.

If this project involves clinical procedures or administering substances it is a condition of Ethics approval that all relevant SOPs published on the department communities pages are fully complied with.

Please advise us if there are any changes to the research during the life of the project. Minor changes can be advised using the Minor Amendments Form on the Ethics Website, but substantial changes may require a new application to be submitted.

Many thanks,

Ethics Officer

Appendix B

Congregational Interviews and Consultations

Interviews

Names of Interviewees and Interview Number	Date/s	Names of Interviewees and Interview Number	Date/s
1. Jasmin	7/10/16	16. Belinda	9/1/18
2. Kirsty	9/10/16	17. Peter	9/1/18
3. Terry	19/10/16	18. Jake	7/2/18
4. Caspian	25/10/16 & 11/4/18	19. Duncan	13/2/18
5. Bill	7/3/17 & periodic breakfast meetings	20. Katerina	13/2/18
6. Lynda	19/3/17 & 10/4/18	21. Ben	16/2/18
7. Lucy	4/10/17 & 4/4/18	22. Morgan	16/2/18
8. Debbie	10/10/17 & 24/4/18	23. Venessa	16/2/18
9. Mark	10/10/17 & 24/4/18	24. Reanna	16/2/18
10. Drummond	24/10/17	25. Stacey	20/3/18
11. Jessica	24/10/17	26. Gary	20/3/18
12. Jerry	13/11/17	27. Becky	4/4/18
13. Tamsin	14/11/17	28. Desmond	23/4/18
14. Adrian	21/11/17	29. Lisandra	23/4/18
15. Beverley	6/12/17	30. Leah	22/7/18

Formal Consultations

Formal Congregational Consultations	Date
Consultation Group 1	1/7/18
Consultation Group 2	2/8/18
Consultation Group 3	5/6/18
Consultation Group 4	8/7/18
Leadership Consultation	21/9/18

Appendix C

Sample Interview Questions

Members'/Leaders' Interview Questions (50 Minutes)

Preliminary questions:

- How long have you been coming to this church?
- Which church did you go to before?
- Is this church similar to your old one?
- What attracted you to this church?
- Why did you start coming to this church?
- What have I assumed in this question—value-neutral critique?

Main Questions:

- Formal preamble on research.
- How does this church compare to your old one? (For new members.)
- **Phase 1:** Can you tell me about your views of mission/outreach/evangelism? (Look at church literature. What language do they use in there?)

Possible Prompts:

- What you can remember from the past?
- Now compared to the past?
- What is the congregation's view of mission?
- (Show motto) Tell me about what this means to you. How well does the motto of the church reflect you?
- Imagine you had to write a motto. What would yours be?

Phase 2: Have you noticed any changes, for instance, in outreach?

Possible Prompts

- For you?
- For your family?
- In what you do on the church's premises?
- In what you do outside its premises?
- In how you seek to witness?
- How others engage in witnessing?
- In what is taught or preached?
- How the church is led or run?
- In what the church does?
- How you decide what God might want you to do?
- How the church decides what God might want it to do?

Phase 3: Overall, how do you feel about all this change?

Appendix D

Qualitative Data

This appendix provides qualitative data that has arisen from the coding process of raw data. It focuses on the testimonies of Phoenix's members and a leader, all of which are related to their perceptions and ordinary theologies of the impact of *Missio Dei* theology on the church.

D1: *Jessica:* And for me you see it's that a lot of these people who are coming I know because of their kids, so through school I know those families already, and I think there's another thing going on with them. I've got a relationship with those families who I then try to say "Well, how about coming to the allotment" kind of thing, so it's a kind of a crossover between my work and my church. It can be quite difficult because I can't be overtly a Christian at work.

D2: *Jake:* I think it was probably about a year and a half ago. So we'd had the plot for probably six months or so. And it was, we ran some summer sessions for kids and families throughout the summer. And we'd had quite a busy session, and we'd had about seventy or eighty kids, so it was busy. I think it was Jessica who actually said, she was sat down doing some planting over there, I think she actually said, "This is church." And that was an important moment for us as a group or community, that "This is church."

D3: *Becky:* And you know people can just give ideas, and Bill can say "That's a great idea." Youth work . . . it's so open and you can go and help whenever you want. You can go and help out in almost any ministry you want to. And if God spiritually challenges you to do something I think there's more freedom.

D4: *Jake:* No one is asking, "What are you doing? You have to tell us." There's freedom to experiment and be ourselves. A lot of that is the pastor. He lets us be free. You know he's very good at seeing people's gifting.

D5: Desmond: Yeah, I think so, it was a fresh kind of start, you know, not having to think of everything and do everything. It was like there was a community of people who were, you know, doing stuff.

Lisandra: And doing good stuff, because I think we were leaders by default really, because church was always at our house. I think we probably had some of those giftings, but we were slightly reluctant. If you had said to me, you know, "Tell me, how many years have you been essentially leading a house church?," really without much of a vision, it was really leading a glorified house group. We managed to pull the house group into Phoenix, which was really good. So they all came with us. So, Peter and all of them came.

D6: Lynda: I've been in the church for the last nineteen years, but in the last ten years it has changed massively. You wouldn't recognize it from ten years ago. I think that the way it has changed is that about ten years ago it was felt that you had to come into church to hear about God, to hear about Jesus, and if you wanted someone to hear about Jesus, then they would have to come to church with you to hear about him. And now what is different is that we are all missionaries, all on God's mission, all going around telling people about Jesus. Actually we need them to meet Jesus before they come to church.

D7: Beverley: There was opposition at church. It was hell. Not from Bill—other people who couldn't see the point. And you know they said, "What's this got to do with God?," and "It's a pity that it's not more evangelistic." A lot of those people have left now. But there was loads of opposition.

D8: Bill discussed the resistance he had encountered at first to setting up Phoenix's Bible school, during a breakfast meeting we had in the first quarter of the year in 2017. He explained how at first [in 2011] he had handpicked a few men and women who showed interest in learning more about the Bible and how to engage in outreach. He shared his notes from a B.Th course he had been doing at a Bible college. This gave him the idea of trying to set up a Bible school in Phoenix. He explained that he had encountered a lot of scepticism from the church's elders at first, and they refused to give permission for a Bible school. However, after about a year the elders changed their minds. This is what *Isaac* said about it:

> So you know in the early days of the Bible school, when Bill started explaining it to the eldership team, we were like "We don't get it. You are going to have to explain it again so we can

get it." Until we as leaders got it we couldn't possibly think that the congregation were going to get it.

D9: Desmond: When I think back a few years ago to literally have people standing up during a service saying "The Great Commission isn't for everyone." It was like, they said, 'The Great Commission just applied to those group of people back then and not to everyone." And I thought, "Do people have that opinion? Is that even an opinion?"

D10: Bill discussed the challenges that the leadership team faced as they tried to utilize the pastoral skills of members in order to visit the church's older people, during a breakfast meeting I had with him in the second quarter of the year in 2018. He explained that longstanding members expected the senior pastor to visit them. These members seemed to feel that only a visit from the official paid minister counted as a real pastoral visit. A visit from a volunteer, even if they had been trained by the church to engage in pastoral work, did not seem to count as a visit. Bill explained that this put a lot of pressure on the senior minster and it was a problem which was proving hard to find a solution to.

Appendix E

Congregational Questionnaire

God's Mission and God's People

Questionnaire (Survey)

God's Mission in the Witness and Life of the Church

This piece of research is seeking to discover how the theological idea that God is a missionary God might be influencing your faith-community to further develop its own missional identity and to see itself as a participant in God's mission in its local neighborhood, or in the broader life experiences of members in their work and home lives. The researcher (Andrew R. Hardy) will use the gathered data to complete a doctorate in practical theology at Roehampton University. The Latin phrase *Missio Dei* means "mission of God."

What the researcher is interested in finding out is: How are your church's beliefs and practices being influenced by obtaining a vision of itself as a community of people who want to help others in their neighborhood, as well as in their church's community, to get to know this God who is seeking to form a faith-based relationship with them?

Please take a few minutes to complete this questionnaire, which is designed to find out what you believe about the mission of God and your participation in that mission. The questionnaire is anonymous and the answers you give will be treated confidentially, so you can feel free to express your opinions. There are no right or wrong answers. We are interested in what YOU feel and believe. You will need to read the short passage below before you progress to answering some questions.

For most questions all you need to do is circle or tick a single response. It's very important that you answer ALL THE QUESTIONS IN EACH SECTION, even if it is hard to decide. Don't spend too long on each one: your first answer is usually the best. The questionnaire will take ten minutes to complete.

Thank you for your time and help.

Rev. Andy R. Hardy

(Researcher)

About You and the Church:

1. For how long have you been part of Phoenix?

- Less than six months
  - 6–11 months
  - 1–2 years
  - 3–5 years
  - 6–10 years
  - 11–20 years
  - 21–30 years
  - 31–40 years
  - 41–50 years
  - More than 50 years

2. Which church denomination would you most identify with, prior to this church?
   - Another FIEC church
   - Pentecostal
   - Independent
   - Anglican

- Charismatic/new church
- Orthodox
- Asian church
- Baptist
- Brethren
- Methodist
- URC
- Roman Catholic
- African church
- Chinese church
- Other

3. On average, over the last year, how frequently have you attended the Sunday Services?

- Three times a month or more
- Twice a month
- Once a month
- Less than once a month

4. Are you a member of this church?
☐ Yes ☐ No

5. Do you hold any positions of responsibility in the church? (For this question tick all the boxes that apply):

- None
- Ministry leader
- Musician
- Sunday school teacher
- Youth group leader
- Bible study leader (not house group)
- House group leader

- Deacon
- Pastor/Elder

6. Do you attend one of the church house groups?
   ☐ Yes   ☐ No
If Yes, how often do you attend?:

- Always, or nearly always
- About half the time
- Infrequently

7. On average, over the last year, how frequently have you attended the Sunday evening services?

- Three times a month or more
- Twice a month
- Once a month
- Less than once a month

8. This church is "evangelical." What do you understand "evangelical" to mean?

9a. Please answer the following questions in terms of what you have thought or believed just up until and prior to doing this questionnaire .(Indicate your answers by placing a tick in the relevant boxes.)   YES   NO

Have you heard of the term "mission of God" (Latin, *Missio Dei*)?

(If you answer No, then please do not continue with this survey but return it to Andy Hardy, but ensure you tick No)

APPENDIX E

Please answer the following questions in terms of what you have thought or believed just up until and prior to doing this questionnaire. (Indicate your answers by placing a tick in the relevant boxes.)	YES	NO

9b. Would you say you understand what the term "mission of God" means?

9c. Would you say that your understanding of the "mission of God" has inspired you to think or act in new ways in terms of how you seek to share your faith?

9d. Did you first hear the term "mission of God" in this church during the time of the present pastor and leadership team?

9e. Would you say that the teaching or preaching of the present pastor and leaders who have done a ForMission college degree have given you an understanding of what it means to believe that God has a mission?

9f. Would you say that the teaching or preaching of the present leaders who have not done a ForMission college degree have given you an understanding of what it means to believe that God has a mission?

9g. Have you heard the term "mission of God" referred to by members of this church during the time of this pastor?

9h. Have you heard the term "mission of God" referred to in a house group of this church during the time of this pastor?

10a. Please indicate all the sources where you have heard or read about the term "mission of God" below by ticking the relevant boxes.	
This church (Current Pastor and Leaders)	Sermon(s)/teaching (This church, 2009–17)
Another church	Sermon(s)/teaching (previous pastor(s), pre-2008)
Christian event	Christian magazine
Christian TV	Journal
Christian radio	Book
Worship song/hymn	Church newsletter
Phoenix in-house training course(s)	Church notices
Life group or house group (this church)	Life group or house group (another church)
Visiting preacher	Website or web source (i.e., Facebook, etc.)

Family member | Friend or work colleague
The Bible and Bible notes | Devotional book
A Bible commentary or dictionary | College or University
Theology Program | Other:

> 10b. Please rank in order of importance the most influential sources that have helped you to meaningfully understand the term "mission of God." Only choose a maximum of five out of the options below, where "1" placed in a relevant box to the right of a category is the most influential, "2" the next most influential, until you get to the least influential 5th option, *if you have that many.*

This church (Current Pastor and Leaders) | Sermon(s)/teaching (This church, 09–17)
Another church | Sermon(s)/teaching (previous pastor/s pre-2008)
Christian event | Christian magazine
Christian TV | Journal
Christian radio | Book
Worship song/hymn | Church newsletter
Phoenix in-house training course(s) | Church notices
Life group or house group (this church) | Life group or house group (another church)
Visiting preacher | Website or web source (i.e. Facebook, etc.)
Family member | Friend or work colleague
The Bible and Bible notes | Devotional book
A Bible commentary or dictionary | College or University
Theology Program | Other:

About You and the Wider Church

11. Do you attend services at another church more than three times a year?

    ☐ Yes ☐ No

If Yes, please write church name below:

12. Have you gone to any of the Christian events/conferences listed below in the last year? (For this question please tick all the boxes that apply.)

- None
- FIEC conference
- Spring Harvest
- London Men's/Women's conference
- Keswick convention
- Greenbelt
- Other (Please specify)

About You

13. What age group do you belong to?:

- 18–19
- 20–29
- 30–39
- 40–49
- 50–59
- 60–69
- 70–79
- 80+

14. What is your gender?

☐ Male ☐ Female

15. What qualifications do you have? (For this question, please tick all boxes that apply.)

- None
- CSE
- GCSE/O-levels
- GNVQ
- C & G
- A-levels
- AVQ
- HND
- Certificate/Diploma
- Degree
- Professional qualification
- Higher degree

Thank you for helping with this questionnaire

Questionnaire administered by: Rev Andrew Hardy

Upon completion of this questionnaire you may choose not to submit it. If at a later time before the publication of the research in December 2016 you want to withdraw your questionnaire please do so by emailing: andyhardy@formission.ac.uk. All data found on questionnaires will be scanned into PDFs; the hard copies will be shredded. The data will then be electronically stored on one external data storage device. This device will be locked in a safe for ten years and at the end of that period destroyed.

The questionnaire will take about ten minutes to complete and will be given to every church member.

Please note that there is no compulsion or pressure to take part in the project, and that should someone decline to participate or subsequently withdraw, they will not be adversely affected. Please complete the consent form that is included with this questionnaire.

Investigator Contact Details:

Rev Andrew Hardy
Student

Appendix F

Field Notes Template

File Name:	
Title:	
Date:	

What happened? (Thick Description of Day's Activity.)
This is for accurately describing what happened during the day. Answer "who, what, when, where, why, how" and try to stick to "facts" to create a *verbal snapshot* of what happened. This includes noting direct quotes and snippets of conversations. Things to look out for: detailed factual information about what is occurring. The focus should be on "thick description" of all aspects of the site and the individuals. This includes a physical description of the site and the individuals, events and activities that are occurring, and social interactions between individuals.
NOTES

Reflections/Reflexivity
Reflect on the day's experiences, writing about how "I" might have influenced events, what went wrong (and what "I" could do differently next time), and how "I" feel about the process. Describe how you are reacting and feeling about what you are observing, as well as initial interpretations about what you are observing.
NOTES

Emerging Questions/Analysis
Note questions "I" might ask, potential lines of inquiry, and theories that might be useful. This is where "I" start to do some analytical work.

APPENDIX F

NOTES

Future Action
This is a "to-do" list of actions. Include a timeframe alongside each point.
TO-DO LIST AND TIMELINES

Appendix G

Summary of Missional Projects

THIS APPENDIX PROVIDES INFORMATION about the aims of the missional projects of Phoenix church. It also helps to explain a little of the background to each project.

Missional Initiatives

Description of Missional Initiative	Number of Members Involved	Year of Launch	Missional Aims
Community Support Group (the lonely and those with mental health issues)	3	2015	This group met once a week on Wednesdays in the church's function rooms opposite to the working men's club, and later next door to the new church building which was opened in late February 2018. Attendees were able to socialize with peers, as well as have a meal. The congregants involved in the group, with Bill's support, would talk with attendees and pray for them. There was a short piece from the Bible read to them, and then group members would sing some worship songs or contemporary secular popular songs. None of these attendees went to the church's Sunday morning services.

Missional Café	5	2016	The café was located in the estate which was close by to the working men's club. The estate was among the top 5 percent of the poorest city suburbs in Britain. Patrons came from the estate, being made up of lonely people and mothers with their toddlers. The café aimed to provide their clients with quality food and beverages. The café was one of the shops that were all housed in a terraced row. The aim was for staff to take time to serve customers, as well as to listen to them and at times to pray for them. Congregants also engaged in what they called gospel gossiping with clients and some of them came to embrace a Christian faith. The café project did not aim to get clients to attend Phoenix church, but several young men who were converted began to attend its services on Sunday mornings. The café project coordinator explained that it was their goal to actually make the café into a Christian spiritual support community in its own right, rather than seeking to attract people to the local church.
Missional Allotment 1	6	2013	This allotment was located nearby the church and sought to fulfill several missional goals. Congregants sought to influence other locals who used the allotment about their faith when opportunities permitted them to do this. The main goal of the allotment was to support other local missional projects by providing grown produce for them to use. For example, produce was provided for the missional café, as well as a Christian homeless project in the city. The coordinator of the project explained that the team believed that they were seeking to meet the needs of the poor, as well as seeking to provide a Christian presence and witness to others who used the allotment.

SUMMARY OF MISSIONAL PROJECTS 213

Missional Allotment 2 and Church Plant	12	2014	This allotment was located in another ward of the city. It was considered to be a kind of church-planting project. The team that led this project met every Friday to care for the allotment, as well as to seek to interact with locals from the neighborhood. Like allotment project 1, a key aim was to be a Christian influence to locals. This project also hosted fieldwork opportunities for teachers and children from a local nearby school. Children and teachers came to the allotment periodically and were given opportunities to care for the church allotment, as well as being given talks by the congregants about nature, creation, and the Creator. The missional team also hosted special events at the allotment, which had up to about eighty local parents and children attending them. At these special events, children would be able to help in the allotment, play games in a field opposite the allotment, and hear Bible stories and be prayed for. The coordinator of this project explained that the allotment was a rather tongue-in-cheek kind of church-planting project. The team of members who supported it considered it to be a church-planting project because of its clear Christian ethos and missional practices that were making a visible impact on locals.
Missional Allotment 3 (Church Car Park)	10	2018	This allotment was interestingly located in the garden strips that surrounded the new church building that had been opened in late February 2018. It was part of a national project, known as Incredible Edible, that sought to provide opportunities for local needy people in the community to pick produce that was grown in the allotment. Signage around the church explained that locals were free to pick whatever they were in need of without needing to make payment. Some church members would care for the allotment directly after Sunday morning services. They often spoke to passersby who were at times intrigued by what was being done. Locals picked produce and also at times engaged in spiritual conversations with church members at work in the allotment. This allotment was started during 2018, and it was hard to assess its impact on the church or locals. However, it shared similar aims to the other two allotment projects.

Missional Summer Children's Club	20	2009	This summer club took place in a city park near Phoenix. It was led and hosted by members from Phoenix, as well as some helpers from other churches. It lasted for one week, but required a lot of preplanning in the year leading up to the event. The married couple who were responsible to coordinate the event (both Phoenix members) organized social events, musical events, and dinners throughout the year to raise the £10,000 required to run the event. It had been going on for about nine years. The couple also trained volunteers and made sure that crafts, games, and other resources were gathered in order to run the event. About 200 local children attended this event every year. It consisted of games, Bible stories, face painting, live worship, and prayer. The aim was to meet children in the natural context of the local park their families used. The team sought to share their faith with these children and their families. Like other projects, the aim was to influence people to become Christians, as well as to provide opportunities for locals to get to know local Christians. Some families that attended were also Christians, so it was possible for locals to get to know children that belonged to Christian families. Apparently some locals also visited churches as a result of this summer event. I did not meet any of them during my time of research at Phoenix.
14 House Groups	80	2009–2018	It may seem strange to include house groups as a missional initiative given that they often only include Christians and do not seek to include locals who do not espouse a Christian faith. However, in the context of Phoenix these fourteen house groups were launched over the nine-year period by Bill and his team. The goal was to focus members' attention on praying for people in their neighborhoods, as well as to seek to influence those showing interest in matters of faith. Hence these groups were an important part of the leadership team's strategy to help members to begin to focus on mission in the community, rather than hosting prayer meetings in Phoenix's small church hall. About five of the house groups took the further step of having locals come to their actual house groups in order to share in their spiritual life. I met at least fifteen newcomers to Phoenix who attended Sunday morning worship services who were either exploring the Christian faith or who had embraced it who also attended a house group.

Appendix H

Churches of Christ Background

FCC IS PART OF a family of congregations called, variously, Disciples of Christ or Churches of Christ.[1] These churches first emerged in the early nineteenth century, later becoming a worldwide movement.[2] They trace their origins to both the United Kingdom and the USA.[3] In the United Kingdom, Churches of Christ began as a "cooperative" meeting of congregations in 1842.[4] FCC currently has forty-eight member churches. In the USA, Churches of Christ is much larger and traces its origins to the work of three Christian leaders: Barton Stone, and Thomas and Alexander Campbell. Stone and the Campbells were originally Presbyterian ministers.[5] Churches of Christ has become known as a denomination although the founders resisted labels of this type.[6] Stone and the Campbells' ecclesiological convictions posited that all churches were part of the one universal church of Christ, which resonates with Free Church Catholic Ecclesiology (cf. §1.3).[7] I share this conviction.

Churches of Christ is part of what is termed the "Restoration Movement."[8] Those like myself who aver a theology of restoration es-

---

1. Cf. FCC, "Home Page"; Olbright, "Churches of Christ," 212–20; Holloway and Foster, *Renewing God's People*, 7, 11, 49, 61.

2. Cf. Holloway and Foster, *Renewing the World*, 15–24.

3. Cf. Olbright, "Churches of Christ," 212–20; Holloway and Foster, *Renewing God's People*, 7, 11, 49, 61; Thompson, *Let Sects and Parties Fall*.

4. Cf. Thompson, *Let Sects and Parties Fall*, 13–32.

5. Cf. Thompson, *Let Sects and Parties Fall*, 13–20.

6. Cf. Hughes, *Reviving the Ancient Faith*, 11.

7. Cf. Hughes, *Churches of Christ*, 5.

8. Cf. Holloway and Foster, *Renewing the World*, 17–19.

pouse the theological conviction that the universal church of Christ was never intended to be disunited and fragmented.[9] The diverse assortment of denominations and traditions of more recent history (the twentieth century) are considered to be far from the ideal of one united body of Christ.[10] Hence, an aspiration is to try to restore the unity of the Christian movement. I, as well as FCC and ForMission college, aver this kind of ecumenism, although I believe that it is not possible to organize a network of churches without putting structures and identifying markers in place. Neither do I believe it is necessary that unity requires the dissolution of denominations. I believe unity can be celebrated because of a common faith in the triune God. These are all common convictions espoused by FCC.

---

9. Cf. Holloway and Foster, *Renewing the World*, 17–19.
10. Cf. Holloway and Foster, *Renewing the World*, 15–19

Bibliography

Akrong, Abraham. "Deconstructing Colonial Mission - New Missiological Perspectives in African Christianity." In *Christianity in Africa and the African Diaspora: The Appropriation of a Scattered Heritage*, edited by Afe Adogame et al., 63–75. London: Continuum, 2011.

Alexander, Estrelda. "Introduction." In *Philip's Daughters: Women in Pentecostal-Charismatic Leadership*, edited by Estrelda Alexander and Amos Yong, 1–16. Eugene, OR: Pickwick, 2009.

Ammerman, Nancy T., et al., eds. *Studying Congregations: A New Handbook*. Nashville: Abingdon, 1998.

Anderson, Ray S. *The Shape of Practical Theology: Empowering Ministry with Theological Praxis*. Downers Grove, IL: IVP Academic, 2001.

Anselm of Canterbury. "Proslogion." In *The Major Works*, edited by Brian Davies and G. R. Evans, translated by M. J. Charlesworth, 82–104. New York: Oxford University Press, 1998.

Aquinas, Thomas. "Summa Theologica." http://www.ccel.org/ccel/aquinas/summa.

Arthur, Eddie. "*Missio Dei* and the Mission of the Church." https://www.wycliffe.net/more-about-what-we-do/papers-and-articles/missio-dei-and-the-mission-of-the-church/.

Astley, Jeff. "Ordinary Theology and the Learning Conversation with Academic Theology." In *Exploring Ordinary Theology: Everyday Christian Believing and the Church*, edited by Jeff Astley and Leslie J. Francis, 45–54. Farnham, UK: Ashgate, 2013.

———. *Ordinary Theology: Looking, Listening and Learning in Theology*. Farnham, UK: Ashgate, 2002.

Astley, Jeff, and Lesslie J. Francis. *Exploring Ordinary Theology: Everyday Christian Believing and the Church*. London: Routledge, 2013.

Bacchiocchi, Samuel. *Divine Rest for Human Restlessness: A Theological Study of the Good News of the Sabbath for Today*. Rome: The Pontifical Gregorian University Press, 1982.

Ballard, Paul, and John Pritchard. *Practical Theology: Christian Thinking in the Service of Church and Society*. 2nd ed. London: SPCK, 2006.

Banks, Robert. *Reenvisioning Theological Education: Exploring a Missional Alternative to Current Models*. Grand Rapids: Eerdmans, 1999.

Barfoot, Cas H., and Gerald T. Sheppard. "Prophetic vs. Priestly Religion: The Changing Role of Women Clergy in Classical Pentecostal Churches." *Review of Religious Research* 22 (1980) 2–17.

Barns, Ian. "Reimagining the Gospel as Public Truth." In *Theology in Missionary Perspective: Lesslie Newbigin's Legacy*, edited by Mark T. B. Laing and Paul Weston, 155–71. Eugene, OR: Pickwick, 2012.

Baroni, Laura, et al., eds. "Defining and Classifying Interest Groups." *Int Groups ADV* 3 (2013) 141–51.

Barrett, Lois Y., et al. *Treasure in Clay Jars: Patterns in Missional Faithfulness*. Grand Rapids: Eerdmans, 2004.

Bassham, Rodger C. *Mission Theology 1948–1975: Years of Worldwide Creative Tension, Ecumenical, Evangelical, and Roman Catholic*. Pasadena, CA: William Carey Library, 1979.

Bauckham, Richard. "Mission as Hermeneutic for Scriptural Interpretation." In *Reading the Bible Missionally*, edited by Michael W. Goheen, 28–44. Grand Rapids: Eerdmans, 2016.

Beaver, R. Pierce. "The History of Mission Strategy." In *Perspectives on the World Christian Movement*, edited by Ralph D. Winter and Steven C. Hawthorne, 58–72. Rev. Ed. Pasadena, CA: William Carey Library, 1992.

Bebbington, David W. *Evangelicalism in Modern Britain: A History from the 1730s to 1980s*. London: Routledge, 2005.

Becker, Penny Edgall. *Congregations in Conflict: Cultural Models of Local Religious Life*. Cambridge: Cambridge University Press, 1999.

Becker, Penny Edgall, et al., eds. "Straining at the Tie that Binds: Congregational Conflict in the 1980s." *Review of Religious Research* 34 (1993) 193–209.

Benner, David G. *Spirituality and the Awakening Self: The Sacred Journey of Transformation*. Grand Rapids: Brazos, 2012.

Bennett, Zoe. "Britain." In *The Wiley-Blackwell Companion to Practical Theology*, edited by Bonnie J. Miller-McLemore, 475–84. Oxford: Wiley-Blackwell, 2014.

Berger, Teresa. "Feminist Ritual Practice." In *The Oxford Handbook of Feminist Theology*, edited by Mary McClintock Fulkerson and Sheila Briggs, 525–43. Oxford: Oxford University Press, 2012.

———. "Prayers and Practices of Women: Lex Orandi Reconfigured." *Yearbook of the European Society of Women in Theological Research* 9 (2001) 63–67.

Berry, Jan N. "Transforming Rites: The Practice of Women's Ritual Making." PhD Thesis. University of Glasgow, 2006.

Bevans, Steven B. *Models of Contextual Theology*. Maryknoll, NY: Orbis, 2012.

Bevans, Steven B., and Roger P. Schroeder. *Prophetic Dialogue: Reflections on Christian Mission Today*. Maryknoll, NY: Orbis, 2011.

Bielo, James S. *Words upon the Word: An Ethnography of Evangelical Group Bible Study*. New York: New York University Press, 2009.

Bird, Michael F. "Incorporated Righteousness: A Response to Recent Evangelical Discussion Concerning the Imputation of Christ's Righteousness in Justification." *JETS* 47 (2004) 253–75.

Bliese, Richard H. "Developing Evangelical Public Leadership for Apostolic Witness: A Missional Alternative to Traditional Pastoral Formation." In *The Missional Church and Leadership Formation: Helping Congregations Develop Leadership Capacity*, edited by Craig Van Gelder, 72–96. Grand Rapids: Eerdmans, 2009.

Boa, Kenneth. *Conformed to His Image: Biblical and Practical Approaches to Spiritual Formation.* Grand Rapids: Zondervan, 2001.
Bockmuehl, Klaus. *Listening to the God Who Speaks: Reflections on God's Guidance from Scripture and the Lives of God's People.* Colorado Springs, CO: Holmers and Howard, 1990.
Bohache, Thomas. *Christology from the Margins.* London: SCM, 2008.
Bolt, John. "Eschatological Hermeneutics, Women's Ordination, and the Reformed Tradition." *Calvin Theological Journal* 26 (1991) 370–88.
Bosch, David J. *Transforming Mission: Paradigm Shifts in Theology of Mission.* Maryknoll, NY: Orbis, 2000.
Bouyer, Louis. *The Spirit and Forms of Protestantism.* San Francisco: Ignatius, 2017.
Braaten, Carl E. "The Kingdom of God and Life Everlasting." In *Christian Theology: An Introduction to its Traditions and Tasks,* edited by Hodgson, P. and King, R., 328–52. 3rd ed. London: SPCK, 2008.
Branson, Mark Lau. "A Missional Church Process: Post-intervention Research." *Journal of Religious Leadership* 13 (2014) 99–132.
Branson, Mark Lau, and John F. Martinez. *Churches, Cultures and Leadership: A Practical Theology of Congregations and Ethnicities.* Downers Grove, IL: IVP Academic, 2011.
Brierley Consultancy. "Where Is the Church Going?" https://www.brierleyconsultancy.com/where-is-the-church-going.
Briggs, John A. Y. "Tambaram Conference." In *Evangelical Dictionary of World Missions,* edited by A. Scott Moreau, 928–29. Grand Rapids: Baker, 2000.
Bryman, Alan. *Social Research Methods.* 3rd ed. Oxford: Oxford University Press, 2008.
Bullard, Scott W. *Re-membering the Body: The Lord's Supper and Ecclesial Unity in the Free Church Traditions.* Eugene, OR: Cascade, 2013.
Cameron, Helen et al. ed. *Talking about God in Practice: Theological Action Research and Practical Theology.* London: SCM, 2010.
———. *Theological Reflection for Human Flourishing: Pastoral Practice and Public Theology.* London: SCM, 2012.
Canlis, Julie. *Calvin's Ladder: A Spiritual Theology of Ascent and Ascension.* Grand Rapids: Eerdmans, 2010.
Cartledge, Mark J. "Pentecostal Experience: An Example of Practical Theological Rescription." *Journal of the European Pentecostal Theological Association* 28 (2008) 21–34.
———. *Testimony in the Spirit: Rescripting Ordinary Theology.* London: Routledge, 2010.
Cavaness, Barbara L. "Leadership Attitudes and the Ministry of Single Women in Assemblies of God Missions." In *Philip's Daughters: Women in Pentecostal Charismatic Leadership,* edited by Estrelda Alexander and Amos Yong, 112–30. Eugene, OR: Pickwick, 2009.
Charmaz, Kathy. *Constructing Grounded Theory: A Practical Guide through Qualitative Analysis.* London: SAGE, 2011.
Chou, Hui-Tzu Grace. "The Impact of Congregational Characteristics on Conflict-Related Exit." *Sociology of Religion* 69 (2008) 93–108.
Clark, David B. *Breaking the Mould of Christendom: Kingdom Community, Diaconal Church and the Liberation of the Laity.* Peterborough, UK: Epworth, 2005.

Clark Moschella, Mary. "Ethnography." In *The Wiley-Blackwell Companion to Practical Theology*, edited by Bonnie J. Miller-McLemore, 224–33. Oxford: Wiley-Blackwell, 2014.

Coate, Mary Anne. *Clergy Stress: The Hidden Conflicts of Ministry*. London: SPCK, 1990.

Collicutt, Joanna. *The Psychology of Christian Character Formation*. London: SCM, 2019.

Collins, Peter. "Religion and Ritual: A Multi-Perspectival Approach." In *The Oxford Handbook of the Sociology of Religion*, edited by Peter B. Clarke, 671–87. Oxford: Oxford University Press, 2011.

Cormode, Scott. "Cultivating Missional Leaders: Mental Models and the Ecology of Vocation." In *The Missional Church and Leadership Formation: Helping Congregations Develop Leadership Capacity*, edited by Craig Van Gelder, 99–119. Grand Rapids: Eerdmans, 2009.

Cray, Graham. *Mission-Shaped Church*. London: Church House, 2004.

Croft, Steven. *Transforming Communities: Re-imaging the Church for the 21st Century*. London: Darton, Longman and Todd, 2002.

Cronshaw, Darren. "Australians' Reenvisioning of Theological Education: In Step with the Spirit?" *Australian ejournal of Theology* 18 (2011) 223–35.

———. "Reenvisioning Theological Education and Missional Spirituality." *JATE* 9 (2012) 9–27.

———. "Reenvisioning Theological Education, Mission and the Local Church." *Mission Studies* 28 (2011) 91–115.

Crumbley, Deidre Helen. "Sanctified Saints – Impure Prophetesses: A Cross-cultural Reflection on Gender and Power in Two Afro-Christian Spirit-Privileging Churches." In *Philip's Daughters: Women in Pentecostal-Charismatic Leadership*, edited by Estrelda Alexander and Amos Yong, 74–94. Eugene, OR: Pickwick, 2009.

Darsih, Endang. "Learner-Centred Teaching: What Makes It Effective." *Indonesian EFL Journal* 4 (2018) 33–41.

Daubert, Dave. "Vision-Discerning vs. Vision-Casting: How Shared Vision Can Raise Up Communities of Leaders Rather than Mere Leaders of Communities." In *The Missional Church and Leadership Formation: Helping Congregations Develop Leadership Capacity*, edited by Craig Van Gelder, 147–72. Grand Rapids: Eerdmans, 2009.

Davey, John. *Burnout: Stress in the Ministry*. Leominster, UK: Gracewing, 1995.

Davies, Noel A. "Ecumenism." In *The Routledge Encyclopedia of Missions and Missionaries*, edited by Jonathan J. Bonk, 127–31. London: Routledge, 2010.

Davies, Noel, and Martin Conway. *World Christianity in the 20th Century*. London: SCM, 2008.

Davies, Saunders. "Mission and Spirituality for Life." In *Mission and Spirituality: Creative Ways of Being Church*, edited by Howard Mellor and Timothy Yates, 27–42. Sheffield, UK: Cliff College Publishing, 2002.

Davis, Caroline Franks. *The Evidential Force of Religious Experience*. Oxford: Clarendon, 1989.

D'Costa, Gavin. *Christianity and World Religions: Disputed Questions in the Theology of Religions*. Chichester, UK: Wiley-Blackwell, 2009.

Dehmlow Dreier, Mary Sue, ed. *Created and Led by the Spirit: Planting Missional Congregations*. Grand Rapids: Eerdmans, 2013.

———. "Planting Missional Congregations: Imagining Together.'" In *Created and Led by the Spirit: Planting Missional Congregations*, edited by Mary Sue Dehmlow Dreier 3–26. Grand Rapids: Eerdmans, 2013.

De Wit, Hans. ed. *Through the Eyes of Another: Intercultural Reading of the Bible*. Elkhart, IN: Institute of Mennonite Studies, 2004.

Drane, John. *Do Christians Know How to Be Spiritual? The Rise of New Spirituality, and the Mission of the Church*. London: Darton, Longman and Todd, 2005.

Dreyer, Jaco S. "Knowledge, Subjectivity, (De)Coloniality, and the Conundrum of Reflexivity." In *Conundrums in Practical Theology*, edited by Joyce Ann Mercer and Bonnie J. Miller-McLemore, 90–109. Leiden: Brill, 2016.

Dreyer, Wim A. "Missional Ecclesiology as Basis for a New Church Order: A Case Study." *HTS Teologiese Studies/Theological Studies* 69 (2013) 1–5.

Engelsviken, Tormod. "*Missio Dei*: The Understanding and Misunderstanding of a Theological Concept in European Churches and Missiology." *International Review of Mission* 92 (2003) 481–97.

Espinoza, Benjamin D. "The Shaping of Things to Come: Innovation and Mission for the 21st-Century Church." *Christian Education Journal* 10 (2013) 464–67.

Faggioli, Massimo. *Vatican II: The Battle for Meaning*. New York: Paulist, 2012.

Faith Survey. "Christianity in the UK." https://faithsurvey.co.uk/uk-christianity.html.

Fee, Gordon D. *Paul, the Spirit, and the People of God*. Peabody, MA: Hendrickson, 1996.

Fergusson, David. "Ecumenism and the Doctrine of the Trinity Today." In *The Oxford Handbook of The Trinity*, edited by Gilles Emery and Matthew Levering, 547–58. Oxford: Oxford University Press, 2011.

Fiddes, Paul S. *Participating in God: A Pastoral Doctrine of the Trinity*. Louisville: Westminster John Knox, 2000.

FIEC. "Beliefs." (2016). https://fiec.org.uk/who-we-are/beliefs.

———. "Who We Are." (2016). https://fiec.org.uk/who-we-are.

———. "Women in Ministry." (2016). https://fiec.org.uk/who-we-are/beliefs/women-in-ministry.

Flett, John G. *The Witness of God: The Trinity, Missio Dei, Karl Barth, and the Nature of Christian Community*. Grand Rapids: Eerdmans, 2010.

Flynn, James. "Testimony in the Spirit: Rescripting Ordinary Pentecostal Theology." *Pneuma* 34 (2012) 275–76.

Foss, Sonja K. *Rhetorical Criticism: Exploration and Practice*. 3rd ed. Long Grove, IL: Waveland, 2004.

Foster, Richard. *Streams of Living Water: Celebrating the Great Traditions of Christian Faith*. London: Fount, 1999.

Francis, Lesslie John. "Caring for Clergy in Crisis." *Parson and Parish* 156 (2001) 11–16.

Franke, John. "Teaching Missional Theology." http://wrfnet.org/resources/2008/04/teaching-missional-theology.

Franklin, Patrick S. "Missionaries in Our Own Back Yard: Missional Community as Cultural and Political Engagement in the Writings of Lesslie Newbigin." *Didaskalia* 25 (2015) 161–90.

Frederickson, Scott. "The Missional Congregation in Context." In *The Missional Church in Context: Helping Congregations Develop Contextual Ministry*, edited by Craig Van Gelder, 44–64. Grand Rapids: Eerdmans, 2007.

Frost, Michael, and Alan Hirsch. *The Shaping of Things to Come: Innovation and Mission for the 21st-Century Church*. Grand Rapids: Baker, 2013.

Fuller, Leanna K. *When Christ's Body Is Broken: Anxiety, Identity, and Conflict in Congregations*. Eugene, OR: Pickwick, 2016.

Gaines, Timothy R. "Politics, Participation, and the *Missio Dei* in the Thought of Miroslav Volf and the Wesleyan Tradition." *Wesleyan Theological Journal* 47 (2012) 72–89.

Galdas, Paul. "Revisiting Bias in Qualitative Research: Reflections on Its Relationship with Funding and Impact." *International Journal of Qualitative Method*, 16 (2017) 1–2.

Garrett, Robert I. "Missional Church—A Vision for the Sending of the Church in North America." *Southwestern Journal of Theology* 42 (2000) 126–27.

Gehring, Roger. W. *House Church and Mission: The Importance of Household Structures in Early Christianity*. Peabody, MA: Hendrickson, 2004.

Gibbs, Eddie, and Ryan K. Bolger. *Emerging Church: Creating Christian Community in Postmodern Cultures*. London: SPCK, 2006.

Giddens, Anthony. *Sociology*. 6th ed. Cambridge, UK: Polity, 2012.

Gill, James J. "Burnout—A Growing Threat in Ministry." *Human Development* 1 (1980) 21–27.

Gladwin, Ryan R. "Testimony in the Spirit: Rescripting Ordinary Pentecostal Theology." *Practical Theology* 5 (2012) 353–55.

Goheen, Michael. *"As the Father Has Sent Me, I Am Sending You": J. E. Lesslie Newbigin's Missionary Ecclesiology*. Zoetermeer, Netherlands: Boekencentrum, 2000.

———. *The Church and Its Vocation: Lesslie Newbigin's Missionary Ecclesiology*. Grand Rapids: Baker Academic, 2018.

Graham, Elaine. "Frailty and Flourishing." *Practical Theology* 4 (2011) 333–38.

Graham, Elaine, and Heather Walton. "A Walk on the Wild Side: A Critique of the Gospel and Our Culture." *Christian Movement* 33 (1991) 1–7.

Graham, Elaine, et al. *Theological Reflection: Methods*. London: SCM, 2005.

Gray, James, ed. *W. R.: The Man and His Work: A Brief Account of the Life and Work of William Robinson, M.A., B.Sc., D.D., 1888–1963*. Birmingham, UK: Berean, 1978.

Greene, Collin, and Martin Robinson. *Metavista: Bible, Church and Mission in an Age of Imagination*. Milton Keynes: Authentic, 2008.

Gregersen, Niels Henrik. "Introduction." In *Incarnation: On the Scope and Depth of Christology*, edited by Niels Henrik Gregersen, 1–14. Minneapolis: Fortress, 2015.

Grenz, Stanley J. *Rediscovering the Triune God: The Trinity in Contemporary Theology*. Minneapolis: Fortress, 2004.

Grenz, Stanley J., and Smith, Jay T. *Created for Community: Connecting Christian Belief with Christian Living*. Grand Rapids: Baker Academic, 2014.

Grudem, Wayne. *Systematic Theology: An Introduction to Biblical Doctrine*. Nottingham, UK: IVP, 2007.

Guder, Darrell L., ed. "Investigating Theological Formation for Apostolic Vocation: Presidential Address." *Missionalia* 37 (2009) 63–74.

———. *Missional Church: A Vision for the Sending of the Church in North America*. Grand Rapids: Eerdmans, 1998.

Guest, Matthew. *Evangelical Identity and Contemporary Culture: A Congregational Study in Innovation*. Eugene, OR: Wipf & Stock, 2008.

Haldar, Dipankar. "Towards Convergence of Ecumenism and Evangelicalism in Post-Edinburgh-1910 Era: Quest for Faithful Christian Witness to People of Other Faiths." http://www.edinburgh2010.org/fileadmin/files/edinburgh2010/files/Resources/UBS%20Haldar%20-%20Convergence%20Ecumenical%20Evangelical.pdf.

Hammersley, Martyn, and Paul Atkinson. *Ethnography: Principles in Practice*. 2nd ed. London: Routledge, 2005.

Hanciles, Jehu J. *Beyond Christendom: Globalization, African Migration, and the Transformation of the West*. Maryknoll, NY: Orbis, 2008.

Hancock, Thomas E., et al. "Attempting Valid Assessment of Spiritual Growth: A Survey of Christ-centered Living." *Christian Education Journal* 2.1 (2005) 129–53.

Hardy, Andrew. "Ethnography and Understanding Power Encounters." In *Power and the Powers: The Use and Abuse of Power in Its Missional Context*, edited by Andrew Hardy et al., 75–92. Eugene, OR: Cascade, 2015.

———. "John's Gospel and Discipleship." In *Missional Discipleship After Christendom*, edited by Andrew Hardy and Dan Yarnell, 46–74. Eugene, OR: Cascade, 2018.

———. *Pictures of God: Shaping Missional Church Life*. Watford, UK: Instant Apostle, 2016.

Hardy, Andrew, et al. *Power and the Powers: The Use and Abuse of Power in the Missional Context*. Eugene, OR: Wipf and Stock, 2015.

Harris, Tania. "Hearing God's Voice: The Role of Revelatory Experience in Ministry and Mission among Australian Pentecostals." Unpublished Paper, 2018.

———. "Where Pentecostalism and Evangelicalism Part Ways: Towards a Theology of Pentecostal Revelatory Experience." *Asian Journal of Pentecostal Studies* 23 (2020) 31–56.

Harvey, Barry, and Bryan C. Hollon, eds. "Series Preface." In *Free Churches and the Body of Christ: Authority, Unity, and Truthfulness*, edited by Jeffrey W. Cary, ix–xii. Eugene, OR: Cascade, 2012.

Hastings, Ross. *Missional God, Missional Church: Hope for Re-Evangelizing the West*. Downers Grove, IL: IVP Academic, 2012.

Healy, Nicholas M. *Church, World and the Christian Life: Practical-Prophetic Ecclesiology*. Cambridge: Cambridge University Press, 2000.

Henderson Callahan, Sharon. "Forming Lay Missional Leaders for Congregations and the World." In *The Missional Church and Leadership Formation: Helping Congregations Develop Leadership Capacity*, edited by Craig Van Gelder, 120–46. Grand Rapids: Eerdmans, 2009.

Heneise, Michael T. "A Critical Evaluation of Lesslie Newbigin's Theology of Mission in the Light of Western Pluralism." *Journal of European Baptist Studies* 4 (2004) 40–55.

Hermans, C., and Schoeman, W. J. "Survey Research in Practical Theology and Congregational Studies." *Acta Theologica* 22 (2015) 45–63.

Heron, John. *The Facilitator's Handbook*. London: Kogan Page, 1989.

Hiebert, Paul G. *The Gospel in Human Contexts: Anthropological Explorations for Contemporary Missions*. Grand Rapids: Baker Academic, 2009.

———. *Transforming Worldviews: An Anthropological Understanding of How People Change*. Grand Rapids: Baker Academic, 2008.

Hiebert, Paul G., and Eloise Hiebert-Menses. *Incarnational Ministry: Planting Churches in Band, Tribal, Peasant, and Urban Societies*. Grand Rapids: Baker, 1995.

Hilber, John W. "Diversity of OT Prophetic Phenomena and NT Prophecy." *The Westminster Theological Journal* 56 (1994) 243–58.
Hills, Sarah A. "A Theology of Restitution as Embodied Reconciliation: A Study of Restitution in a Reconciliation Process in Worcester, South Africa." PhD Thesis. Durham University, 2014.
Hirsch, Alan, and Tim Catchim. *The Permanent Revolution: Apostolic Imagination and Practice for the 21st-Century Church*. San Francisco: Jossey-Bass, 2012.
Hoekendijk, Johannes C. "The Church in Missionary Thinking." *International Review of Mission* 41 (1952) 324–36.
Hogg, William. *Ecumenical Foundations*. New York: Harper and Brothers, 1952.
Holloway, Gary, and David A. Foster. *Renewing God's People: A Concise History of Churches of Christ*. Abilene, TX: Abilene Christian University Press, 2006.
———. *Renewing the World: A Concise Global History of the Stone-Campbell Movement*. Abilene, TX: Abilene Christian University Press, 2015.
Holmes, Colin, and David Lindsay. "In Search of Christian Theological Research Methodology." *SAGE Open* 8.4 (2018) 1–9.
Holmes, Pamela. "The Spirit, Nature, and Canadian Pentecostal Women: A Conversation with Critical Theory." In *Philip's Daughters: Women in Pentecostal-Charismatic Leadership*, edited by Estrelda Alexander and Amos Yong, 185–234. Eugene, OR: Pickwick, 2009.
Holmes, Peter R. *Trinity in Human Community: Exploring Congregational Life in the Image of the Social Trinity*. Milton Keynes: Paternoster, 2006.
Holmes, Steven R. *The Holy Trinity: Understanding God's Life*. Milton Keynes: Paternoster, 2012.
Holt, Mack P. "Calvin and Reformed Protestantism." In *The Oxford Handbook of Protestant Reformations*, edited by Ulinka Rublack, 214–32. Oxford: Oxford University Press, 2017.
Honderich, Ted, ed. *The Oxford Companion to Philosophy*. Oxford: Oxford University Press, 1995.
Hopewell, James F. *Congregation: Stories and Structures*. Philadelphia: Fortress, 1987.
Horrell, J. Scott. "Toward a Biblical Model of the Social Trinity: Avoiding Equivocation of Nature and Order." *JETS* 47 (2004) 399–421.
Hughes, Nic J. "1995–1996 Newbigin Sermons from Holy Trinity Brompton, London (Sermon on Individual Prayer)." https://newbiginresources.org/individual-prayer/.
Hughes, Richard Thomas. *The Churches of Christ*. 2nd ed. Westport, CT: Praeger, 2001.
———. "Life in the Spirit: An Overview of Lesslie Newbigin's Pneumatology of Mission." *The Ashbury Journal* 68 (2013) 95–105.
———. *Reviving the Ancient Faith: The Story of Churches of Christ in America*. Grand Rapids: Eerdmans, 1996.
Hull, John M. *Towards the Prophetic Church: A Study in Christian Mission*. London: SCM, 2014.
Hunsberger, George R. *Bearing the Witness of the Spirit: Lesslie Newbigin's Theology of Cultural Plurality*. Grand Rapids: Eerdmans, 1998.
———. "Introduction: The Church between Gospel and Culture." In *The Church Between Gospel and Culture: Emerging Mission in North America*, edited by George R. Hunsberger and Craig Van Gelder, xiii–xix. Grand Rapids: Eerdmans, 1996.

Hurtado, Larry W. *Lord Jesus Christ: Devotion to Jesus in Earliest Christianity.* Grand Rapids: Eerdmans, 2003.

Hussain, Ashatu. "The Use of Triangulation in Social Science Research: Can Qualitative and Quantitative Methods be Combined?" *Journal of Comparative Social Work* 1 (2009) 1–12.

Inge, John. *A Christian Theology of Place.* Farnham, UK: Ashgate, 2003.

Jackson, Eleanor. "'And the Truth Shall Set You Free': Lesslie Newbigin's Understanding of 'Truth' as Illustrated by His Life and Work." In *Theology in Missionary Perspective: Lesslie Newbigin's Legacy,* edited by Mark T. B. Laing and Paul Weston, 102–24. Eugene, OR: Pickwick, 2012.

Jackson-Jordan, Elizabeth Ann. "Clergy Burnout and Resilience: A Review of the Literature." *Journal of Pastoral Care and Counselling* 67 (2013) 1–5.

Johnston, William. *Mystical Theology: The Science of Love.* London: Harper Collins, 1995.

Jones, E. Stanley. "Where Madras Missed the Way." *The Christian Century* 56 (1939) 86–89.

Kaggwa, Robert. "Mission and the Spirit." In *Mission and Spirituality: Creative Ways of Being Church,* edited by Howard Mellor and Timothy Yates, 43–66. Sheffield, UK: Cliff College Publishing, 2002.

Kaiser, Christopher B. "From Biblical Secularity to Modern Secularism: Historical Aspects and Stages." In *The Church between Gospel and Culture: The Emerging Mission in North America,* edited by George R. Hunsberger and Craig Van Gelder, 79–112. Grand Rapids: Eerdmans, 1996.

Karkkainen, Velli-Matti. *Christology: A Global Introduction: An Ecumenical, International, and Contextual Perspective.* Grand Rapids: Baker Academic, 2003.

———. "The Church in the Post-Christian Society between Modernity and Late Modernity: Lesslie Newbigin's Post-Critical Missional Ecclesiology." In *Theology in Missionary Perspective: Lesslie Newbigin's Legacy,* edited by Mark T. B. Laing and Paul Weston, 125–54. Eugene, OR: Pickwick, 2012.

———. *The Holy Spirit: A Guide to Christian Theology.* Louisville: Westminster John Knox, 2012.

———. *An Introduction to Ecclesiology: Ecumenical, Historical and Global Perspectives.* Downers Grove, IL: IVP Academic, 2002.

———. *Pneumatology: The Holy Spirit in Ecumenical, International, and Contextual Perspective.* Grand Rapids: Baker Academic, 2002.

———. *Trinity and Religious Pluralism: The Doctrine of the Trinity in Christian Theology of Religions.* Aldershot, UK: Ashgate, 2004.

———. *Trinity and Revelation: A Constructive Christian Theology for the Pluralistic World.* Vol. 2. 4 vols. Grand Rapids: Eerdmans, 2014.

———. *The Trinity Global Perspectives.* Louisville: Westminster John Knox, 2007.

Kelebogile, Thomas Resane. "A Critical Analysis of the Ecclesiology of the Emerging Apostolic Churches with Special Reference to the Notion of the Fivefold Ministry." *Researchgate* (2008) 136–213. https://www.researchgate.net/publication/279652158.

Kelly, Brian M. "Testimony in the Spirit: Rescripting Ordinary Pentecostal Theology." *Canadian Journal of Pentecostal Charismatic Christianity* 4.1 (2013) 69–70. https://journal.twu.ca/index.php/CJPC/article/view/102/80.

Kenneson, Philip D. "Nicholas Lash on Doctrinal Development and Ecclesial Authority." *Modern Theology* 5 (1989) 271–300.
Kim, Kirsteen. *Joining in with the Spirit: Connecting World Church and Local Mission*. London: Epworth, 2009.
Kimball, Dan. *The Emerging Church: Vintage Christianity for New Generations*. Grand Rapids: Zondervan, 2003.
Kimmel, Allan J. *Ethical Issues in Behavioral Research: Basic and Applied Perspectives*. Oxford: Blackwell, 2007.
Kirk, J. Andrew. *What Is Mission?: Theological Explorations*. London: Darton, Longman and Todd, 1999.
Koet, Bart K. "Dreams and Revelations: Food for Theological and Philosophical Thought." In *Dreams and Spirituality: A Handbook for Ministry, Spiritual Direction and Counselling*, edited by Kate Adams et al., 3–15. London: Canterbury, 2015.
Kossie-Chernyshev, Karen. "Looking Beyond the Pulpit: Social Ministries and African American Pentecostal-Charismatic Women in Leadership." In *Philip's Daughters: Women in Pentecostal-Charismatic Leadership*, edited by Estrelda Alexander and Amos Yong, 61–73. Eugene, OR: Pickwick, 2009.
Kreider, Alan. *The Change of Conversion and the Origin of Christianity*. 1999. Reprint, Eugene, OR: Wipf and Stock, 2007.
Laing, Mark T. B., and Paul Weston, eds. *Theology in Missionary Perspective: Lesslie Newbigin's Legacy*. Eugene, OR: Pickwick, 2012.
Lash, Nicholas. "Considering the Trinity." *Modern Theology* 2 (1986) 183–96.
Latourette, Kenneth Scott. "By Way of Inclusive Retrospect." In *Perspectives on the World Christian Movement*, edited by Ralph D. Winter and Steven C. Hawthorne, 22–32. Rev. ed. Pasadena, CA: William Carey Library, 1992.
Lausanne Movement. "The Lausanne Movement's Unique Calling." https://www.lausanne.org/about-the-movement.
Lawler, Michael. "Faith, Praxis, and Practical Theology: At the Interface of Sociology and Theology." *Horizons* 29 (2002) 199–224.
Legrand, Dorothee. "Phenomenological Dimensions of Bodily Self-Consciousness." In *The Oxford Handbook of the Self*, edited by Shaun Gallagher, 204–27. Oxford: Oxford University Press, 2013.
Long, D. Stephen. *Saving Karl Barth: Hans Urs von Balthasar's Preoccupation*. Minneapolis: Fortress, 2014.
Lonsdale, David. "The Church as Context for Christian Spirituality." In *The Blackwell Companion to Christian Spirituality*, edited by Arthur Holder, 239–53. Chichester, UK: Blackwell, 2011.
Louth, Andrew. *Introducing Eastern Orthodox Theology*. London: SPCK, 2013.
Love, Curtis R., and Cornelius J. P. Niemandt. "Led by the Spirit: Missional Communities and the Quakers on Communal Vocation Discernment." *HTS Theological Studies* 70 (2014) 1–9.
Ma, Julie C. "Changing Images: Women in Asian Pentecostalism." In *Philip's Daughters: Women in Pentecostal-Charismatic Leadership*, edited by Estrelda Alexander and Amos Yong, 203–14. Eugene, OR: Pickwick, 2009.
Macchia, Frank D. "Pentecostal and Charismatic Theology." In *The Oxford Handbook of Eschatology*, edited by Jerry L. Walls, 280–94. Oxford: Oxford University Press, 2008.

MacIlvaine, W. Rodman. "How Churches Become Missional." *Bibliotheca Sacra* 167 (2010) 216–33.
Mager, Robert. "Action Theories." In *The Wiley-Blackwell Companion to Practical Theology*, edited by Bonnie J. Miller-McLemore, 255–66. Oxford: Wiley-Blackwell, 2014.
Martin, David. "Undermining the Old Paradigms Rescripting Pentecostal Accounts." *Pentecostal Studies* 5 (2006) 18–38.
Martinson, E. Terri. "Characteristics of Congregations That Empower Missional Leadership: A Lutheran Voice." In *The Missional Church and Leadership Formation: Helping Congregations Develop Leadership Capacity*, edited by Craig Van Gelder, 175–208. Grand Rapids: Eerdmans, 2009.
McClendon, James W. *Biography as Theology: How Life Stories Can Remake Today's Theology*. Nashville: Abingdon, 1974.
McClendon, James W., and James M. Smith. *Convictions: Defusing Religious Relativism*. Eugene, OR: Wipf & Stock, 1994.
McClintock Fulkerson, Mary. *Historical Theology: An Introduction to the History of Christian Thought*. 2nd ed. Chichester, UK: Wiley-Blackwell, 2013.
———. *Places of Redemption: Theology for a Worldly Church*. Oxford: Oxford University Press, 2010.
McKnight, Scot. *Kingdom Conspiracy: Returning to the Radical Mission of the Local Church*. Grand Rapids: Brazos, 2014.
McGrath, Alister, E. *Historical Theology: An Introduction to the History of Christian Thought*. 2nd ed. Chichester: Wiley-Blackwell, 2013.
McNeal, Reggie. *Missional Communities: The Rise of the Post-Congregational Church*. San Francisco: Jossey-Bass, 2011.
Mercer, Calvin. "Jesus the Apostle: 'Sending' and the Theology of John." *JETS* 35 (1992) 457–62.
Mercer, Joyce Ann, and Bonnie J. Miller-McLemore, eds. *Conundrums in Practical Theology*. Leiden: Brill, 2016.
Mobsby, Ian. *God Unknown: The Trinity in Contemporary Spirituality and Mission*. Norwich, UK: Canterbury, 2012.
Moltmann, Jurgen. *The Crucified God*. London: SCM, 2001.
———. *God in Creation: An Ecological Doctrine of Creation*. London: SCM, 1985.
———. "Is God Incarnate in All That Is?" In *Incarnation: On the Scope and Depth of Christology*, edited by Niels Henrik Gregersen, 119–32. Minneapolis: Fortress, 2015.
———. *Theology of Hope*. London: SCM, 2002.
———. *The Trinity and the Kingdom of God*. London: SCM, 1981.
Moynagh, Michael. *Church in Life: Innovation, Mission and Ecclesiology*. London: SCM, 2017.
Moynagh, Michael, and Philip Harrold. *Church for Every Context: An Introduction to Theology and Practice*. London: SCM, 2012.
Murray, Stuart. *Church after Christendom*. Carlisle, UK: Paternoster, 2004.
———. *Post-Christendom*. Carlisle, UK: Paternoster, 2004.
Neill, Stephen. *A History of Christian Missions*. London: Penguin, 1990.
Neu, Diann L. "Women-Church Transforming Liturgy." In *Women at Worship: Interpretations of North American Diversity*, edited by Marjorie Proctor-Smith and Janet Walton, 163–78. Louisville: Westminster John Knox, 1993.

Newbigin, Lesslie. "Can the West Be Converted?" *Princeton Seminary Bulletin* 6 (1985) 25–37.

———. "Can the West Be Converted?" *Evangelical Review of Theology* 11 (1987) 355–68.

———. "The Cultural Captivity of Western Christianity as a Challenge to a Missionary Church." In *A Word in Season: Perspectives in Christian World Missions*, edited by Eleanor Jackson, 66–79. Grand Rapids: Eerdmans, 1994.

———. "Evangelism in the Context of Secularization." In *A Word in Season: Perspectives on Christian World Missions*, edited by Eleanor Jackson, 148–57. Grand Rapids: Eerdmans, 1994.

———. *Foolishness to the Greeks: The Gospel and Western Culture*. London: SPCK, 1986.

———. "The Gospel and Our Culture: A Response to Elaine Graham and Heather Walton." *Modern Churchman* 34 (1992) 1–10.

———. "The Gospel as Public Truth." *The Gospel and Our Culture Newsletter* 9 (1991) 1–2.

———. *The Gospel in a Pluralist Society*. Grand Rapids: Eerdmans, 1989.

———. *The Household of God: Lectures on the Nature of the Church*. London: SCM, 1953.

———. *The Light Has Come: An Exposition of the Fourth Gospel*. Edinburgh: Handsel, 1987.

———. *Mission and the Crisis of Western Culture*. Edinburgh: Handel, 1989.

———. "The Missionary Dimension of the Ecumenical Movement." *Ecumenical Review* 14 (1962) 207–15.

———. "Missions in Ecumenical Perspective." https://newbiginresources.org/1962-missions-in-an-ecumenical-perspective/.

———. *One Body, One Gospel, One World: The Christian Mission Today*. London: SCM, 1958.

———. *The Open Secret: An Introduction to the Theology of Mission*. London: SPCK, 1995.

———. *The Other Side of 1984: Questions for the Churches*. Geneva: World Council of Churches, 1983.

———. *Proper Confidence: Faith, Doubt and Certainty in Christian Discipleship*. London: SPCK, 1995.

———. *The Relevance of Trinitarian Doctrine for Today's Mission*. CWME Study Pamphlets 2. London: Edinburgh House, 1963.

———. *The Reunion of the Church: A Defence of the South India Scheme*. 2nd ed. London: SCM, 1960.

———. "The Sending of the Church—Three Bible Studies." *New Perspectives on World Mission and Unity* 1 (1984) 1–14.

———. "The Trinity as Public Truth." In *The Trinity in a Pluralistic Age: Theological Essays on Culture and Religion*, edited by Kevin J. Vanhoozer, 1–8. Grand Rapids: Eerdmans, 1997.

———. *Truth to Tell: The Gospel as Public Truth*. London: SPCK, 1991.

———. "What Is 'A Local Church Truly United?'" *Ecumenical Review* 29 (1977) 115–28.

Niemandt, Cornelius J. P. "Five Years of Missional Church: Reflections on Missional Ecclesiology." *Missionalia* 38 (2010) 397–412.

———. "Trends in Missional Ecclesiology." *HTS Teologiese Studies/Theological Studies* 68 (2012) 1–9.

Olbright, Thomas H. "Churches of Christ." In *The Encyclopedia of the Stone-Campbell Movement*, edited by David A. Foster, 212–20. Grand Rapids: Eerdmans, 2004.

Ott, Craig, and Stephen Strauss, with Timothy C. Tennent. *Encountering Theology of Mission: Biblical Foundations, Historical Developments, and Contemporary Issues*. Grand Rapids: Baker Academic, 2010.

Paas, Stefan. "A Case Study of Church Growth by Church Planting in Germany: Are They Connected?" *International Bulletin of Mission Research* 42 (2018) 40–54.

———. "The Discipline of Missiology in 2016: Concerning the Place and Meaning of Missiology in the Theological Curriculum." *Calvin Theological Journal* 51 (2016) 37–54.

———. "Leadership in Mission: The Reformed System of Church Governance in an Age of Mission." *Calvin Theological Journal* 50 (2015) 110–25.

Paas, Stefan, and Alrik Vos. "Church Planting and Church Growth in Western Europe: An Analysis." *International Bulletin of Mission Research* 40 (2016) 243–52.

Papanikolaou, Aristotle. "Contemporary Orthodoxy Currents on the Trinity." In *The Oxford Handbook of The Trinity*, edited by Gilles O. P. Emery and Matthew Levering, 328–38. Oxford: Oxford University Press, 2014.

Partington, Gary. "Qualitative Research Interviews: Identifying Problems in Technique." *Issues in Educational Research* 11.2 (2001) 32–44. https://ro.ecu.edu.au/ecuworks/4368/.

Perrin, Ruth H. *The Bible Reading of Young Evangelicals: An Exploration of the Ordinary Hermeneutics and Faith of Generation Y*. Eugene, OR: Pickwick, 2016.

Petra, Basilio. "Christos Yannaras and the Idea 'Dysis.'" In *Orthodox Constructions of the West*, edited by George Demacopoulos and Aristotle Papaniklaou, 161–80. New York: Fordham University Press, 2013.

Phillips, Elizabeth. "Charting the 'Ethnographic Turn': Theologians and the Study of Christian Congregations." In *Perspectives on Ecclesiology and Ethnography*, edited by Pete Ward, 95–106. Grand Rapids: Eerdmans, 2012.

Pinnock, Clark H. *Flame of Love: A Theology of the Holy Spirit*. Downers Grove, IL: IVP Academic, 1996.

Proctor-Smith, Marjorie. *In Her Own Right: Constructing Feminist Liturgical Tradition*. Nashville: Abingdon, 1990.

Rae, Murray. "The Congregation as Hermeneutic of the Gospel." In *Theology in Missionary Perspective: Lesslie Newbigin's Legacy*, edited by Mark T. B. Laing and Paul Weston, 189–202. Eugene, OR: Pickwick, 2012.

Raiter, Michael. "Missional Church—A Vision for the Sending of the Church in North America." *The Reformed Theological Review* 58 (1999) 50–51.

Randall, Ian M. "Mission in Post-Christendom: Anabaptist and Free Church Perspectives." *Evangelical Quarterly* 79 (2007) 227–40.

Raser, Harold E. "Compassion: Being the Hands and Feet of God." In *Missio Dei: A Wesleyan Understanding*, edited by Keith Schwanz and Joseph Coleson, 158–67. Kansas City: Beacon Hill, 2011.

Rempel, John D. "Sacraments in the Radical Reformation." In *The Oxford Handbook of Sacramental Theology*, edited by Hans Boersma and Matthew Levering, 298–312. Oxford: Oxford University Press, 2015.

Rich, Hannah. *Growing Good: Growth, Social Action and Discipleship in the Church of England*. London: Theos, and the Church Urban Fund, 2020.

Robinson, Martin, and Dwight Smith. *Invading Secular Space: Strategies for Tomorrow's Church*. London: Monarch, 2003.
Roebuck, David G. "'Cause He's My Chief Employer': Hearing Women's Voices in a Classical Pentecostal Denomination." In *Philip's Daughters: Women in Pentecostal-Charismatic Leadership*, edited by Estrelda Alexander and Amos Yong, 38–60. Eugene, OR: Pickwick, 2009.
Rogers, Andrew P. *Congregational Hermeneutics: How Do We Read?* Farnham, UK: Ashgate, 2015.
———. "Ordinary Biblical Hermeneutics and the Transformation of Congregational Horizons Within English Evangelicalism: A Theological Ethnographic Study." PhD Thesis. King's College London, 2009.
Ross, Cathy. "Hospitality: The Church as 'A Mother with an Open Heart.'" In *Mission on the Road to Emmaus: Constants, Context, and Prophetic Dialogue*, edited by Cathy Ross and Steven B. Bevans, 67–84. Maryknoll, NY: Orbis, 2015.
Roxburgh, Alan J. *Missional Map-Making: Skills for Leading in Times of Transition*. San Francisco: Jossey-Bass, 2010.
———. *The Sky Is Falling: Leaders Lost in Transition*. Eagle, IA: ACI, 2005.
Roxburgh, Alan J., and Fred Romanuk. *The Missional Leader: Equipping Your Church to Reach a Changing World*. San Francisco: Jossey-Bass, 2006.
Ruthven, Jon. "On the Cessation of the Charismata: The Protestant Polemic of Benjamin B Warfield." *Pneuma* 12 (1990) 14–31.
Sanford, John A. *Ministry Burnout*. London: Arthur James, 1982.
Sarisky, Darren. "The Meaning of the *Missio Dei*: Reflections on Lesslie Newbigin's Proposal that Mission Is of the Essence of the Church." *Missiology* 42 (2014) 257–70.
Schleiermacher, Friedrich. *The Christian Faith*. Edited by H. R. Mackintosh and J. S. Stewart. 1821. Reprint. Berkeley: Apocryphile, 2011.
Schreiter, Robert J. *Constructing Local Theologies*. Maryknoll, NY: Orbis, 1985.
Searle, John R. "The Irreducibility of Consciousness." In *Philosophy of Mind: A Guide and Anthology*, edited by John Heil, 700–708. Oxford: Oxford University Press. 2011.
Shah, Alpa. "Ethnography? Participant Observation, a Potentially Revolutionary Praxis." *University of Chicago Press Journal* 7 (2017) 45–59.
Shaw, Perry. *Transforming Theological Education: A Practical Handbook for Integrative Learning*. Cumbria, UK: Langham, 2014.
Sheldrake, Philip. *Spaces for the Sacred*. London: SCM, 2001.
Sheridan, Timothy M., and H. Jurgens Hendriks. "The Emergent Church Movement." *Deel* 53 (2012) 312–23.
Silverman, David. *Doing Qualitative Research*. 4th ed. London: Sage, 2017.
Slee, Nicola. *Women's Faith Development: Patterns and Processes*. Aldershot, UK: Ashgate, 2004.
Smith, Charles Frederick. *An Evangelical Evaluation of Key Elements in Lesslie Newbigin's Apologetics*. Fort Worth, TX: Southwestern Baptist Theological Seminary Press, 1999.
Smith, Collin Miller. "The Protest of Christ and the Death within God: An Analysis of Moltmann's Departure from Classical Theism in the Crucified God." *Perspectives in Religious Studies* 45 (2018) 15–26.

Smith, James K. A. *Desiring the Kingdom: Worship, Worldview, and Cultural Formation.* Vol. 1. 2 vols. Grand Rapids: Baker Academic, 2009.
———. *Imagining the Kingdom: How Worship Works.* Vol. 2. 2 vols. Grand Rapids: Baker Academic, 2013.
Song, Choan-Seng. "Freedom of the Human Spirit from Captivity: The Task of Religious Communities in the Postmodern World." In *Contextuality in Reformed Europe: The Mission of the Church in the Transformation of European Culture,* edited by Christine Lienemann-Perrin, 15–34. Amsterdam: Rodopi, 2004.
Spencer, Stephen. *SCM Studyguide: Christian Mission.* London: SCM, 2007.
Stache, Kristine. M. "Leadership and the Missional Church Conversation: Listening in on What Leaders in Four Denominational Systems Have to Say." In *The Missional Church and Leadership Formation: Helping Congregations Develop Leadership Capacity,* edited by Craig Van Gelder, 209–38. Grand Rapids: Eerdmans, 2009.
Stanley, Brian. "Activism as Mission Spirituality: The Example of William Carey." In *Mission and Spirituality: Creative Ways of Being Church,* edited by Howard Mellor and Timothy Yates, 67–82. Sheffield, UK: Cliff College Publishing, 2002.
Stanley, Susie C. "Wesleyan/Holiness and Pentecostal Women Preachers: Pentecost as the Pattern of Primitivism." In *Philip's Daughters: Women in Pentecostal-Charismatic Leadership,* edited by Estrelda Alexander and Amos Yong, 19–37. Eugene, OR: Pickwick, 2009.
Stetzer, Ed. *Planting Missional Churches: Your Guide to Starting Churches that Multiply.* Nashville: B and H Academic, 2016.
Stevens, R. Paul. *The Abolition of the Laity: Vocation, Work and Ministry in a Biblical Perspective.* Milton Keynes: Paternoster, 1999.
Suurmond, Jean-Jacques. *Word and Spirit at Play.* London: SCM, 1994.
Swinton, John, and Harriet Mowat. *Practical Theology and Qualitative Research.* London: SCM, 2013.
Tanner, Kathryn. "Incarnation, Cross, and Sacrifice: A Feminist-Inspired Reappraisal." *Anglican Theological Review* 86 (2004) 35–56.
———. "Social Trinitarianism and Its Critics." In *Rethinking Trinitarian Theology: Disputed Questions and Contemporary Issues in Trinitarian Theology,* edited by Robert J. Wozniak and Giulio Maspero, 368–86. London: T. and T. Clark, 2012.
Tavast, Timo. "Challenging the Modalism of the West: Jenson on the Trinity." *Pro Ecclesia* 19 (2010) 355–68.
Tennent, Timothy C. *Invitation to World Missions: A Trinitarian Missiology for the Twenty-first Century.* Grand Rapids: Kregel, 2010.
Terry, John Mark. "Indigenous Churches." In *Evangelical Dictionary of World Missions,* edited by A. Scott Moreau, 483–85. Grand Rapids: Baker, 2000.
Thatcher, Adrian. "Theology, Happiness, and Public Policy." In *Theology and Human Flourishing: Essays in Honour of Timothy J. Gorringe,* edited by Mike Higton et al., 251–64. Eugene, OR: Cascade, 2011.
Thiessen, Joel, et al. "What Is a Flourishing Congregation? Leader Perceptions, Definitions, and Experiences." *Religious Research Association* 4 (2018) 1–25.
Thiselton, Anthony C. *Systematic Theology.* London: SPCK, 2015.
Thomas, John M. "The Role of the Church as a Cultural Critic in the Missiology of Lesslie Newbigin." *Missio Apostolica* 15 (2007) 94–102.
Thompson, David M. *Let Sects and Parties Fall: A Short History of the Association of Churches of Christ in Great Britain and Ireland.* Birmingham, UK: Berean, 1980.

Thompson, Iain. "Ontotheology? Understanding Heidegger's *Destruktion* of Metaphysics." *International Journal of Philosophical Studies* 8 (2000) 297–327.

Thompson, Judith, et al. *SCM Studyguide: Theological Reflection*. London: SCM, 2008.

Trokan, John. "Models of Theological Reflection: Theory and Praxis." *Journal of Catholic Education* 1 (1997) 144–58.

Tueno, Guerin. "Built on the Word: The Theology and Use of the Bible in the Australian Anglican Fresh Expressions of Church." Doctoral Thesis, Durham University, 2014.

Turner, Max. *The Holy Spirit and Spiritual Gifts*. Peabody, MA: Hendrickson, 2005.

Turner, Victor. *The Forest of Symbols: Aspects of Ndembu Ritual*. New York: Cornell University Press, 1967.

———. *The Ritual Process: Structure and Anti-Structure*. New York: Routledge, 2017.

Tye, Michael. "Philosophical Problems of Consciousness." In *The Blackwell Companion to Consciousness*, edited by Susan Schneider and Max Velmans, 17–31. 2nd ed. Oxford: Wiley-Blackwell, 2017.

Van Gelder, Craig. "How Missiology Can Help Inform the Conversation about the Missional Church in Context." In *The Missional Church in Context: Helping Congregations Develop Contextual Ministry*, edited by Craig Van Gelder, 12–43. Grand Rapids: Eerdmans, 2007.

———. *The Missional Church and Leadership Formation: Helping Congregations Develop Leadership Capacity*. Grand Rapids: Eerdmans, 2009.

———. *The Missional Church in Context: Helping Congregations Develop Contextual Ministry*. Grand Rapids: Eerdmans, 2007.

———. "Theological Education and Missional Leadership Formation: Can Seminaries Prepare Missional Leaders for Congregations?" In *The Missional Church and Leadership Formation: Helping Congregations Develop Leadership Capacity*, edited by Craig Van Gelder, 11–44. Grand Rapids: Eerdmans, 2009.

Van Gelder, Craig, and Dwight J. Zscheile. *The Missional Church in Perspective: Mapping Trends and Shaping the Conversation*. Grand Rapids: Baker Academic, 2011.

———. *Participating in God's Mission: A Theological Missiology for the Church in America*. Grand Rapids: Eerdmans, 2018.

Van Gennep, Arnold. *The Rites of Passage*. New York: Routledge, 2004.

Volf, Miroslav. *After Our Likeness: The Church and the Image of the Trinity*. Grand Rapids: Eerdmans, 1998.

———. *Exclusion and Embrace: A Theological Exploration of Identity, Otherness, and Reconciliation*. Nashville: Abingdon, 1996.

Wachsmuth, Melody J. "Mission and the Reformation: Lessons from the Reformers and Anabaptists." *KAIROS* 11 (2017) 143–54.

Wagner, J. Ross. "*Missio Dei*: Envisioning an Apostolic Reading of Scripture." *Missiology* 37 (2009) 19–32.

Wainwright, Geoffrey. "Contemporary Ecumenical Challenges from the Legacy of Lesslie Newbigin." In *Theology in Missionary Perspective: Lesslie Newbigin's Legacy*, edited by Mark T. B. Laing and Paul Weston, 277–89. Eugene, OR: Pickwick, 2012.

Ward, Pete. *Introducing Practical Theology: Mission, Ministry, and the Life of the Church*. Grand Rapids: Baker Academic, 2017.

———. *Participation and Mediation: A Practical Theology for the Liquid Church*. Canterbury, UK: SCM, 2008.

———. *Perspectives on Ecclesiology and Ethnography*. Grand Rapids: Eerdmans, 2012.

Ware, Frederick L. "Spiritual Egalitarianism, Ecclesial Pragmatism, and the Status of Women in Ordained Ministry." In *Philip's Daughters: Women in Pentecostal-Charismatic Leadership*, edited by Estrelda Alexander and Amos Yong, 215–34. Eugene, OR: Pickwick, 2009.

Warner, Robert. *Reinventing English Evangelicalism, 1966–2001: A Theological and Sociological Study*. Milton Keynes: Paternoster, 2007.

Watkins, Clare. *Disclosing Church: An Ecclesiology Learned from Conversations in Practice*. London: Routledge. 2020.

Watts, David, et al.. *Edward Jeffreys, Healing Evangelist: His Story, Movement, and Legacy*. Stourbridge, UK: Transformation, 2017.

Webb, Stephen H. "Eschatology and Politics." In *The Oxford Handbook of Eschatology*, edited by Jerry L. Walls, 500–517. Oxford: Oxford University Press, 2008.

Weller, Susan C., et al. "Open-Ended Interview Questions and Saturation." *PLoS ONE* 13 (2018) 1–18.

Wells, Samuel. *Incarnational Mission: Being with the World*. London: Canterbury, 2018.

Wesley, David. "The Church as Missionary." In *Missio Dei: A Wesleyan Understanding*, edited by Keith Schwanz and Joseph Coleson, 19–28. Kansas City: Beacon Hill, 2011.

Weston, Paul. "Ecclesiology in Eschatological Perspective: Newbigin's Understanding of the Missionary Church." In *Theology in Missionary Perspective: Lesslie Newbigin's Legacy*, edited by Mark T. B. Laing and Paul Weston, 70–87. Eugene, OR: Pickwick, 2012.

———. "Lesslie Newbigin: His Writings in Context." In *Theology in Missionary Perspective: Lesslie Newbigin's Legacy*, edited by Mark T. B. Laing and Paul Weston, 10–18. Eugene, OR: Pickwick, 2012.

———. *Lesslie Newbigin, Missionary Theologian: A Reader*. Grand Rapids: Eerdmans, 2006.

White, Peter. (2015). "A Missional Study of Ghanaian Pentecostal Churches: Leadership and Leadership Formation." *HTS Teologiese Studies/Theological Studies* 71 (2015) 1–8.

Wigner, Daniel E. "Spiritual Borrowing: Appropriation and Reinterpretation of Christian Mystic Practices in Three Emergent Churches." PhD Thesis, Durham University, 2014.

Wilkinson, Michael. "Testimony in the Spirit: Rescripting Ordinary Pentecostal Theology." *Pentecostal Studies* 12 (2013) 252–53.

Williams, Daniel H. *Evangelicals and Tradition: The Formative Influences of the Early Church*. Milton Keynes: Paternoster, 2005.

Witherington, Ben, III. *Jesus the Seer: The Progress of Prophecy*. Minneapolis: Fortress, 2014.

———. "The Trinity in Johannine Literature." In *The Oxford Handbook of the Trinity*, edited by Gilles Emery and Matthew Levering, 69–79. Oxford: Oxford University Press, 2014.

Woodhead, Linda. "Why so Many Women in Holistic Spirituality?: A Puzzle Revisited." In *A Sociology of Spirituality*, edited by Kieran Flanagan and Peter C. Jupp, 115–26. Farnham, UK: Ashgate, 2010.

Woolnough, Brian, and Wonsuk Ma, eds. *Holistic Mission: God's Plan for God's People*. Oxford: Regnum, 2010.

Wozniak, Robert J., and Giulio Maspero, eds. *Rethinking Trinitarian Theology: Disputed Questions and Contemporary Issues in Trinitarian Theology*. London: T. and T. Clark, 2012.

Wright, Christopher J. H. *The Mission of God's People: A Biblical Theology of the Church's Mission*. Grand Rapids: Zondervan, 2010.

Wright, N. T. *Paul: Fresh Perspectives*. London: SPCK, 2005.

Wright, Walter C. *Relational Leadership: A Biblical Model for Leadership Service*. Milton Keynes: Paternoster, 2008.

Yarnell, Dan. "Imitation of Christ and Pauline Discipleship (*Imitatio Christi*)." In *Missional Discipleship after Christendom*, edited by Andrew Hardy and Dan Yarnell, 75–91. Eugene, OR: Cascade, 2018.

Zizioulas, John D. *Being as Communion*. London: Darton, Longman and Todd, 2013.

———. *The Eucharistic Communion and the World*. London: T. & T. Clark, 2011.

www.ingramcontent.com/pod-product-compliance
Lightning Source LLC
Chambersburg PA
CBHW051635230426
43669CB00013B/2311